# Praise for *Wild Yoga*

"Rebecca Wildbear understands mysticism as a wildly complex and important dimension of life, one we moderns have ignored and even dispelled. She is a mystic, as we all are. Reading *Wild Yoga* has convinced me that mysticism is not something we learn so much as uncover, rediscover. We need not do this alone. With Rebecca Wildbear as a guide — in the physical wilderness, and now on the page — we deepen our knowledge that we all embody the sacred in nature, which holds the key to both our survival and our evolution. This fills me with hope."

— **Brooke Williams**, author of *Mary Jane Wild: Two Walks and a Rant*

"Yoga practice has always been about cultivating a deeper connection with nature. And yet, as our culture has become increasingly disconnected from the natural world, so too has the yoga world. In this refreshing book of storytelling and practice, Rebecca Wildbear vividly invites us back to the place where yoga, care for the Earth, and humanity are interwoven, a place where we can dream of a livable future on Earth."

— **Amy Ippoliti**, coauthor of *The Art and Business of Teaching Yoga*, yoga teacher, and Earth advocate

"In *Wild Yoga*, Rebecca Wildbear offers a gentle path leading us toward both personal healing and planetary care. Her method is embodied and soulful, informed by Earth's wisdom, supported by yoga practice — and designed to deeply motivate activism. May we follow her lead."

— **Laura Sewall, PhD**, ecopsychologist and author of
*Sight and Sensibility: The Ecopsychology of Perception*

"Rebecca Wildbear is a force of nature. This important and beautifully written book is not only a powerful new way to look at yoga; it's a clear and exhilarating guide to reconnecting to our animal bodies and to the wild nature that is our real home. We all owe a deep debt to Rebecca for writing this profound book."

— **Derrick Jensen**, author of *A Language Older Than Words*

"In this lyrical, honest, and kind book, Rebecca Wildbear invites you through simple and profound practices to deepen your connection to yourself, nature, and the planet. *Wild Yoga* is a timely guide at this inflection point for the Earth, one that will help you find better yoga, or union."

— **Sage Rountree, PhD**, E-RYT 500, author of
*Everyday Yoga* and *Teaching Yoga Beyond the Poses*

"*Wild Yoga* beautifully combines land-based mysticism with a deep and necessary focus on embodiment. Rebecca Wildbear offers up a set of practices to encourage us to show up: to reconnect with our own wild nature, and with the soul of this embattled Earth."

— **Sharon Blackie, MA, PhD**, author of *Hagitude*

"Weaving her personal experiences as a cancer survivor, yoga teacher, and wilderness guide, Rebecca Wildbear charts a journey for all seekers to become 'love warriors for the Earth,' protecting the great forests and waterways of our planet. *Wild Yoga* is a treasure — a brilliant road map for these tumultuous times."

— **Dr. Suzanne Simard**, forest ecologist and author of
*Finding the Mother Tree*

# Wild Yoga

# Wild Yoga

## A Practice of Initiation, Veneration & Advocacy for the Earth

## Rebecca Wildbear

### Illustrations by Sarah E. Brooks

New World Library
Novato, California

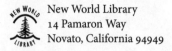

New World Library
14 Pamaron Way
Novato, California 94949

The material in this book is intended for education. No expressed or implied guarantee of the effects of the use of the recommendations can be given or liability taken. The author's experiences used as examples throughout this book are true, although identifying details such as names and locations have been changed to protect privacy.

Wild Yoga® is a registered trademark of Rebecca Wildbear.
Illustrations by Sarah E. Brooks
Text design by Tona Pearce Myers

Library of Congress Cataloging-in-Publication Data

Names: Wildbear, Rebecca, author. | Brooks, Sarah E., illustrator.
Title: Wild yoga : a practice of initiation, veneration & advocacy for the Earth / Rebecca Wildbear ; illustrations by Sarah E. Brooks.
Description: Novato, California : New World Library, [2023] | Includes bibliographical references. | Summary: "Written by a longtime yoga practitioner, *Wild Yoga* helps readers develop a greater awareness of their selves and their environment — their inner and outer worlds — by using a range of yoga and meditation techniques. Includes physical exercises, spiritual practices, and personal narratives to illustrate key concepts"-- Provided by publisher.
Identifiers: LCCN 2022049820 (print) | LCCN 2022049821 (ebook) | ISBN 9781608687978 (paperback) | ISBN 9781608687985 (epub)
Subjects: LCSH: Yoga--Therapeutic use. | Nature, Healing power of. | Spiritualism. | Environmental ethics--Meditations.
Classification: LCC RM727.Y64 W55 2023 (print) | LCC RM727.Y64 (ebook) | DDC 615.8/24--dc23/eng/20221101
LC record available at https://lccn.loc.gov/2022049820
LC ebook record available at https://lccn.loc.gov/2022049821

First printing, February 2023
ISBN 978-1-60868-797-8
Ebook ISBN 978-1-60868-798-5
Printed in Canada on 100% postconsumer-waste recycled paper

New World Library is proud to be a Gold Certified Environmentally Responsible Publisher. Publisher certification awarded by Green Press Initiative.

10    9    8    7    6    5    4    3    2    1

For the beloved Earth
~ oceans, whales, forests, songbirds, mountains, bears, rivers, salmon ~
in praise of your sanctity and with reverence for your wisdom.

# Contents

# Awakening from the Edge of Death

The coastal dirt road heading south ends in Punta Banco, Costa Rica. I awaken at dawn to the distant songs of an abundance of birds and take in the vibrant colors and shapes of palm trees, red hibiscus flowers, and a pair of scarlet macaws. Looking out toward miles of untouched tropical rain forest and the vast expanse of the ocean beyond, I feel held by the salty sea's moist, warm air. My eyes fill with tears as mist surrounds the trees.

Once it was like this everywhere: humans living *within* nature, the natural world permeating us. I attune to the songs of insects and animals, the crashing of waves, the toucan screeching in the morning, squirrel monkeys swinging through the canopy in the afternoon, and the ylang-ylang tree offering its scent at dusk. Gently swaying in a hammock, my body relaxes in the rain forest's night sounds. Its ever-changing chorus is loudest after sunset. Cicadas buzz, and many crickets and katydids rub their wings together.

Living in the embrace of rain forest and ocean as the resident yoga teacher at an off-grid eco-farm, I unlearn separation and distraction and remember an old way of listening. Nature and my body speak to me. In truth, they always have. Now I am present enough to hear them.

I have not always been in tune with my body. But once, an illness forced me to listen. I was twenty-one and a semester away from college graduation when I received a cancer diagnosis. Non-Hodgkin's lymphoma had created a nine-centimeter tumor in two lymph nodes in front of my heart. Chemotherapy and radiation were my prescriptions, with a 33 percent chance I could be cured.

After college, I had wanted to travel abroad or live on a ship, but my plans fell away. I held my emotions in until the doctor said I could not return to summer camp in the mountains because the risk of infection was too high. I wept. I would miss the rivers and forests.

As editor of the college newspaper, an A student, and a leader on campus, I valued *doing* things over simply *being*. Of course, doing has value, but I was out of balance. I barely inhabited my body, driving myself like a machine and spending little time in nature, which I had loved so much as a child. Later, I would discover a doing born out of listening.

Being bald felt strange — the skin on my head touched my pillow, and strangers on the street stared at me. Without eyelashes, I blinked a lot to keep out dust. After each chemotherapy treatment, intense nausea and vomiting often made me wonder if death had arrived. Not knowing how long I would live brought my attention to the blossoming of buds and the shimmer of sun on the lake. I relished the dark clouds and gusts of wind of an approaching storm and the sudden bolts of lightning, rumbles of thunder, and pouring rain. Slowly, I began noticing a mysterious presence within me. I wondered if it was God or the Divine. It felt sacred and evoked a surprising joy. I felt loved and began to see beauty in simple moments, each breath a gift.

After nine months, my cancer retreated. I glanced in the mirror at the stubble of hair growing on my head. Two-year, then five-year checkups passed. The tumor did not return. But I had begun to move to the rapid beat of mainstream culture again to work and survive. I was losing the connection to my own sacred heart that I had found while ill. Yet in the wilderness, I felt connected to what I loved most — nature. Everything enchanted me: the night sky, a rushing river, looking into the eyes of deer. In my midtwenties, I went on a fifty-day Wilderness Leadership Semester with the Colorado Outward Bound School. I became a wilderness guide and therapist, partnering with nature to support others in deepening their own connection.

*Yoga* means "union" and comes from the Sanskrit root *yuj*, meaning "to join together." My body, mind, and spirit were not united when I was diagnosed with cancer. I overfocused on everyday tasks and pushed myself to achieve while longing for divine union. When I was ill, I connected to something sacred inside myself. I could feel it even when I was not in nature. Once I was well, I wanted to find this again. Following my longing for the sacred has directed my life and who I have become.

My personal story, it turns out, was interwoven with ecological devastation. Throughout my time at college, I had walked on farmlands and parks and along roads and railway lines that surrounded the campus, where one of the most widely used weed-killing products in the world was deployed extensively. Humans exposed to glyphosate herbicides have a 41 percent increased risk of developing non-Hodgkin's lymphoma.[1] Later, in the rain forest, I felt safe from the poisons our culture inflicts.

I first went to Costa Rica to participate in yoga teacher training after five cold winters as a wilderness therapist in Utah, meeting with groups in freezing temperatures around a smoky fire. Yoga taught me to nurture myself and listen within, and I returned to Costa Rica for twelve winters. My body began to relax and vibrate as I moved in pleasurable ways. New channels of communication opened within me and between me and the natural world. My asana practice deepened. My movements became a prayer of communion with the universe.

## Wild Yoga

Wild Yoga is an embodied practice to help us love ourselves, deepen our relationship with the natural world, and stretch our consciousness. Nature can inspire our movements, align us with our instincts, initiate us into living our soul's purpose, and guide us in tending the well-being of all life. Our bodies are sacred. Marrying the healing practice of yoga — strength, flexibility, relaxation, presence — with reverence for nature, Wild Yoga catalyzes our curiosity to explore our dreams and the mysteries of life and to grow our capacities to live in reciprocity with the Earth.

Asana is the physical practice of yoga, relating to the poses or postures of yoga. Today asana is synonymous with yoga, but it is only one component. Moving our bodies and bringing them into the shapes of particular poses is valuable. Yet the more profound purpose of yoga has always been to become more fully ourselves, deepen our awareness of and relationship with the world, and inspire our actions. For more than five thousand years, spiritual seekers have asked, "Who am I?" and "What should I do while I'm here?" The Bhagavad Gita, or "The Song of God," a Hindu scripture written between 400 BCE and 200 CE, is one of the first yogic texts and takes place on a battlefield.[2] Arjuna, a disillusioned Pandava warrior, and his brothers are exiled from their kingdom, Hastinapura, fighting their cousins to get it back. Krishna, an avatar of the Hindu god Vishnu, helps Arjuna navigate the two paths, contemplation and action, so that his spiritual life can guide him in the world.

Drawn from ancient yogic principles, the philosophy of Wild Yoga emerged mainly through my experience. In this book, I balance the principles of Wild

Yoga with practices and invite you, the reader, to go on a consciousness-altering journey. To expand your perception so you can seek the guidance of greater intelligence. To cultivate your capacity to perceive animals and plants, soils and rivers, as alive and conscious beings with whom you can relate. To listen to your body, the more-than-human world, and dreams and connect with your soul's purpose. These practices can alter the way you live. By enhancing your ability to receive the messages of your body, nature, soul, and dreams, they aim to guide you in how to live as a vital member of the Earth community in service to the world.

In this book, I blend personal growth with environmental and social justice to offer tools to engage with the perils of ecological devastation. Our wellness and our planet home are linked. The Earth needs people who can live their purpose and honor and advocate for the natural world.

Each chapter builds on the previous one, asking increasingly more of you. Immersing yourself in the readings and carrying out the suggested practices will help prepare you for the next chapter, the next step. Spend as long as you need in earlier chapters before moving on to later ones. Take your time.

Get professional help if you need to before engaging further. You are responsible for determining your own mental and emotional preparedness and limitations and the level at which it is healthy for you to engage with these practices, which can be intense and challenging, especially those in later chapters. Ask for support. Be compassionate with yourself.

If you do not feel sufficiently emotionally resourced or have a mental illness or chemical addiction, consider sticking with the practices in the first few chapters rather than moving on.

In part I, I encourage you to return to your instinctual nature, to deepen into your body and listen to the animate natural world. Feel the flow of your heart and receive the love of trees. Welcome your ferocity and listen to your dreams. Live into your wild-bodied nature and root yourself in a relationship with the Earth.

In part II, I invite you to open up to the mystery of what you love and grieve. Experience longing and vulnerability, descend into darkness, and deepen your imagination. Then, let go and be sung back to life from the heart of the living planet and the mystery of your soul and dreams. Sing your note in the universe and join in the world's symphony.

In part III, I guide you to cultivate your erotic nature, listen to your muse, and offer yourself to the world by praying in the dark, dreaming for the world, and protecting wild places. Stretch your consciousness, sense the wisdom of forests and rivers, and offer yourself as a love warrior for the Earth.

The branches of a tree grow from a trunk, and the tributaries of a river flow into the source. I have explored many branches and tributaries. A variety of ancient yogic traditions take a multipath approach. For example, the Bhagavad Gita mentions three paths:

- Karma yoga, a call to action and selfless service.
- Bhakti yoga, cultivating love and devotion.
- Jnana yoga, which strengthens our intellect and provides wisdom.

Each chapter of *Wild Yoga* offers practices to deepen imaginative listening and stretch your awareness. I aim to open you to unordinary ways of perceiving and awaken your inherent connection with the place we all most deeply belong to: the Earth.

In this book, I share aspects of my own story to demonstrate the principles and practices of Wild Yoga and help you gain the understanding, tools, and motivation to embark on your journey, one that not only fulfills you but also tends to the vitality of life. Sharing my personal stories with you — traumas, heartbreaks, challenges — makes me feel vulnerable. Yet I have chosen to tell them because they may offer a place of resonance and ignite the potential to discover/uncover some of your hidden strengths. So many people have been taught to hide their vulnerabilities and act like everything is "fine." Yet facing our pain and discomfort is part of growing, maturing, and being alive. Mysteries are unveiled amid the rupture of what is most precious. I hope reading my stories will give you the courage to be with your tender places.

For most of my adult life, I have witnessed the power of the natural world to heal and transform. As a guide for Animas Valley Institute in Durango, Colorado, and a teacher of Wild Yoga since 2006, what I have experienced in the field is beyond what science or the rational mind can fathom. The Earth is extraordinarily generous, a healer and lover with magic beyond explanation. I call the Earth "she" because she is our mother — the giver of life, food, clothing, shelter, and song. She taught me how to love and has shown me that love is the foundation of any practice.

I encourage you to spend more time in wild places as you engage with the practices in this book if you are fortunate enough to have access. I will offer alternatives if you do not. Wherever we are, we can call the wilderness into our bodies through our imagination, connect to our instinctual nature, and remember the wildlife that once lived underneath cities and towns. Even in

wild places, our minds can imprison us and keep us distracted and disconnected from our bodies. The "work harder" mentality has found me pushing
myself rather than listening to my body. At its core, yoga asana invites us to
inhabit our bodies, so we can love and listen to ourselves and be present with
the world around us.

Some practices in this book invite you to wander in the wilderness. Being
in nature is powerful. Yet there are dangers: extreme temperatures, sun, rain,
insects, snakes and other animals, human predators, and getting lost. Talk to
park rangers or locals to inquire about potential risks in your area. Know your
limits. Do not wander far if you do not have experience navigating the wilderness. Perhaps bring a phone or tracking device for emergencies. Since these
devices are often unreliable, tell someone where you'll be and when you'll be
back. You are responsible for taking care of yourself.

Each chapter of this book concludes with a yoga pose that supports the
theme of the chapter and an illustration drawn by Sarah E. Brooks to help you
visualize the pose. Yoga asana practice provides excellent benefits. However, if
you suffer from an injury or medical condition that may put you at risk, con-
sult a professional and consider whether the poses suit you. You are responsible for gauging your physical limitations. If you are new to asana, working
with a yoga teacher to gain awareness before attempting more challenging
poses would be wise. It is better to build your agility slowly rather than force
or strain yourself. Adjust the postures and do what feels right for you. Stop
whenever you need to. If you experience pain, listen to your body, alter the
pose, or stop altogether. Be gentle with yourself.

Through simple movements that engage the beginner, enhanced by creative concepts that inspire the seasoned yogi, Wild Yoga aims to unite body,
mind, and spirit and invite us to live from our souls. I created Wild Yoga
in partnership with the rain forests of Costa Rica, the red rock canyons of
Utah, and the mountains of Colorado. As I listened for what these wild places
wanted to reveal, I was often surprised by the words that arose through me or
how I sensed each ecosystem influencing my movements. Can you remember
any of the wild places where you have been? What did you notice while there?

Listening is a way we can give back. We can revere nature and resist the
dominant culture by choosing to value life on the planet more than profits
or business as usual. Wild Yoga emerged from the revelations of my dreams,
soul, and experiences in nature. The deep ecology movement, Bill Plotkin's
Soulcraft, Don Stapleton's Self-Awakening Yoga, and other practices and

philosophies also inform Wild Yoga.[3] Marrying self-development with Earth stewardship, cultural revolution, and sacred activism, Wild Yoga aims to serve humans and all life on the planet, including more-than-humans and the future beings of all species.

I dedicate this book to the Earth as a prayer for the healing and restoration of forests, mountains, oceans, and rivers through the awakening and nurturing of our inherent wild nature. May these teachings, stories, and practices offer a path to open your heart to what is most sacred. May they ground you in love and strength. May they restore your relationship with the Earth so that you and your dreams, mystery, and muse may live in cocreative reciprocity with life on the planet.

# Part I

# THE WILD

*I want to live in the twilight country of my wildish self,*
*a deer leaping into moons of light as if summoned,*
*seeking some reason to fall down closer to the earth.*

— RENI FULTON, "MY WILDISH SELF"[1]

# CHAPTER ONE

# Listen to the Intelligence of Your Body

The pool appears on the beach at low tide. I immerse myself and alternate between floating in its calm waters and sitting on the sandy bottom. Mesmerized, I gaze at the waves crashing on nearby rocks. The sea expands to the horizon, and the sun shines on the water. Pelicans fly by in a V; some swoop down and dive for fish. The breeze smells of salt. I speak to the ocean: "You are beautiful. I love you. What can I give you?"

A response arises through the spontaneous movements of my body. I surrender to the tide pool's ebb and flow, gently moving back and forth. I play with balancing on my hands in Crow Pose (Bakasana). Squatting, I place my hands on the sand and bring my knees onto the back of my arms. I come onto my tippy-toes and balance as my feet rise. I hold the pose until I fall, splashing into the water and onto the sand. Wading into waist-deep water, I go vertical and stand on my hands in Handstand (Adho Mukha Vrksasana). My head is underwater. I fall, landing with a gentle splash.

I feel called to the rocks at the edge of the pool. Falling on them while doing poses would hurt. I admire their solidity. They hold their place amid ever-changing currents. I climb atop one and stand in Tree (Vrksasana) and then Dancer (Natarajasana). Both are balancing poses. It is challenging to do these poses on a rock while waves are rolling in. In Tree Pose, I shift my weight onto one leg. Slowly, I place the sole of the opposite foot onto the inner thigh of my standing leg. Then, I move into Tree Pose on the opposite leg. In Dancer, I again shift my weight onto one leg. Lifting the back heel of the opposite leg toward my buttocks, I bend my knee, pull my back heel up toward the sky, and reach forward with my opposite hand. I have done these poses many times on solid ground. Remaining steady on the rocks, surrounded by the chaos of waves, strengthens my capacity to find balance.

Each particular being I am drawn to — tree, water, rock — inspires me to experience it more intimately, and I respond differently to each. For example, when the ocean calls me, I enter the surf and dive under the crashing waves. Once I am out deep enough, in the middle of rolling waves, I float perpendicular to them, offering myself. As they move over me, tiny bubbles emerge after each one breaks. The bubbles touch my skin, caressing me.

After a while, I swim back to the shore and step into the tide pool. And then I climb back onto the rock. Soon I find myself in a Wild Yoga flow, moving from tide pool to sand to ocean to rock. First, I listen to what each place wants to show me. Then, my body moves in response. The tide pool, rock, sand, and ocean take me in. They receive me.

## Return to the Body

To be truly alive is to live from within our body, fully aware. Children, like animals, naturally inhabit their bodies with wonder, joy, and innocence. As a child, I loved to swim in the ocean near my grandparents' home on the Jersey shore. With sand in my toes, salt on my tongue, and the sound of waves intermingled with the cries of seagulls, I knew that I was alive and a part of a grand and exquisite world.

Our dominant culture trains us to be disembodied. Separating our minds from our bodies makes humans less healthy but more docile and obedient to external power structures. When we begin school, we are taught to sit at a desk most of the day. We learn to fall out of our bodies and into our heads, to let our minds rule. We are taught that our thoughts make us intelligent. To survive in school, we learn to ignore our bodies' wishes and impulses, be disciplined, and sit quietly. We go on living our lives from our heads. Losing touch with our bodies disconnects us from ourselves. Tragically, that is what is considered healthy and sensible in our society.

Yoga asanas, the body postures of yoga, have the power to call us back home. To bring us back into the body and show us that being there is essential. I participated in my first asana class in my senior year of college. Through cancer, my body had been showing me that it was no longer willing to live as the servant of my mind. Still recovering from a thoracic-section biopsy surgery, I found the asana class painful and did not try yoga again for many years.

I played soccer and basketball in elementary and high school. I felt strong and graceful maneuvering a ball with feet or hands to the goal or basket. After college, I ran a marathon, joined a US Masters Swimming team, and swam 4.4 miles across the Chesapeake Bay.

Yoga asana was not like sports. It asked more of me. I tried asana again in my late twenties and committed to participating in a weekly class. I longed to be more flexible but usually encountered my stiffness. I felt humbled. My asana practice asked me to show up on my mat and be present with my body exactly as it was. I became aware of the places that felt painful or tense and noticed where I felt disconnected. I aimed to be gentle with myself and accept my inadequacies and discomfort.

Coming back into my body was difficult. I thought the monthlong yoga teacher training in Costa Rica would help me become more flexible, but after a week, my hamstrings were screaming. Trying to force them loose had made them tighter. I stumbled back and forth from my dorm room to class on the jungle trails. Something needed to bend, and it would not be my hamstrings. When I slowed down and reminded myself that yoga is not about accomplishing poses, I relaxed and let go of my expectations. My muscles stretched more easily as my movements began to come from within. In some moments, I felt beautiful as I flowed from pose to pose — like how I imagined the trees, ocean, and moon feel when they are shining brightly.

My asana practice was a choice to return to my body. To accept and listen to it. Yoga is the willingness to show up and attend. Some days, I simply lie on my mat in my yoga practice. I am tired and want stillness. Other days, I need to turn on music, stretch, and feel strong. Listening to your body is vital. Each of us is unique and called to move differently. Yoga helps us cultivate a deep and loving relationship with ourselves. Simple movements and poses can foster flexibility and strength as much as challenging ones.

Yoga taught me how to live at a loving pace with my body. In Costa Rica, the moist heat of the tropics forced me to slow down and embrace my body as an intimate companion. Sometimes I can still get disconnected and become overly immersed in work or other things I need to do. When I lie on my yoga mat and tune in, often the first responses to arrive are silent tears. These tears seem to express gratitude, as if my body is saying, "Thank you for taking the time to be with me."

Connect with your body. Go outside and find a place to lie on the ground. Or, if you are inside, imagine yourself in a wild place. For example, if you are near a beach, do beach yoga. Lie on your back in the sand or insulate yourself with a mat, towel, or sarong. Move in any way your body wants, or be still. Perhaps rock your head side to side as you let your opposite hip rise off the ground and then thump down. Roll onto your belly into Sphinx Pose (Salamba Bhujangasana). Raise your upper body and relax your pelvis and legs with wrists and palms flat on the Earth. Or lift your arms and legs to fly in Superman Pose (Viparita Shalabhasana). Imagine yourself flying over the ocean. What sensations, emotions, or images arise? What wants to happen next? Notice how this place influences you.

## Connect to Nature

Nature lives in perpetual asana. Tree branches, trunks, and roots inhabit unique shapes in a dance with wind, sun, and soil. Monkeys climb, birds flutter, and dolphins ride waves. Yoga poses originated from yogis witnessing nature. Ancient yogis were trying to find the path to restore us to our instinctual nature. Many poses are named after animals. In the wilderness, we can remember how to inhabit our bodies. I feel my body within the body of Earth, deepening my connection to myself and the wild world.

Nature shows us how to do Wild Yoga. Walk in the forest or sit in the desert and watch what trees, rocks, and animals do. Living at the edge of Tucson, Arizona, I watched the javelinas as they wandered near my home. Their movements followed a rhythm — walking, pausing, lifting a leg, and holding it midair. In Alaska, I spent time with the brown bears. They would fish from a boulder — moving their heads back and forth to survey the water, diving in to catch salmon, climbing back on the rock — or play with their young along the shore. Sometimes I embodied the movements I saw. I wanted to understand these animals, discover the motions of my body, and create poses. Each of us can play and pray like the original yogis, trying to find the shapes of our wild nature.

Some movements flow, shifting us from one pose to the next in a fluid meditation, like my flow from the tide pool to rocks to the ocean. When we are in a flow, we can witness how our body wants to move and let it direct us. Allowing your body to move you is the deepest yoga asana. If you can't tell what your body wants, begin by exploring the poses I offer at the end of each chapter, and then ask your body if there is another way it wants to move. When our body directs our movements, they become prayer. Our body is a doorway to the sacred. We may feel ourselves touching Spirit.

Connect to the transpersonal — Earth, Spirit, Mystery — through the presence and motion of your body. Begin with the Earth. Notice where you feel drawn: Is it to the contact of rock, sand, or grass? Or to the sounds of wind, rain, or birds? We can understand wild places by listening to them through our bodies. I have done yoga asana in rain forests and canyons, on rivers and mountains. When we are fully present in our bodies, the places we inhabit can influence our awareness and communicate with us through the spontaneous movements of our bodies. Their energies can enter us and speak through us. Each wild place where we do yoga affects us differently. We can come to know each ecosystem and ourselves and sense the sacred communion between us.

Go out into nature. Or imagine yourself in a wild place. Perhaps do tree yoga: climb into the branches of a tree and notice how your arms and legs intertwine with the tree. Or do rock yoga: balance atop a rock and witness the landscape. Maybe balance in Tree Pose or Dancer. If you are new to yoga, begin with basic Tree Pose. Place the toes of one foot on the ground while resting that heel on your opposite ankle.

Notice how the presence of each place influences your movements and practice. Try practicing yoga in water — a lake, river, ocean, or swimming pool. Choose a safe place. If you are near the sea, do ocean yoga. Do Lotus (Padmasana), Half Lotus (Ardha Padmasana), or Squat Pose (Malasana) in the sand close to the surf. Wait for the waves to reach you. Once they arrive, notice how the sand shifts beneath you. *If the ocean is a safe place for you, swim in it.* Dive under a wave. Float an inch under the surface, perpendicular to a rolling wave. Feel it roll over your body. If the waves are big, float a few inches under the surface. Surf. Swim toward the shore as a wave approaches you from behind. Once it catches you, bring your arms forward over your head and connect your hands. Stay straight. Ride the wave to the shore or roll to the side to pull out. If you can't be with the ocean, go there in your imagination and listen to the sounds.

If you live in a city and cannot get anywhere wild, connect to the natural world wherever you are. Look up at the sky and see if you can feel a connection with the sun, moon, or stars. Feel the breeze or rain on your skin and commune with the trees, plants, or animals near you. Remember the wilderness that lived on the land before it became a city. Imagine what and who once lived there. Be in your body and imagination as you move.

## Attune to the Body

Many of the stories of our dominant Western culture brainwash us into thinking of the body as less than the mind. The Bible tells a tale about the Fall, when humans left their bodies and moved into their heads. Some recognize the story of Adam and Eve as a metaphor for what occurred over millennia in many cultures. Adam and Eve were living in Eden, eating anything they wanted until they ate from the forbidden Tree of Knowledge. This gave them the capacity to think, but they lost the ability to live at one with creation. They covered their naked bodies in shame and exited Eden. When we are in our bodies, at one with nature, we are in touch with intelligence more significant than our minds. We must return, individually and culturally, to listening to our bodies and the Earth, so we can learn, grow, and create in partnership with their wisdom.

Begin by slowing down and attuning to your body. Two yoga teachers central to my life, Brahmanand Don Stapleton and his wife, Amba, created a skit to demonstrate the power the mind can have over the body and offer a way to restore balance. Don and Amba and other yoga teacher trainers at Nosara Yoga Institute, including me, would perform the skit to show people how to reattune to prana, the life force within. We each played a part: Body, Mind, Prana.

In the skit, the Body is happy, following its natural inclinations — eating, sleeping, playing, loving. We can see this behavior in children and puppies. However, when the Mind tells the Body to work harder — gather different food, do extra stuff — the Body gets overwhelmed.

"Relax," Prana tells the Body. "Live in alignment with your natural rhythms. Relaxation is more important than food."

I remember this wisdom when I feel stressed, as many of us do in an unhealthy and traumatizing cultural environment. I lie on my mat and close my eyes, narrowing my focus to my body and breath. I remember my love for and commitment to my body.

Some cultures seem to have maintained a sense of connection with their bodies and the natural world. But even if we don't come from those cultures, we can restore the relationship between our bodies and nature. In my early thirties, I enacted a ceremony in a giant juniper tree in a red rock canyon. I apologized to my animal body for ignoring her to conform to the wishes of others. "I love you," I told her, vowing to listen to her needs and feelings and expressing a desire to get to know her.

## The Mystery Within

There are many ways to listen to our body besides yoga asana. I have studied and practiced Hakomi, a body-centered experiential psychotherapy developed by Ron Kurtz that combines somatic awareness with exploring core beliefs.[1] I have trained in Somatic Archaeology, a bodywork created by Ruby Gibson that unearths memories to heal the past and create a new myth.[2] I engage in body-centered meditation, body prayer, and dance and have developed a way of listening to the body that I call "Listening to the Mystery Within." What arises inside us can be as mystical as a dream. A waking dream is happening within us all the time, often outside our conscious awareness. We can tune in. One of my clients, Faith, told me that she spent years in psychotherapy in her early adulthood healing from an abusive childhood. Her body felt like a dangerous place. She engaged in practices of listening to her body and nature for years. Now she wanders along the coastline near her home in Washington, dancing and communing with the sea. She paints pictures of the images that arise when she listens to her body and makes altars for the ocean of seashells and driftwood.

"I trust my body," she told me. "It heals and guides me and helps me create."

No matter who we are, we can learn to listen to our bodies and track the sensations, memories, images, movements, and words that arise unbidden. We may not know what they mean, but we can honor whatever comes and try to understand. All sorts of things — intergenerational traumas, personal myths, future potentialities — can be locked inside us. As we listen, clues about our pain, emotions, addictions, or life circumstances may be unveiled. Or we may be taken deeper still, receiving revelations about our relationship to the world, our mythic purpose, or our ancestors. By listening, we can connect to the mysteries of life. As we move in our bodies with the images that come, we explore, learn, and invite more.

My friend Doug was initiated by the revelations of his body. Once, he shared a childhood story with me about his father forcing him to return to a job that he had as a teenager. His boss was emotionally abusive. He had quit after his boss verbally attacked him and other employees and demanded they work overtime.

"You don't turn down work," his father said. "Go back and get your job."

In his midforties, Doug developed painful and debilitating pelvic spasms. He had always been a hard worker, but now he could not work, and he began listening to his body. The images that came to him in his dreams and waking experiences were of women. He explored each vision, noticing a felt sense of the feminine in his body. No matter our sex or gender, we each possess qualities of the archetypal masculine and feminine. We need both to live in balance. However, the aspects themselves can vary. For Doug, the feminine was intuitive and heart-centered. As he integrated his feminine side, Doug slowed down, listened to his feelings, and nurtured himself.

The terms *masculine* and *feminine* have gone out of favor, even as archetypal energies that live in everyone and the universe. Yet these opposing energies have always existed, whatever we choose to call them. The Chinese refer to them as *yin* and *yang*. Doug's body gave him a visual and physical sense of his inner feminine, and she let him know he had suppressed her. As he listened and spent time with the images, the pain in his pelvis guided him to imagine what it might be like to be a woman. His pain diminished when he brought his inner masculine and feminine into balance.

The mainstream culture denigrates the feminine and the qualities of the archetypal feminine: nurturing, receptive, interior, gestational, and mysterious. Most people suppress the feminine. Naming her seems necessary, so we remember how precious she is. Listening to the wisdom of our bodies and the Earth is archetypally feminine, as are many of the practices of Wild Yoga. These practices are as necessary for men as they are for women. An essential aspect of the healthy masculine is reverence and respect for the feminine. Healthy cultures honor the feminine. The practices of Wild Yoga are valuable for every human, whatever their sex or gender. The Earth needs all of us to listen.

## Wild Yoga Practices for Listening to the Intelligence of Your Body

I have included practices and yoga asana at the end of this chapter, as I do for all the chapters in this book, to invite readers to integrate these teachings. Yoga asana is key to exploring the practices of Wild Yoga. All ability levels are welcome. Those who do yoga may be familiar with the poses, yet the variations and deep imagination explorations bring a new dimension. I offer basic instructions for those new to asana. Remember to gauge your physical limitations and be gentle with yourself. Go slow; stop if you are experiencing pain. Do each pose alone or as part of a flow. Follow the wisdom of your body.

As you engage in the practices in each chapter, be patient with yourself. To listen in the ways that I am inviting takes time. Don't give up. Be present with whatever is happening. Seek to create a loving relationship with your body and nature.

- Choose a moment in your day, perhaps first thing in the morning. Lie down. Notice what you feel. Turn on your favorite song or soak in the silence. See whether your body prefers to move or be still. Remain still until a movement arises. Notice *how* your body wants to move — perhaps by remembering poses from a yoga class or by making up movements.
- After witnessing your body in the practice above, ask your body how it wants to move and listen for a response. If nothing comes, be patient and keep asking. If the slightest urge to move arises, follow it. Notice what happens next. Are you called to stop or move differently? Follow the urges of your body.
- Then, lie still and notice without judgment how your body feels. Close your eyes. Breathe deeply. Imagine a wild place is holding you. Scan your body from toes to head, focusing your attention on each part of your body in turn. Notice if you feel any sensations. Stay out of your mind. Imagine your body is speaking. What do you hear it say?
- Engage in a daily body movement practice like yoga, dance, or tai chi. As you move, accept your body as it is. If you want to explore more about Wild Yoga using a video, you can watch the twenty-two-minute video *Embody Your Wholeness* at rebeccawildbear.com (or on You-Tube: youtube.com/watch?v=vpWYCuW4Phs&t=2s).[3] Embody the poses that feel comfortable.
- Heal your relationship with your body by journaling. Imagine a conversation between your mind and body and listen to the needs and wishes of each. Ask your body questions. How does it feel? What does it want? Be curious to understand more.
- Experience the world through childlike eyes: wander in nature and imagine you are seeing it for the first time. Connect to a sense of wonder. Notice where you are drawn and how nature influences the way you move. What sensations, images, or emotions arise? Do you feel the place receiving you or revealing something? Journal about what you discover.

## *A Yoga Pose for Listening to the Intelligence of Your Body*

### HAPPY BABY POSE

I encourage you to spend time in nature and explore the poses of Wild Yoga outside. Or, if you are not able, do them inside by remembering or imagining a wild place.

Happy Baby Pose (Ananda Balasana) is a hip opener. It energizes the body, releases the lower back and sacrum, stretches the hamstrings, soothes the spine, and calms the brain. This pose can relieve stress, tension, and fatigue while awakening a childlike curiosity. In addition, regular practice of this pose reduces stiffness in your lower back and hips and helps ease back pain.

*To get in the pose:*

- Lie on your back on the ground (or on a bed if you need extra cushioning). Exhale and bend your knees into your belly while squeezing your perineum (the area between your anus and your scrotum or vulva). Press your tailbone into the ground.
- Inhale and grip the outside edges of your feet with your hands or place your first two fingers around your big toes. If you can't reach your feet, hold your knees instead or loop a yoga strap around the soles of your feet and hold one end in each hand.

- Open your knees slightly wider than your torso and bring them toward your armpits. Keep pressing your tailbone toward the floor to protect your lower back.
- Position each ankle directly over your knees, so your shins are perpendicular to the floor.
- Flex through your heels and gently push your feet into your hands (or fingers or yoga strap).
- Explore the pose by moving however your body wants. Notice what feels pleasurable or evokes curiosity.
- Release your feet, knees, or the strap to come out of the pose.

While in Happy Baby Pose, imagine gravity as the Earth's way of loving you. Let your body be as heavy as it is. Relax into the Earth's embrace. Rest and receive nourishment. Be still or explore movement — follow your body's impulses. Imagine yourself as a newborn babe, having just arrived in your human body for the first time. What do you notice? Ask your body: What feels good? Play. Perhaps roll from side to side.

Close your eyes and listen more deeply. Track whatever arises. Perhaps slide your hands down to your knees and roll again from side to side. Let your nose turn toward the floor as you roll onto each side and release your neck. Move as slowly as you like. Imagine breath and gravity moving you. Invite feelings of ease and relaxation. How little effort can you put forth? Attend to the sensations you feel within your body and listen for what they may reveal.

Playing in Happy Baby Pose invites us to be at home, relaxed in our bodies, experiencing our connection to the Earth. Yet that's just a start — our relationship with the natural world can grow. There is more the trees, water, and rocks can show us, if we are willing to listen. In the next chapter, we will learn how to deepen our perception and offer our attention to nature, so that we may receive its wisdom and guidance.

## CHAPTER TWO

# Deepen Your Ecological Perception

I descend into an ancient canyon in southern Utah. Lying down on a slab of rock next to a creek, I listen to the sound of flowing water and look up at the blue sky. The leaves of the cottonwood and aspen trees surrounding me are starting to turn gold. The afternoon sun is slipping behind the canyon walls.

"Please help me encounter my soul," I say to the trees and the water. "I want to serve the world."

At thirty years old, I had quit my job, moved out West, and come into this canyon to participate in a ceremony of deep listening, a three-day solo fast. My whole life, I had preferred being in nature; I backpacked, rock climbed, kayaked, and mountain biked. I became a wilderness guide and a wilderness therapist. Even so, I yearned to be closer to nature. I wanted to have a relationship with forests and oceans similar to the one I had as a child.

A gray rock glimmers in the distance, calling me to hike up to the perch where it sits on a red rock wall. On the way up, I step on rocks and walk through dry washes, careful to avoid the cryptobiotic soil, the living crusts that hold the desert together, which took thousands of years to form. Once atop the cool rock, I close my eyes and relax, knowing this is where I will fast.

Each day, I look at the red rock walls and down into the stunning canyon below, asking aloud, "What is my purpose?" The desert's response is silence. Sometimes I hear the flap of a raven's wings. Or the call of a mourning dove. Words form in my mind: "You're not ready."

On the third and final day, my body feels weak from not eating. I hike down to the bottom of the canyon to place a rock on a stone pile to signal I am okay to a quester on the other side of the canyon. He left a stone yesterday to let me know he is safe. My heart is beating rapidly. It scares me. On the way back up, I stop every few feet to rest. I wonder, *Could I have a heart attack?* Suddenly I am reminded of when I had cancer. I remember the pressure of the tumor in front of my heart and how difficult it was to breathe. Finally, back at the gray rock, I collapse. Exhausted, I listen, mesmerized by the pounding of my heart — loud, strong, fast.

"What is my purpose?" I ask softly, looking at the juniper and piñon trees covering the canyon. I no longer expect an answer.

"Brave Heart," a nearby piñon whispers. I feel disarmed.

"No, that's a movie." My response is fast, but too late to stop the flood of memories, images, and emotions. Seeing flashes of moments when I was brave makes me feel overjoyed. I dared to speak and take risks. Remembering times when I turned away in fear stirs up feelings of regret. I am unsure who Brave Heart is, but I want to be her.

After my solo, I often wake up in the middle of the night. *How will I live this vision?* I write poetry, tears silently falling. *Is my heart unraveling, or is it coming back to life?*

## Restore Animistic Perception

Listening to the Earth can give us the most essential instructions in our life. I have witnessed many people who have received visions that enabled them to devote their lives to what matters. This may be hard to believe if you have never experienced it. Most people are directed by their egoic minds. The ego can make things happen, but it often does not know what is worth doing. Our ego can accomplish tasks or get others to like us. Yet it may not know who we were born to be or what the Earth wants.

Ancient and present-day cultures of indigenous and nature-based peoples experience the Earth as animate. Animism, one of the oldest belief systems in the world, suggests that soul and spirit exist in humans, animals, plants, and rocks. All of us are the descendants of indigenous peoples somewhere. Our ancestors saw the cosmos as ensouled. It is in our DNA to perceive mountains, rivers, and oceans to be as alive as thunder, wind, and stars. We can reawaken this inherent capacity and "revive animistic perception" with the aid of our wild imaginations, posits writer Geneen Marie Haugen.[1] "The imaginal and animate worlds are related, if not wildly the same."

Some say those who ascribe human characteristics to animals and forces of nature anthropomorphize. But this term dismisses the intelligence of trees, elk, and ravens. Unfortunately, most people fail to see that other beings besides humans have an essence, an inner life. Instead, the dominant culture teaches us to perceive nature as a lifeless commodity. This misperception is at the foundation of our ecological crisis.

In *The Lost World of the Kalahari*, Laurens van der Post writes about living among the Bushmen of the Kalahari Desert. He describes how shocked they were that he could not hear the stars.[2] They thought he must be joking or lying. Once they realized he honestly could not hear them, they concluded he must be ill and expressed great sorrow. For the Bushmen knew that anyone who cannot listen to nature must have the gravest sickness of all.

We must choose to look at and relate to the world as if it is ensouled. Then, we'll see the intelligence of bears, forests, the ocean, and the sun. We can regard nature as alive, engage in a direct conversation, share our most potent questions, feelings, and longings, and listen for a response. New and ancient potentialities can emerge when we sense beyond the fragmented stories our colonized world urges us to live. We may feel grief and rage at the ongoing destruction of so many beloved wild places. Or we may be cracked open to the most healing, enriching, and mysterious encounters of our life, rife with surprising and visionary potentialities.

Yoga aims to awaken us to our relationship with everything. Humanity often forgets about the natural world, but the core of Wild Yoga is the capacity to feel the Earth's body as an extension of our own, to sense that we reside *within* her. We can listen to her, seek her guidance about who we are called to be, and learn more about who she is and what she needs. We can become reciprocal and participatory partners in her creation.

## Listener of Sorrows

Early on a three-day solo fast, Adam spoke to the land about his longing to raise a family. Later, sleeping in a hammock under cottonwoods, he was awakened by loud snorting. A band of javelinas was coming toward him. Slowly, they quieted and settled beneath him. He loved being in their nest.

Throughout the days, a lizard stayed close, looking him in the eyes and doing push-ups.

"Patience," he heard.

A Gila monster walked straight toward him while he was in ceremony.

"Go slow. Take your time. Be ferocious," Adam heard.

A field of humming bumblebees sounded like monks praying. He felt them calling him to return to his Buddhist roots and sat down to meditate.

One day, a turkey vulture came with a massive cut on one wing. Adam felt sad. The vulture's wound reminded him of his own. He cried and began to remember the suffering of his Korean ancestors. He grieved for them.

A black butterfly landed on a branch nearby. Adam saw patterns of blue and orange on the butterfly's wings as they slowly fluttered. As he watched the butterfly, Adam heard a voice inside him. It was like a thought, but not anything Adam would ever think. He heard he was to be *a listener of sorrows*.

"I loved connecting to nature," Adam told me after his solo, "but listening to sorrows does not appeal to me."

Once home, Adam had little time to listen. As the coach of several organizations, he held multiple jobs, and his wife worked a lot too. Months turned into years. He and his wife tried to get pregnant, but they could not.

While hiking one day, Adam heard the rustle of leaves behind him. He turned around and saw a deer watching him. Adam remembered the vulture's wing and the black butterfly. The awe and wonder he had felt on his solo suddenly returned. His eyes filled with water.

He realized he needed to change his life, to have time to listen to nature. So he and his wife reduced their expenses and their workloads. He enacted a ceremony in the wilderness, under the oak tree near where the deer had come. He retold the story of his solo fast.

"It'll take time for me to understand you," he said, "but I'll keep listening."

## Replant Yourself in Nature

Children are enchanted by the flutter of hummingbird wings, the colors of wildflowers, and the sounds of a rushing river. They feel amazement and curiosity and sense their innate connection to the natural world. Do you remember the wonder you felt when you first climbed trees, floated in the water, or watched birds? Recall your favorite moments. Look at the wild world around you now through the eyes of your child self.

I spoke to trees and rocks when I was young. I knew they had feelings and lives, but like most children, I was taught that this perception was just my imagination, not real. I spent most of my time outside, sitting in the branches of a maple or pine tree in my suburban neighborhood. Some days I walked down an avenue of giant tulip trees, hidden in the backyards of two rows of houses, to the grounds of a historic mansion. My grandparents' home bordered the New Jersey Pine Barrens. My uncle took my brother and me hiking, and I marveled at how much life a forest could hold. I loved walking in the dark soil of the swamp with giant ferns growing under white cedar trees.

Studies show that children today spend far less time playing outdoors than previous generations and are more attuned to computers and video games than to the cycles of the Earth. Author Richard Louv coined the phrase "nature-deficit disorder": the idea that humans, especially children, are being mentally and emotionally harmed by not spending enough time in the wild world.[3] Modern culture's disassociation from the Earth isn't new. Yet research shows the disconnect is worsening due to parental fears about their children's safety, too much screen time, and a loss of wild places. Chellis Glendinning calls the systematic removal of our lives from the natural world by the dominant paradigm of Western civilization our "original trauma."[4]

I worked as an elementary school counselor in my midtwenties and created lessons for children to connect to nature, taking them outdoors whenever possible. Some children told me that sitting at a desk all day depressed them, but when they were outside, they felt alive. I worked as a wilderness therapist for fifteen years with anxious, addicted, depressed, and angry teenagers and young adults. My clients lived in the wilderness for two or three months and learned how to cook, make a shelter, share their feelings, and lead the group. Some felt so much healthier that they did not want to leave. In one study, 81 percent of wilderness therapy clients claimed their treatment was effective a year after discharge, while 17 percent said they were still struggling.[5]

Nature is more than our healer. She is our deepest place of belonging. For the last few decades, I have guided others to reattune their perceptions — sensing, feeling, imagination — to listen to the Earth. Our wholeness comes from rooting in the rhythms of nature. We tend to our psyches not by ridding ourselves of pathology, but by replanting ourselves in the Earth and inviting her to guide us.[6] We need to respect her as a living and breathing being with whom we can and must commune. Yet how can people who do not see the Earth as sentient come to perceive that she is?

In this chapter, I combine author Laura Sewall's ideas about ecological perception with my own experiences in nature. I share altered variations of the five perceptual practices she recommends in her essay "The Skill of Ecological Perception" and turn them into six practices.[7] Three approaches are introduced immediately below, and three more are detailed a bit later in the section "Partner with the Earth."

First, be mindful. Increase your capacity to pay attention to the natural world. People commonly go out in nature and stay in their thinking minds — solving problems, listening to a podcast, making plans. Leave technology behind and get out of your head. Be truly present. Imagine you are looking at a wild place for the first time. Learn to be open and receptive to the natural world wherever you are. Slow down. Notice, with all of your senses, who or what is around you. Are there trees, flowers, water, or sunlight? Take note of the colors, textures, and shapes. Observe the movement of wind or water or the dynamics of shadow and light. "Focused attention produces a richness of color," writes Laura Sewall, "a depth of sensory experience, and often means the difference between seeing and not seeing."[8] Bring your full attention to the world around you. What draws you in or makes you curious?

Second, go to the places that call you. Notice which beings or ecosystems bring you most alive. Spend time in these places, maybe for a few hours, a day, or the whole night. Sit in a forest, prairie, or wetland. Take in what and who is around you — trees, a stream, or a red-tailed hawk. Be present with all your senses. Feel the quality of light or temperature on your skin. Track whatever arises inside you. What does this place awaken in you? What do you feel, sense, or imagine? Notice who or what draws your attention and how you feel in their presence.

Third, fall in love with a wild place or a nonhuman, something as small as a ladybug or more immense than a mountain. What is it like to be with the one you love? Does it soften your facial muscles or bring a gentle smile to your lips? Feel your capacity to love nature grow. Look at the wild world with "love eyes." Find a place on the land where one being meets another: ants crawling on bark, the wind touching the leaves, the river lapping the shore. Notice where day meets night. Or the stars and moon offer the sky back to the sun. Perceive the relationship between things — where mountain encounters desert, the ocean meets forest, tree roots mingle with soil. Where one place meets another, look for the love in the space between them. Let the visual beauty touch you.[9]

These practices are best in the wild. Yet Kabir, a man I guided online, lives in Mumbai, India, and found a way to do them in the city. He had lived in Mumbai his whole life and walked by one lone tree in his area without paying attention. Then, for the first time, Kabir decided to sit with it. Looking and listening, he felt drawn to put his hands on the trunk. Others were around. Surprisingly, he became enchanted with the tree and did not worry about what others thought. Connecting to the tree elated him. He began to return each week, walking several blocks to sit with the tree and listen.

## Partner with the Earth

Listening does not always lead to understanding. The messages we receive from nature can be hard to decipher. Six months before my solo quest in the canyon, I wandered in an oak-hickory forest near the Blue Ridge Mountains to listen and see who or what might want to speak with me. I was participating in a five-day Soulcraft Intensive led by the Animas Valley Institute, and the guides had urged us to have a conversation with nature.[10]

I heard barking and looked up, captivated. A squirrel with big brown eyes and a curious face looked straight into me only ten feet from my head. His barking was persistent and emphatic, unlike any I had heard or seen. He maintained eye contact, then moved up and down the tree and along several branches, still barking, before returning to where we met. He seemed neither upset nor injured. He was not trying to get me to leave. Instead, he was trying to communicate something. I just did not know what. I wondered, *Could he be talking to someone else?* There were no other squirrels or animals in sight. His barking went on for more than an hour. Being with him, I felt enlivened. I thanked him aloud.

A couple of weeks later, a red fox appeared walking at dusk on the farm where I lived in West Virginia. He stopped, stared at me from far across the pond, and then howled mournfully. His cry pierced me. After a while, he quieted, turned, and walked on.

"He was probably scared of you," someone said later.

"He was unlike any other fox," I responded. "It was extraordinary."

What were the squirrel and red fox saying?

"Perhaps they were noticing and welcoming your presence in the wild world?" my Soulcraft guide, Lauren, suggested.

I remembered Mary Oliver's poem "Wild Geese" and wondered if the squirrel and red fox had been calling out to me "harsh and exciting — / over and over announcing [my] place / in the family of things."[11] Being with them made me feel seen and like I belonged.

Deepening our ecological perception develops our capacity to live in partnership with the Earth. This is imperative for the survival of humans, the biosphere, and all of life. Speaking and listening to the Earth is foundational, and our imagination helps us. Too bad many are taught to put it away, like an outgrown toy in grade school. Imagination can link us to intuition and an innate emotional affiliation with all living organisms, activating biophilic love for the wild and catalyzing a yearning to be close to and care for nature.

To get started, imagine what it would be like if you were a tree, a canyon wall, a river, or a bobcat. Sense yourself covered in bark or fur. Perceive the world through the eyes of these others. Experience the changing of the day or season. Merge with one of them in your imagination. Or choose another being. Does a mountain feel solid? A river fluid? Experience the world as they might. How does time pass from the point of view of a one-hundred-year-old tree? Or mountains that are several millennia old? Observe human activity from their perspective — roads, cities, cars. See if you can grasp what Sewall calls "timescales far beyond that of a human lifetime."[12]

Amala lives in Lhasa, Tibet, and can rarely be in the wild. As part of an online class, she went on the roof of her apartment complex to wander on the land. She could see a river underneath her building and through the city. She closed her eyes and imagined what it would be like to be the river, moving under and around different buildings and providing water. Soon, she found herself traveling back in time in her imagination, hundreds of years. She could sense trees, grasses, and animals — Tibetan antelopes, bears, snow leopards, wild yaks, sheep, gazelles, and red deer. As the river, she remembered when her waters nourished an entire ecosystem.

After merging with another in your imagination, return to being human. Prepare for a second practice. Feel the rise and fall of your breath and blood pulsing through your veins. Become aware of the shape of your body. Sense yourself as a cell within the Earth's body, a part of her. How are you called to move or be present? Recognize how you are in communion with the natural world and live within and are wholly dependent on it. Feel yourself in an intimate union — like you are every day, whether you realize it or not. Remember how she nourishes you, providing the food you eat, the materials of your clothing, and your home. Lie on the ground. Feel how you are constantly intermingling with and nourished by the Earth. "Being within and 'wholly dependent upon' the body of the Earth," says Sewall, "requires a kind of communion or exchange not unlike that shared with a lover."[13]

For a third practice, talk and listen to the more-than-human world. Speak to trees, rain, or rocks with words, song, movement, or silence. Do not expect a response, but leave space for the possibility. A reply may come as a sign, synchronicity, dream image, vision, memory, or emotional sensation. Listen with all your senses, intuition, feeling, and imagination. Notice what arises within you while in a particular place. Awaken to your visionary or imaginal self, so you can receive images from the Earth through your deep imagination. If none come, invite them. Speak aloud about your longing to receive a vision. Ask the Earth what she wants you to see. Wait. Be curious and willing to be surprised. Notice any shifts in the world around you or in your perception. Be open to whatever comes. If a response seems mysterious, you are on track.

Deep imagery has intelligence. Eligio Stephen Gallegos calls it "a dimension with its own integrity."[14] Our mind can influence our creativity, writing, and art. Yet when we listen to the deep imagination, images do not come from our minds. They arise unbidden in night dreams or daydreams, in the liminal space at the edge of consciousness, and often they do not make sense to our rational mind. We can tell they come from our deep imagination partly because we would not have consciously thought of them. We honor these waking dreams by being receptive to what bubbles up through the Earth into our psyche. We do not analyze or interpret them. Instead, we seek to live and be guided by the mysteries we receive.

Six months after my solo, I did a ceremony to accept the name Brave Heart. I did not understand who she was, but I kept listening as I embodied who I imagined her to be. I did and said things differently. I went to places and had conversations I sensed she might have. I aimed to be more courageous. Embodying what comes to us through listening to nature and our deep imagination alters our life. Meaning comes after we act on what we have been given. Listening for and manifesting these visions is a way we partner with the Earth.

## Wild Yoga Practices for Deepening Your Ecological Perception

Be present to the beauty of the natural world. Invite a conversation. It may take time to understand. Keep listening.

- Remember the connection you had to nature as a child, the places and beings that were the most significant. Did you spend time with trees or lakes? Were you more drawn to rivers or thunderstorms? Close your eyes and return to them in your imagination. Journal about what you discover. Offer gratitude.
- Go on a wander in nature and look at everything with wonder, through the eyes of your child self. Notice what places or beings draw you the most. Do you prefer to be atop a mountain or under a forest canopy? Would you wish to be with the ocean or on a prairie? Where would you go now if you could be anywhere?

- Replant your psyche in nature. Imagine looking at a wild place for the first time. Be present with all your senses. Go to the places that call you. Track what arises inside you. Fall in love. Perceive the relationship between things, where one place meets another.
- Partner with the Earth. Feel yourself as a cell in the body of Earth. Imagine what it would be like to perceive the world through the eyes of nonhumans. Talk to nature. Notice what arises within you as you listen for a response. Invite images to come from the Earth.
- Wander in nature and regard the world as ensouled. Observe what attracts, repels, or scares you. Notice where you feel called to go. Imagine all the beings in nature as alive. Introduce yourself aloud. Tell them what you see in them. Offer praise or a song, dance, or prayer. Listen for a response with all your senses, feeling, and imagination.
- Wander until something calls you. You may feel attraction, repulsion, allurement, terror, or surprise. Or it may seem like you have an umbilical cord pulling you closer. Once the being finds you, tell it what you experience in its presence. Share your most profound questions or longings. See what happens next. Offer gratitude.

## *A Yoga Pose for Deepening Your Ecological Perception*

### YOGA SQUAT POSE

Yoga Squat Pose elongates the spine, strengthens the core, opens the hips, and enhances balance. It helps undo the adverse effects of chair sitting. You might be in this pose while making a fire, cleaning, or spinning pottery. Children often inhabit Squat Pose as they move and play.

*To get in the pose:*

- Start from a standing position with your feet parallel and slightly wider than your hips.
- Bend your knees and gently lower your pelvis toward the Earth. Turn your feet outward as you bring your hips lower than your knees. (If you need support, you can hold on to something stable, like a tree. If your mobility is limited, you can lower your pelvis onto a yoga block or stool instead.)
- Keep your spine vertical and your head reaching away from your pelvis. Perhaps lean slightly forward. If your heels come off the floor,

place a rolled towel or mat under them for support (or rocks or sticks if you are in nature).

- Bring the backs of your arms against your inner shins and lift your chest to lengthen your spine. (If it is too hard to find balance, you can keep holding on instead.)
- Press your hands together into Prayer Pose at your heart. (Do only this part if you have no mobility in your lower limbs.)
- Relax your shoulders and breathe slowly and deeply.
- Return to standing to come out of the pose.

In Yoga Squat Pose, we are upright on our feet, instead of relaxed into gravity like in Happy Baby Pose. Yet we bring our pelvis, our center of gravity, close to the Earth. Alert and flexible, we are ready to respond. Here, it is easy to sense ourselves as animals.

If you like, flow into other variations from Yoga Squat Pose. For example, tuck your head beneath your torso, curl inward, or twist to either side. Place your hands on the ground, jump like a frog, or hop like a rabbit. If you are an adept yogi familiar with Crow Pose, move into it or call in your strength and power with another arm-balancing pose.

Play in Yoga Squat Pose. Perhaps imagine yourself as a monkey swinging through the jungle. Place one hand on the Earth while reaching the other toward the sky. Look up at the hand that is stretching toward the sky. Switch arms, moving them back and forth in unison with your breath. Imagine traveling through the jungle on vines.

Engage in Yoga Squat Pose in stillness. Imagine your feet in the ground, your spine extending into the soil. Your body is planted on the Earth and reaching for the sky. Feel your spine moving through the crown of your head, rising into the stars. Sense yourself as a cell within the Earth's body. Notice if any images, memories, feelings, or sensations arise.

Yoga Squat Pose invites us to take root. As we are nourished by the Earth, we may awaken to the flow of our inner river, our heart aroused. Transported back to the high perch of my solo fast, I lie on the large gray rock and listen to my heart's unmistakable, rapid pounding. The inner river calls us. It needs to flow freely. Our hearts are the ground from which intimacy with ourselves and the world can grow. In the next chapter, we will explore this.

## CHAPTER THREE

# Flow in the River of
# Your Heart Waters

A couple of weeks after my solo fast, I backpack six miles into a canyon in Arizona. Rock walls covered with petroglyphs and cliff dwellings remind me of those who came before. That night, lying in my tent, I can't sleep. Listening to the song of a meandering creek, I am drawn to wander in the dark. Images of tarantulas, rattlesnakes, and scorpions fill my mind. I'm afraid. Yet I want to embody the vision I received — to be Brave Heart. Finally, I unzip my tent and step out.

Soon, I find myself at the edge of a large pool beneath a rock wall. Sitting there, I speak of my longing to free the dam within my heart. Stars glimmer in the still water. A memory flashes from my solo fast: trying to crack my heart open, I had picked up a heavy rock and tossed it on several rock surfaces.

"Please let me feel my heart," I had said.

My heart had felt imprisoned behind a protective shell. I'd hoped cracking the rock would break open my heart, but instead I'd collapsed on the ground in exhaustion.

Now, at the pool's edge, I long to be Brave Heart, but how will that happen if I can't feel my heart? So I speak to the rock wall, the creek, the spirits of ancient ancestors, the cottonwoods, and anyone listening.

"Please let me free the dam of my emotions and cry," I say.

A few tears come. I offer them to the creek and watch them fall into the water. The wind and water respond in gusts and ripples. The light of the stars swirls in moving water.

I make rhythm with two small rocks, one red and one white. Words flow from my lips as my heart mingles with the song and the creek. I speak aloud to the canyon and the pool of water:

An ache in my chest keeps me from sleeping.
Is it heartbreak, longing, or love?

I survived by burying my feelings.
My sensitivity has grown tough.
Let the dam crumble,
Let the river flow free.
Let me cry for the Earth and all her people.

The following day, I return to the pool and look for the red and white rocks. I had left them at the edge of the pool the night before, but now they sit elegantly atop a rock a few feet offshore, surrounded by water. Red and yellow flowers have been placed underneath them. My heart races. Who did this? I have not seen any other humans, and the land is accessible only through a six-mile hike. Could it be the inhabitants of the canyon? Or the spirits of ancestors? Had they heard me? My eyes fill with water. This feels magical and touches me deeply. Mysterious things happen when we are in tune with the living world. They may be clues about the unfolding life we are called to live.

## Deconstructing the Dam

The canyon waters helped me open my heart. Water, our lifeblood, moves in and through us. Born in the womb, we are about 60 percent water. Rivers show us how to flow. But just as they can be dammed, our hearts can become locked up too. Now, when I witness the refreshment rivers bring to those whose paths they cross, I remember to embrace the flow within my heart. Our tender vulnerabilities are precious ingredients of our humanity.

After the river inside me began to flow, I encountered the part of me who is sad in a dream. This one had been hidden most of my life. She held truths that were too painful to feel. Now she began sharing them with me.

A year after my solo fast, I returned to the large rock high in the canyon where I was given the name Brave Heart. In a ceremonial twenty-four-hour solo fast, I honored the inner protectors that surrounded my heart. Their voices were harsh. That is how they kept me from my heart. Their advice: "Shut up. Do not upset anyone. Stay home. Do not take risks. Do not make a mistake. Do not be spontaneous. Do not be a fool. Work hard. There is no time for play. Hide. Be small. Do not show yourself. Be quiet. Do not speak. Do not get close to people. Never say what you feel. Do not feel. Be tough."

"I miss my heart," I told these symbolic rock protectors. "I want to feel." Placing the rocks in a circle around a red *Castilleja* flower, symbolizing my heart, I honored each protector. Then I picked up the flower and cradled it in my hand.

"I love you," I said, creating a nest and placing the flower inside. "I want you to feel nourished and cared for."

I invited the woman inside me who was sad into the ceremony. "Thank you for holding my tears," I said. "Please help me open my heart."

I dug a shallow hole in the ground, pulled up my shirt, and placed my bare belly on the soil. I did not expect tears because they rarely came, but I invited them. Soon, a surprising flood poured through my eyes, and guttural sobs racked my body. I had never cried like this. I am not sure what I was sad about. Perhaps everything. It felt good to release the pain.

Most humans are taught to cut themselves off from feeling, just as we learn to separate from our bodies and the Earth. Yet being with our emotions is the ground from which intimacy with ourselves and everything else grows. Our heart is a wild creature. There is potency in its softness. The heart feels what it feels, even if our mind tries to convince it otherwise. Living from our hearts, we come to know joy and love as well as disappointment and grief.

Return to your heart. Care for it. Wild Yoga is a practice of loving ourselves. Notice when you are shut down. Attune to what your heart needs. Lie on your yoga mat. Place your hands over your heart and ask, "What are you feeling?" Listen. Breathe. Relax.

## Heart Waters

I am on a four-day solo fast in the La Sal Mountains in Utah in late June. Heart-shaped rocks are everywhere. I make an altar for them almost two years after I made the nest for my heart. Splotches of snow cover the gray peaks in the distance. I see the bright red crowns of flickers everywhere and love watching the unique rhythm of their flight.

A few days earlier, I had dreamed I was about to get married, but I was not sure to whom. Each day now, I ask the land who this person is, and heart-shaped rocks appear in varying sizes and colors. Memories come too, along with the stones, of times I ignored my feelings and did what others wanted or stayed in unhealthy situations. I realize I have abandoned my heart for much of my life. Yet that is who the dream wants me to marry: my heart.

I flash back to the red rock canyon where I received the name Brave Heart and where I made the nest for my heart a year later. On the second anniversary, I returned again. In another ceremonial twenty-four-hour solo fast, I dug a small hole near where I had made the nest with the *Castilleja* flower. I placed offerings in it — beads of jade, ruby, and amber; blood and hair. I slept nearby, and when I awakened in the morning, to my surprise, it was empty. The beads were gone.

My heart leaped. Was it the inhabitants of the canyon? The spirits of ancestors? I was in awe and deeply touched. It felt like something had received my gift and maybe appreciated it.

Later, lying on the large gray rock, I began to sing. I often sing when I am alone in nature, but this time a particular song seemed to be coming through me — a song bringing my soul's longing to life.

> You say my name is Brave Heart, so teach me how to love.
> Teach me how to love, Earth, teach me how to love.

> Teach me how to give love in the way a being calls.
> Teach me how to feel love, that warm glow inside.
> Teach me how to receive love and accept a helping hand.

> You say my name is Brave Heart, so teach me how to love.
> Teach me how to love, Earth, teach me how to love.

> I don't want to live in fear of hurting or being hurt.
> Although that may happen, I want to live in love.
> Love that comes and love that goes, like a house with an open door.

> You say my name is Brave Heart, so teach me how to love.
> Teach me how to love, Earth, teach me how to love.

> Teach me to forgive, Earth, that miracle you live each day.
> I want to forgive myself, Earth, for all that I am not.
> I want to cherish life, Earth; feel all the beauty that surrounds.

> You say my name is Brave Heart, so teach me how to love.
> Teach me how to love, Earth, teach me how to love.

Now, in the La Sal Mountains in Utah on my four-day solo fast, I sing to the flickers, the robin redbreasts, the chipmunks, red ants, butterflies, and deer. I sing to the place where I sleep, which I call the enchanted forest. It called me to solo here. Each night, the fragrance of spruce permeates the dark grove, and I lie in my sleeping bag praising these trees.

One night, I have trouble falling asleep. I feel nauseous, and this reminds me of when I had chemotherapy. The night before, I had dreamed about a bald woman who looked like me when I had cancer more than ten years earlier. In the dream, I had kicked her out of my tarp. Now, in my imagination, I invite her back in. She has come to make me aware of how cancer hurt me. I always focused on the gifts of my illness, but she reminds me of how it felt to be cut open, have my blood poisoned, and be so nauseous that I thought I was dying.

The spruce grove holds us. The next night, the bald woman reminds me that cancer had been in front of my heart and came partly from pushing myself, believing I was worthy of love only if I earned it — helping others, working hard. I invite the young child of me and feel tender as I hold and listen to her.

On the third day, a thunderstorm rages, and I feel vulnerable high on the mountain. The lightning strikes are close. With the storm come flashes of other times in my life when I felt powerless. Situations or relationships that hurt my heart and put my well-being at risk. Unconsciously, I had oriented myself around what others wanted in order to love and be loved, make relationships work, and be who society taught me to be. Feeling love had become mixed with pain. I did not trust my longings. My heart is precious, yet somehow, I had learned that giving and receiving love requires me to disregard myself. Now I am being called back home to commit to my heart.

The storm passes, and the sun comes out. A few flickers gather. It is almost sunset. I bathe in a small creek and put on the white lace shirt I bought a few days earlier in a secondhand shop. I create a ceremony and speak vows.

"I'm sorry I did not honor you," I say to my heart. "You are beautiful, and I promise to love and listen to you."

Being with the sadness in my heart brought me back to life. Are there walls around your heart that protect or imprison you? Our hearts seem more willing to share their secrets once they trust we will honor them. Our hearts carry us back to ourselves and teach us what we love.

## Heart Song

Chris heard music coming from the ground on a five-day program near Capitol Reef National Park in Utah. Chris was a musician but had not played his guitar in a while. He picked up a stick, hit it against his hand, and then placed it close to his ear. Chris listened to the vibration: *Wa-ha-esh-wa*. He spoke the sound and loved how the syllables felt coming out of his mouth.

Chris hoped to share his discoveries with his children. But instead, back home, he struggled to find the connection he had felt on the land. Chris worked long hours as a traveling surveyor. He lay awake at night feeling sad and alone, reminding him of his childhood. His parents had often left him with other families or babysitters. Each night, the loneliness haunted him. He comforted his inner hurt child.

"I am with you," he said. "I won't leave."

He found music that soothed him and listened to it. Slowly, his heart began to mend. He wandered into nature to reconnect with *Wa-ha-esh-wa* and returned to where he had first picked up the stick. He found another, hit it against his hand, and placed it close to his ear. He shared the playfulness he felt in nature with his children. They began making music together in the park each weekend. And one day, Chris's guitar called to him. Now that he knew how to listen, songs came to him. He learned how to express the wild sadness of his heart through music.

## Rivers

I am in love with wild water. Oceans and rivers reconnect me to my heart. On my first multiday raft trip, I look up at the stars, planets, and galaxies twinkling in the night sky, framed by the dark silhouettes of red rock walls. We are on the Colorado River in Cataract Canyon. The river glows dark in the moon's light and laps at my toes in the sand.

After I married my heart, I became a river guide so I could spend more time on rivers and develop the skills I needed to navigate safely. Undamming my heart carried me beyond myself to care for the Earth's rivers.

When I get on a river for days at a time, I feel the river digesting me. "Take me in," I say to the river, "so I'll merge with you and return to myself."

Watching water swirl around rocks and ripple over sand, I meld with the flow as we float through mountains, forests, and canyons. I listen to the currents — cascading in playful bubbles, swelling in a loud rush, ebbing in a gentle silence — for clues about what lies ahead.

Our hearts are inextricably linked to the veins and arteries of the Earth. When rivers are imprisoned, we are too. In the United States, there are seventy-five thousand dams over six feet tall, sixty-five thousand over twenty feet, and about two million smaller ones.[1] Dams kill fish and harm ecosystems. Freeing the flow of our hearts can empower us to save rivers, and their liberation revitalizes us.

After two decades of planning, the largest dam removal in US history began in 2011. A friend lives on the Elwha River near Olympic National Park in Washington. She watched the river ecosystem come back to life.[2] Her eyes glowed as she told me about recolonizing fish. They increased in abundance and returned to the sea. Estuaries were recreated, giving habitat to salmon, crabs, clams, and other species. The Elwha River shows us what can happen when we free a river. We need to restore inner and outer rivers, which are inherently connected, to nourish the parched plains of our planet and our lives.

Listening to rivers is a form of Wild Yoga. Guiding a boat, I navigate rocks and currents in wordless communion. The river teaches me how to move within the tumultuous waters of my life. In a graceful dance of will and surrender, I experience life and death potentialities on and off the river. I aim to stay in the flow, navigate safely, and listen to the way the water wants me to go. When my boat flips and I find myself in the silent underwaters, my instinct emerges and propels me to move toward the river's turbulent surface. Heart pumping, I get back in my boat, go with the flow, and engage with whatever comes.

## Wild Yoga Practices for Flowing in the River of Your Heart Waters

Be patient as you open to your heart. If it feels closed, begin by giving it your love.

- Sit or lie in meditation. Notice, without judgment, what you feel in your heart, how you feel physically, and what emotions are present. If you are struggling with what arises, seek a nurturing presence to help — another human or a tree, rock, or mountain. If your mind takes over, bring your attention back to your heart. If it could speak, what would it say?
- Imagine the fortress that protects your heart. Draw or journal about the rocks or walls that keep you safe or imprison you. Create a ceremony to honor your protectors. Remember times when feeling your heart may have been dangerous. Acknowledge how your protectors

have helped. Consider the risks of inviting them to go off duty or keeping them on.

- Contemplate all the ways to nourish your heart. What makes your heart sing? Imagine living in the flow of your heart. Journal about what that would be like. Finish the sentence "If I married my heart, I would _____."

- Sit or lie in a place in nature where you feel held. Tune in to your heart. Ask if any emotions want to be touched or painful experiences want to be remembered. Be present in a loving way with whatever is revealed. Perhaps move your body or make sounds. Allow your emotions to be expressed. Hold and nurture yourself.

- Imagine your heart as a wild creature. What kind of animal might it be? What qualities could it have — quiet, soft, dark, small? Follow this creature. Where would it take you? Move your body to music or in nature or in your imagination. Become the wild animal that is your heart.

## *A Yoga Pose for Flowing in the River of Your Heart Waters*

### SELF-AWAKENING DOLPHIN POSE

Self-Awakening Yoga, a creative learning process created by Don Stapleton, opens "channels of communication between the mind and the body" so we may learn "what the body has to teach us about the workings of prana," the creative life force within.[3] Through a series of movement inquiries, we slow down, strengthen witness consciousness, and move "in the relaxed way the body was designed to move."

Self-Awakening Dolphin Pose is different from the standard Dolphin Pose (Ardha Pincha Mayurasana).[4] Self-Awakening Dolphin Pose brings fluidity to the spine and unlocks our hearts by gently opening our hips, the gateway to our emotions. This pose strengthens our abdominals and supports our backbone, so our body's movements can come from our center. In addition, the rolling flexion and extension of our spine hydrates our vertebral discs. For a visual, watch the Wild Yoga video on my website or YouTube.[5]

*To get in the pose:*

- Sit on the ground and stand your feet on the floor in front of you with your knees upright toward the sky. Plant your hands on the floor behind you. With your feet wider apart than your hips, lower both knees toward the ground on your right side. Your right leg will be staggered in front of your left, making a pinwheel shape, with a little bit of space between your right foot and your left knee.
- Bring your knees upright again and then lower them toward the ground on your left side.
- Bring your knees back and forth from side to side. Then, relax into Pinwheel Pose with your knees toward the ground on your right side.
- Keep both feet flexed as you turn your torso toward your front (right) knee and place your hands there. (If this hurts your knees, or if your hips are too tight, you can modify by keeping your left leg straight. If you can't sit on the ground, do Self-Awakening Dolphin Pose from a chair.)
- Elongate your spine and torso toward the sky and inhale.
- As you exhale, move your torso in a wavelike motion, emphasizing the wave as it rolls through your spine.
- Dive over your knee while keeping your head and heart lifted above your thigh. Then, curl your spine backward, while keeping your chin toward your chest, as you come up. Imagine you are a dolphin diving into the ocean and then sweeping out of the water.
- Sit back and rest in the cradle of your hips before diving again. Continue the movement and coordinate your breath: inhale as your head comes up and exhale as you dive down.
- Allow the movement to get larger and involve more of your body. To facilitate this, imagine drawing a giant circle with the tip of your nose.
- Let the spiraling movement of your torso become hypnotic. Imagine you are a dolphin swimming.
- Let the rocking begin to happen through you rather than by you. Close your eyes, relax your jaw and face, and enjoy the sensations.
- Once you return to stillness, notice how the movement continues to pulse through your muscles and nervous system.
- Bring both knees upright and lower them into Pinwheel Pose on the opposite side. Repeat Dolphin on this side of your body.

• Afterward, scan your body and notice any pulsing or tingling sensations.

In this pose, imagine you are a dolphin moving between water and air, between dark and light. What is it like to move between the worlds? Can you find your way in the flow? Imagine you are a dolphin swimming in a pod with other dolphins. What does it feel like to travel with a cohort of playful friends? Imagine yourself immersed in water. Swim as long as you like.

While sitting upright in the pose, bring one hand to your front knee and scoop the other hand underneath your back heel. Lift your front knee off the ground with your hand. Lower it back. Lift your back ankle off the ground and lower it. Alternate back and forth between lifting your knee and your ankle. This will take you into a rocking motion. Close your eyes and enjoy the sensation of perpetual rocking. Let go of doing the movement and let it move you. Breathe fully. Let your inhale bring you up, and exhale as you sink down. While rocking, imagine yourself as water. On the inhale, rise up like the swell of a wave. On the exhale, fall, bringing your head toward the ground like a crashing wave. Then inhale and swell again, exhale and crash. What does it feel like to be water? Let your breath and gravity move you. As you rise and fall, perhaps imagine yourself as a flowing river.

Next, when your head is up toward the sky, release your hand from your back ankle and plant it on the ground behind you for support. Raise your other arm to shoulder level off the ground and swing your hand from side to side, anchoring your eyes on the movement of your hand. Release your jaw and the muscles of your face. Follow your hand in a relaxed gaze, eyes open or closed. As your arm sways, imagine any stress or tension in your neck or shoulders flying out your fingertips and composting back into the ground. Feel yourself becoming empty of tension. Imagine your fortress of fear crumbling. As you let go, invite yourself to flow in your heart waters.

Self-Awakening Dolphin Pose brings us back into the flow. We let go of restrictive fears, honor our tenderness, and reawaken to the river of life. Yet opening ourselves to the world exposes us to heartbreak and injustice. To engage, we must cultivate the capacity to protect ourselves and those we love. Many creatures in nature were cleverly designed with faculties to be fierce — screeches, barks, claws, fangs, venom, needles, poison. When we are in the flow of our hearts, ferocity can arise in us too. Do you have a fierce desire to care for yourself and those you love? Or a passionate longing to live in a just world? In the next chapter, we will explore the beneficial aspects of ferocity.

# CHAPTER FOUR

# Embody Feral Female Ferocity

One morning, I pick up my yoga mat at the start of class, and a scorpion stings my thumb. I am in the Costa Rican rain forest, and the place is delightful. Exotic flowers — orchids, lilies, bromeliads — brighten every path. Colorful birds are abundant, like resplendent quetzals, scarlet macaws, and a wide variety of hummingbirds. There are hundreds of species of trees. But when I feel the scorpion's sting, I remember the rain forest's ferocity. My thumb throbs for hours, a continual stabbing until it goes numb. Scorpions are tiny and shy, but they act quickly to protect themselves.

Many creatures in the rain forest are fierce. Caterpillars aggregate in nearby trees. My neighbor was once stung by the venous barbs on their skin. A fer-de-lance bit my friend Katie. Considered the most dangerous snake in Central and South America, the fer-de-lance causes more human deaths than any American reptile. Men who clear-cut the rain forest with machetes are their usual victims. Yet fer-de-lances prefer to envenomate animals they can eat. If they use up their venom on predators, they could starve to death. When threatened, the fer-de-lance vigorously wiggles her tail to signal predators to back off. Striking is her last resort.

Katie had been walking in long grass at dusk and never saw the snake. She felt nauseous, checked her feet, and found two tiny puncture wounds on her left heel. In the hospital, Katie befriended the snake in her imagination and painted her. She felt like the snake had initiated her somehow.

A few times, a fer-de-lance has slithered inches from my feet, but none has ever struck me. So many people kill them out of fear. Yet their lives are vital to maintaining balance within the rain forest ecosystem. They are food for hawks, eagles, honey badgers, and other mammals, and in turn, they feed on birds, amphibians, reptiles, rats, and mice.

Mainstream culture is critical of ferocity — anger, force, violence — even though industrial civilization brutalizes nature and people as it expands and exploits. It is legal to destroy lands and species and illegal to protect them. The state maintains itself by physical force. Citizens are scared into being complicit and lured into consuming. The harms inflicted on women are similar to those perpetrated against the planet. Women in mainstream culture are taught to be quiet and submissive and are often demonized if they are fierce. The dominant culture operates through an unspoken hierarchy. Nature and women, and many others, such as poor or indigenous people, are lower in the order. The system of male domination of Western civilization goes largely unnoticed. It is implicit in cultural norms, traditions, education, and religion. It has pervaded for millennia. Those higher on the cultural hierarchy can be violent to those lower. Those lower on the scale are not supposed to be fierce. Aggression shown to those higher in the order by those lower, even to defend themselves or protect nature, is unthinkable and dangerous.[1] If it occurs, society views those who do it as horrible and punishes them.

The feral ferocity of the rain forest is natural. The fer-de-lance and scorpion act boldly to protect themselves, even when threatened by someone higher on the food chain. In my ancestors' Celtic and Norse mythologies, nature-based feminine leadership was expected, and women were the guardians of the Earth. The Cailleach, a divine hag, is a deity of the living Earth. Freyja preserves peace and maintains the cycles of fertility that keep the world in motion. "What if women could, somehow, reclaim the power and respect that women once had?" writes author and teacher Sharon Blackie. "What if we could somehow dismantle the planet-destroying patriarchy, and recreate a world in which we live in balance?"[2] In her book *If Women Rose Rooted*, Blackie calls women to reawaken to their natural power — not only for their well-being but for the love of our threatened Earth.

If humans had feral female ferocity, perhaps we could restore our instinct to protect life. Someone with untamed female ferocity is aware of the subtle and crude dynamics of patriarchal power and does not give in to it, whether they choose to speak or not. With this ferocity, they can respond to injustice from their wild imagination. In the eyes of society, such people may be of lower status, but they know their value and perceive themselves as equal. Typically they are people with deep empathy for the natural world and all who suffer injustice. They dare to act. What if men and women could become allies and honor and embody feral female ferocity within themselves and the world, so they could be a voice for the Earth?

On a twenty-four-hour solo fast in the rain forest, I ask the land to teach me how to be fierce. That night, lying awake in my hammock, I listen to my heart pound in concert with the buzzing of cicadas, the croaking of frogs, and the rummaging of armadillos. The rain forest feels intense, and I am afraid she will consume me. Pumas hunt at night, eating deer, rodents, birds, and reptiles. I fear one could come after me. At first light, the hairs on the back of my neck rise. Someone feels near. I lie still and close my eyes. To my surprise, I see an image of a bear. There are no bears in Costa Rica. I remember that bear has been coming to me in dreams and waking encounters for fifteen years. She has been trying to coax me to embrace my power. I have not seen it because what she asks of me feels too dangerous to conceive. Bear wants me to be fierce. Yet being assertive is risky for women. Girls are not supposed to be stronger or more intelligent than boys. My feminist friends, men and women, acknowledge that men, as a class, hold more power in our society, and women are at a disadvantage. How power operates in our culture affects our relations. Yoga is, in part, about how we relate. A central aspect of Wild Yoga is to unveil power imbalances and listen to the voices not being heard, particularly in the more-than-human world.

After my rain forest solo ends, bear's presence stays with me. Bears defend themselves by fluffing their fur and standing on their hind legs to make themselves look big. They growl, pound their paws on the ground, and charge toward whatever bothers them. No one is fiercer than a bear mama protecting her cubs.

## Bear

The first time bear came to me, I was twenty-four and on a three-day solo fast in the Rocky Mountains. Lying in the dark, afraid, I envisioned a bear crawling under my tarp and eating me. No bear showed up, but years later, after I understood my deep imagination, I realized bear had been pursuing me. A decade later, after many dreams and visitations, she devoured me mythically, asking me to become more like her.

At twenty-nine, just before my then-fiancé and I were married, we legally changed our last name to Wildbear. We both felt more connected to nature than to society. We did not want to follow the tradition of matching our surnames to male lineage. Our wedding cake did not have a plastic bride and groom, but two wooden bears. Alongside our chocolate Labrador retriever, we imagined ourselves as a family of bears.

In my early thirties, a bear was often in my dreams — climbing a tree, walking in a river, looking into my eyes. Once in a dream a bear charged me. As she sped in my direction, I was terrified. Feeling her fur brush my left arm was exhilarating. I felt her power. Spending time with each image, I learned how bear connected to trees and water and how she walked in the world.

Another time, a bear appeared in a mythic dream:

*Fire spreads through the forest as a bear moves toward a giant mother tree. She enters the tree through a fissure in the bark. Later, as I inhabit the cave underneath the tree's roots, I see the bear has descended inside the tree and is in the cave. There is a crack in the cave wall, and the Earth's heart shines through. Its rhythm echoes. A deep pool in the cave feeds a dark underground river.*

Bear is part of my mythos. Bill Plotkin describes mythos as "an identity embodied in a mysterious story that whispers to us in moments of expanded awareness and exquisite aliveness," revealing unique gifts we bring to the world.[3] Our mythos can arise unbidden in our dreams, deep imagination, or encounters in nature. We may not fully understand what it means. It is a living mystery that guides us. After we are aware, we can intentionally tap into and root ourselves in our mythos, alone or engaged in the world. I return to bear in my imagination and witness her moving between the worlds — the underground river, cave pool, tree, burning forest.

In the weeks after my solo in the rain forest, I feel like a bear — swimming in the ocean, walking down the street, doing yoga asana. I have lived in Costa Rica for many winters and loved the warmth, but suddenly I feel too hot, like I have grown a fur coat in the tropics. I wish to be hibernating in the snowy mountains of Colorado, where I live in the summer.

The feminine deities of Norse and Celtic mythology guided my ancestors to be fierce defenders of nature. Bear empowers me. Yet I struggle. My body and psyche feel the effects of being raised as a girl in a toxic masculine society and the ongoing challenges of being a woman trying to live her mythos in a patriarchal world.

## Girls

"I wish I were a boy," I wrote in my journal at age eleven. Girls had to be obedient, stay inside, and wear dresses. Boys ran wild, played sports, and had adventures. No one told me the system saw women as less, but I noticed my mother and grandmothers caring for children, cooking, and cleaning.

In matriarchal, gender-egalitarian societies, caring for children is at the center of cultural life. "Caring for children and cooking aren't less-than activities," said my friend Kristine. "I love cooking and caring for my son." But in Western culture, cooking, cleaning, and being a mother are seen as less important than earning money or being a doctor, lawyer, or engineer. For example, my dad's mom said my grandfather helped her wash dishes when they were first married, until my grandfather's friend came over for dinner and saw him in the kitchen.

"Why are you washing dishes?" the friend asked. "That's women's work."

"From that day on," my grandmother said, "he never washed a dish."

I loved playing sports, but there were no girl's teams until I was in the fourth grade. I assisted my younger brother's soccer team, chasing runaway balls and preparing snacks for the players. They let me play when they didn't have enough boys. Running up and down the soccer field connected me to my body. Being in nature did too, but I rarely had the opportunity to leave my suburban neighborhood and venture into forests, rivers, or mountains. My brother went camping with the Boy Scouts. The Girl Scouts stayed inside, sold cookies, and did crafts.

The boys in my neighborhood let me play football. I often lost, but occasionally my team would be ahead. Some boys would get upset when I caught a pass or scored a touchdown. They didn't want to be beaten by a girl. They would say mean things so that I would lose my focus. "You ugly, flat-chested girl. No boy will ever want you." If that didn't work, they would push me when I was about to catch a pass.

I cut my hair short and wore a baseball cap. Sometimes I was mistaken for a boy. My mom was worried, but it was 1983, and everyone told her that being a tomboy was typical.

"She'll grow out of it," they said.

One day, I rode my bike several blocks away to a different neighborhood where no one knew me. A group of boys was playing basketball. I introduced myself as Johnny and asked to play. I scored a lot of baskets. Being a boy, I was free to play well. No one got upset.

Girls are taught they are less. A 1992 report analyzing more than 1,200 studies on girls and boys in US elementary and secondary public schools concluded that girls were not receiving the same quality or quantity of education as boys.[4] Girls received less attention than boys from classroom teachers. One study found that boys called out answers eight times more often than girls. When girls did call out, teachers typically corrected them: "Raise your hand if you want to speak." African American girls had fewer interactions with teachers than white girls, despite evidence that they frequently attempted to initiate contact.

Most disturbing is that in US schools, sexual harassment of girls by boys — from innuendo to actual assault — is increasing. In one incident, a boy hit a girl in the face.[5] While disciplined, he said he had the right to slap her because she was his girlfriend. School officials report that to be a pervasive position. Many say the problem is not taken seriously, and there is a "boys will be boys" attitude.

Textbooks ignore women's issues, and women are paid less than men. In 1992, women earned sixty-nine cents on the dollar compared to men with equal educational levels, according to a Labor Department analysis. Thirty years later, in 2022, women earn eighty-two cents for every dollar men earn.[6]

Meanwhile, abuse against girls rages worldwide. Over 700 million women currently alive were married as children.[7] Child marriage is legal in 116 countries and in forty-four states in the US. Nearly nine thousand cases of sex trafficking were reported in the United States in 2017, a 13 percent increase from the year prior.[8] Thirteen is the average age of entry into sex trafficking, a multibillion-dollar industry worldwide that uses force, fraud, and coercion to induce people to sell sex in escort services, pornography, and brothels.

## Patriarchy

"Don't use that word," said my friend Ed, a sixty-six-year-old human rights lawyer. "It shuts down the conversation."

"We need to talk about it," responded my friend Zack, a thirty-three-year-old environmental activist. "And dismantle it in ourselves, our communities, and our culture."

The three of us sat at a picnic table on 28th Street in Durango, Colorado, eating lunch next to the Animas River and discussing the "p word": patriarchy.

"Talk about inequality," Ed said. "Address specific problems."

"Not being able to say the word," I observed, "seems key to the problem."

"Men will see you as a feminist, a man-hater." Ed stood up and walked over to throw away his trash.

"Men and women need to be aware of the subtle ways women are deval-ued," Zack pointed out.

"I agree, but it won't happen if you use that word."

"What words will work to get people to care and talk about it?" I asked.

"When I've seen men be condescending to women, I've pointed it out," Zack shared, "but then those men get upset and find fault with me."

Those in power don't want to be challenged. Nor do they want to talk about it. Sometimes I talk to women and ask them how they feel patriarchy has affected them. Many thank me for asking. They seem glad to be permitted to talk about it. Often, they have not been allowed or encouraged to before.

"I struggle to put my finger on it," Emma told me, "until I talk to other women. Sometimes I think it's me. Maybe I'm too sensitive."

Emma worked for a medical association in a small mountain town. A college professor for fourteen years with a master's degree in clinical biology, she told me about her job as we hiked on a trail in the Colorado mountainside.

"You need an emergency medical technician certificate to work here," her boss had told her. But once she had that, they discounted her prior experience and education.

"Men taught the medical courses," she said. "Most did not have a college degree. The information they gave was poorly explained and sometimes dangerously incorrect."

Once, her boss gave the wrong information about what to do in a cardiac emergency.

"I was careful not to discredit him," she explained. "All I said was, 'I'd like to clarify one thing.' Anytime I had something to add, I made sure I spoke in a gentle tone, but my boss would glare at me as if to say, 'How dare you!'"

"Women aren't supposed to know more," I pointed out.

"I stopped saying anything." She sat down on the trail next to a ponderosa pine to drink water. "I kept withering. My boyfriend struggled too. He would tell me stuff but didn't want me to say anything. The men stood up for each other. Those who didn't respect 'the good ol' boys club' were driven out.... The incompetence was scary."

"Like the incompetence harming the Earth," I suggested.

"I knew someone would get hurt one day, and then someone died," she recounted. "Now the medical association is dealing with a wrongful death lawsuit."

For Emma, a competent medical professional, being shut down by men isn't an isolated event. Gender inequality plagues the health care industry. For example, research shows women are more likely to face medical misdiagnosis than men.[9] This is attributed to two main factors: the medical profession's history of distrusting or downplaying women's reports of their symptoms and a lack of scientific medical knowledge about women's health due to their underrepresentation in medical research. These gaps in care cause an increased risk of missed, delayed, and incorrect diagnoses for women.

## The System

The film *The Feminist on Cellblock Y* explores the effects patriarchy has had on the lives of incarcerated men. Looking through the lens of theorists like bell hooks, it follows a classroom of male prisoners who explore what led them to buy into toxic masculinity and become men who glorify violence, objectify women, and overly focus on obtaining money.

"Patriarchy is when the whole culture is telling us to be toxic masculine," explains Richard Edmond Vargas, the twenty-two-year-old inmate who is the class leader.[10] The inmates share how toxic masculinity led them to incarceration, emotional death, loneliness, and bad relationships.

Patriarchy affects us all. On a solo fast, Sam met the young boy inside himself, imprisoned behind a pile of boulders. The boy helped him realize how he had been held captive by the system from a young age.

"Mainstream culture told me who I needed to be," he said, "and it's not who I am."

Sam spent much of his life achieving in school and then in business. He was successful but felt inauthentic. After his solo, he began to slow down and listen to his inner boy.

Being able to see patriarchy seems key to undermining its capacity to endure.

"Men created education," Kathleen told me. A college professor for two decades with a PhD in clinical psychology, she and I ate dinner at her house in Arizona as she shared her view.

"The doctoral process begins by paying homage to the men who came before," she explained. "Going to university is preparing to enter the system." Although her dean and department chair were women, "everything is bowing to the male-defined structure to get tenure. 'Publish in particular journals, serve on university committees.' There's no time to help the world off campus."

Six years earlier, Kathleen's university invited her to teach. Before that, she had worked for nearly a decade at another university.

"They wanted me because of my achievements. Once here, I was told, 'It isn't good to say much your first couple of years.' Women are supposed to be demure. To speak with a certain cadence," she said, mimicking the tone. "There was a woman who openly shared her ideas," Kathleen added, scooping some salad onto her plate. "She was taken down."

Her colleague, Mary, had worked at a university before and was intelligent and highly motivated. Her teaching, service, and scholarship were outstanding. She was on track for tenure — until three other women set out to portray her as irresponsible.

"They were punishing her for challenging the system," Kathleen explained, "for speaking."

In patriarchy, women often punch down on those with less power, usually other women, to gain male approval or raise or maintain their position in the hierarchy.

"I received tenure," Kathleen said. "But after what happened to Mary, I realized I had been silencing myself."

Rich men built the economic system.[11] These privileged few make the rules and reap the significant benefits. Only a small number of men have access to substantial power. Most men find some access to power by dominating women. Patriarchy is about domination. Women in this system are often the targets of male violence. Thirty percent of women worldwide are affected by intimate partner violence.[12] Women suffer the highest rates of severe and repeated domestic violence.[13] Of all the women murdered in the US, about one-third were killed by an intimate partner.[14]

## Ferocity

Dismissal is the most common response when I say something to challenge power. I have also been tone policed, put down, and discredited, and I have silenced myself out of fear or exhaustion or a sense that speaking up would make things worse. Bear teaches me to be stealthy and clever. To risk adverse responses in strategic moments. I seek situations where I can speak the truth and be heard. I do not take what happens personally when power dynamics are at play.

Anger is a natural response when the Earth's or our boundaries are broken. Anger is a sane reaction to structural discrimination, a signal worth listening to. Ferocity is generous. It shows care for our world, as opposed to apathy. When we are fierce, we honor our feelings enough to share them and express love for the world by telling the truth.

Kathleen, the college professor, began to value ferocity after working with a Joan of Arc figure in her dream.

"I thought she was an immature adolescent," Kathleen said, "but she's helping me feel my rage." Kathleen was learning to discern between structures that serve and those that do not as she sought to dismantle unjust systems.

"Imagine what we could do if we didn't have to prove ourselves within these inane systems," she told me. "Perhaps we could address what matters."

Wise ferocity begins with gentleness. Like bears, we can go into the cave, hibernate, and receive a vision to guide our actions. Emma left her job with the medical service after seven years and went on a quest in the wilderness. Every sunset, the light bathed her in an unconditional love beyond any she had known. It mirrored an inner light in the center of her heart, which Emma came to know as her deepest self. Now she cultivates relationships where she can feel her light and speak the truth.

Bear is lovingly fierce. He challenges me to feel anger, listen inside myself to understand what it is about, and then act or speak. Sharing difficult truths is hard. In my early thirties, I began participating in council ceremonies. After I shared, I would beat myself up. *Don't say anything.* I would silence myself. Women who assert their ideas are often disparaged.

In *Rage Becomes Her*, Soraya Chemaly illuminates this dynamic. In a survey of 248 employee performance reviews from 180 managers in the tech field, managers were critical of 58.9 percent of men's behavior and 87.9 percent of women's behavior. Some feedback was helpful, but women were repeatedly reprimanded with comments like "Pay attention to your tone," "Stop being judgmental," "Let others shine," "Step back," and "Be patient." The word "abrasive" was used in 71 of 94 critical reviews received by women. Chemaly posits that women should focus, not on anger management, but on the strategic use of anger.[15]

Bear calls me to write and speak, even in a culture where men wrongly assume they know things and women do not. When I am angry, I find a place to wield an imaginary sword. Dancing on a large rock that overlooks an expanse of the Sonoran Desert, I wave my arm through the air, slicing, cutting, and thrusting. Author Maureen Murdock said, "To destroy the myth of inferiority, a woman needs to carry her own sword of truth, sharpening her blade on the stone of discernment. Because so much of women's truth has been obscured by patriarchal myths, new forms, new styles, and a new language must be developed by women to express their knowledge. A woman must find her own voice."[16]

Closing my eyes, I feel bear navigating the underground river. Living in the echoing heart chamber of the Earth, he maneuvers through the burning forest. "What can I do?" I ask him. Sometimes I hear, "Let it go" or "Focus on what you can change." Other times, he gives me ideas for ways I can engage, speak, or write. My words are my sword.

## Wild Yoga Practices for Embodying Feral Female Ferocity

Strengthen your capacity to call forth your ferocity and find the courage to express it.

- Reflect on wild places or beings you have encountered who are fierce. Remember how you felt in their presence. Imagine what it would be like to be them. Move or breathe as they would.
- Go on a wander in nature. Find a being or place that embodies ferocity. See the world through their eyes. Ask them what they bring to the world.
- Remember fierce places or beings you have encountered in your dreams. How did they make you feel? Reflect on each one. What was unique about their ferocity? Pick a dream being to embody in your imagination. Move as they would. Go on a wander in nature and let them guide you. Imagine what their kind of ferocity could bring to your life.
- Choose an animal that aligns with your sense of ferocity. Wander in nature beside them in your imagination. Where would they go? What would they do? Make sounds — howls, cries, growls. Let this guide you to finding your voice and expressing your ferocity. Notice if the sounds you make want to turn into words or a song or lament.
- Do you have a mythic image that guides you to be fierce? If so, wander, commune, dream, and embody it. Discover what your mythos wants you to bring to the world. If not, wander in nature and ask

your dreams to offer you a guiding image or story about the particular way you are called to be fierce.

- Consider ways you have been devalued if you are a woman or anyone low in the dominant culture's hierarchy. Pay attention to how others are treated. For example, if you are a white woman, you are likely to be treated better than an indigenous or African American woman. Notice how humanity treats nature. Listen to the voices of forest and ocean and mountain. Attune to the everyday violence that is normalized.

- Look around at the abuses no one registers. Why are they overlooked? Do people ignore what is happening or blame others or themselves? Observe similar injustices, like injustice against women and injustice against nature. Call in the animals, dream beings, and mythic images that have guided you to be fierce. Ask them to help you take strategic risks to speak truth to power, organize collectively, and stop the harm.

## *A Yoga Pose for Embodying Feral Female Ferocity*

### WARRIOR I POSE

Warrior I Pose (Virabhadrasana I) will stretch the front side of your body and develop strength in your legs, core, and back. It can help build focus, power, and stability. Begin by feeling the solidity in your body. Imagine jumping your feet apart. Feel your willingness to engage with the world and stand firm.

*To get in the pose:*

- Start in Mountain Pose (Tadasana), facing the long side of your mat. Step or lightly jump your feet three and a half to four feet apart as you exhale.
- Raise your arms perpendicular to the floor (and parallel to each other). Reach your hands toward the ceiling while drawing your shoulder blades down your back, toward your tailbone.
- Turn your left foot in forty-five degrees to the right and your right foot out ninety degrees to the right.
- Keeping your right and left heels aligned, rotate your torso to the

right, squaring the front of your pelvis with the short edge of your mat.

- With your left heel anchored, bend your right knee over your right ankle, so your shin is perpendicular to the floor. Bring your right thigh as close to parallel to the floor as possible.
- Reach up through your arms and lengthen your torso, lifting your rib cage away from your pelvis. Ground your back foot and keep your head in a neutral position as you gaze forward.
- To come out, straighten your right knee, turn your torso and feet toward the long side of your mat, back to your original position, and release your arms.
- Turn your feet to the left and repeat the pose on the opposite side.

Today, patriarchy is waging war. Find the fire within yourself to help empower you to engage. The Bhagavad Gita takes place on a battlefield. Multiple Warrior Pose variations — all described below — build heat and strength and can assist you in imagining alternate ways to interact. After Warrior I, try Humble Warrior, Warrior II, and Reverse Warrior. In all these variations, keep your front knee bent and your shin perpendicular to the ground. Engage your quads. Sink your hips as low as is comfortable. Finally, transition into Warrior III.

To do Humble Warrior (Baddha Virabhadrasana), start from Warrior I Pose, then release your arms and bring them behind your back. Interlace your fingers. Reach your clasped hands down your back and puff up your chest, then bend your upper body to the inside of your right knee. Your clasped hands and arms move up toward the sky. The crown of your head reaches toward the floor.

To transition into Warrior II, turn your hips and torso to face the long side of your mat. Keep your front knee bent and your shoulders over your pelvis. Lower your arms and extend them straight out from your shoulders. You may slide your back foot a slight distance away from your front foot, but keep your front knee above your front foot.

To do Reverse Warrior (Viparita Virabhadrasana), raise your right arm overhead and let your left arm slide down your back leg. Keep a light touch on your left leg. Open your heart to the sky.

Square your hips and return to Warrior I Pose to prepare for Warrior III. Release your arms to your sides. Straighten your right leg and lift your left leg behind you. Bend your upper body forward, keeping your back straight.

Bring your upper body and lifted left leg parallel to the floor. Keep your arms by your sides or swing them ahead in line with your ears, like Superman.

To come out, drop your left foot next to your right and return to Mountain Pose. Then, repeat the sequence on the other side.

Doing Warrior Poses builds stamina. Each variation offers a different perspective. In Warrior I, imagine yourself standing strong, ready to engage with the world. In Humble Warrior, bow to the enemy. Feel your openness to finding a resolution. In Warrior II, approach the situation anew as you open your hips. In Reverse Warrior, engage by exposing your underbelly. In Warrior III, find the inner calm and balance needed to face the outer world. Embodying Warrior Poses increases strength and flexibility and awakens grace in battle.

Make up a Warrior flow of your own. Explore the unique warrior that you are. Notice what movements or positions evoke power. Remember your dreams and encounters with nature. Call in your guides to ferocity. Bring them into your Warrior Poses. Invite them to help you move, imagine, and offer yourself. Change whatever you want. Imagine yourself being as fierce as those you have encountered. Notice how bringing in these images from the depths can empower you. Move, see, and be the warrior. Imagine facing injustice, responding to structural discrimination, or stopping the cruelty inflicted on the natural world. Play and explore what the warrior of you would do.

Warrior Pose helps us feel ferocity and engage with the world's challenges. It can give us the strength and flexibility to face oppression, become guardians of the Earth, or fight for what we care about. Yet ferocity alone is not enough. We need to strengthen our capacity to love in order to engage with the world. Trees are the most loving beings I know. They taught me how to give and receive love. They can help us all. We will explore how in the following chapter.

# CHAPTER FIVE

# Receive the Love of Trees

I embrace a giant ponderosa pine overlooking the Utah desert and breathe in the scent of butterscotch. As I climb and reach for the next branch, the rough texture of the trunk touches my skin. I want to feel close to trees like I did when I was young. Pausing, I wrap my arms around the tree and tuck my nose into the bark. I feel nourished and am transported back in time.

As a child, I lived in trees. The giant ash tree, rising well over one hundred feet in my backyard, was the center of my world. Down the hill in a grove of pines, I played in pine needles, sometimes climbing to the tippy-top of a tree, arms wrapped around the thin tip, the weight of my body gently swaying me from side to side. In summer, I crawled out on the farther branches of the cherry tree, eating more fruit than made it into my basket for Mom's pie. The maple tree in the front yard is where I went to hide. Behind walls of leaves, I could see all, and no one could find me.

Before anyone taught me otherwise, I sensed trees had feelings and inner lives. I knew they were living beings with whom to relate. They looked after me. I felt like they could sense what was happening inside me, more than other humans could. They seemed to understand the secret wounds and traumas of my childhood, the ones my mind did not remember or know how to bear. I felt terrible sometimes, but I didn't know why. The humans around me acted like things were fine, but something felt wrong. I didn't know what it was or how to talk about it. But whenever I was in the trees, I sensed they understood me. As a child, I turned to the smell of pine and bark instead of human skin or voice when I hurt. I climbed into the branches of these elders to be held again and again. I trusted their love and wisdom. They nurtured me.

Although I could receive their love, loving myself was a struggle. In my early thirties, I returned to the trees for help. Feeling their love, I remembered my wounds and developed the capacity to hold myself. Friends and therapists helped too. Yet humans get caught in their dramas. Trees are present and continually listening. Some people judge those who talk about their wounds, yet all people hurt. Those who pretend to be okay are often the most wounded. How could anyone be intact, raised in this culture? Living in it every day? Being loved and held gives us the strength to face what hurts. What happened in our childhood is often buried. As children, we are too busy surviving to feel.

Yoga is about relationships, and love is the foundation. Love is as essential as oxygen. People seek it from others but have difficulty giving it to themselves. The capacity to love heals and enables us to care for others and give to the world. The axiom "Love yourself" rarely comes with instructions. It may feel impossible or exhausting. Many people are taught to buck up rather than to feel, but softening our hearts is essential to love. An affinity for trees is forever inside me. Wild Yoga is rooted in the love of trees.

## Sacred Citizens of the World

Few acknowledge the intelligence of trees. Sacred citizens of the world, trees give us oxygen and inherently understand that they are only as strong as the forest surrounding them. Trees are highly communal and cooperative, sharing nutrients across species. Scientific evidence shows they recognize their kin and favor them with the lion's share of their bounty, especially saplings and those most vulnerable.[1] They care for everyone in their community, sometimes nourishing the stump of a felled tree for centuries. They provide a home to many animals and insects. Linked in an underground tapestry, they nurture the health and well-being of the ecosystem. Yet all over the world — Canada, Alaska, Russia, Brazil, Madagascar, Indonesia, the Philippines — forests are under assault. The equivalent of thirty soccer fields disappears every minute.[2] By treating forests like lumber factories and clear-cutting them for industrial agriculture, our dominant culture is ripping out the lungs of the planet.

In the face of this insanity, it is easy to understand why humans struggle to love themselves and why they may view themselves as raw material, only as valuable as what they can produce or achieve. In college, before I had cancer, I treated myself that way. Love was something to be earned. I became a psychotherapist to hold others the way the trees held me. It was easier to hold others.

And more difficult to love myself, especially when I made a mistake or others were upset with me. In those moments, I would ask the trees for help. I would lean my back against one of their trunks or lie on the ground, looking up at their branches waving in the wind or sparkling in the sun. Then, I began to climb trees again, like I did when I was a child. Wrapping my arms around the trunk, I would stay perched for hours — whispering, singing, resting. I could let go of whatever was going on in my life or my head when I was with trees. In their branches, I could receive their love.

I share my fondness for trees to inspire you to cultivate a relationship with them. Befriend the ones that live near you. Spend time with them. Ask them questions and tell them what you love about them. If you struggle to love yourself, tell the trees and ask them for help. Perhaps sit with your back against their trunk and see if you can feel their support. Imagine your heart connecting to the heart of a tree.

## Apprentice to Trees

When I apprenticed myself to trees in my early thirties, I spoke aloud to them and honored their capacity to love one another and support all of creation. I consciously sought their help, particularly in moments when I was struggling. They reparented me and forever planted my heart in the Earth.

No human parents are perfect, even those who aim to give their child everything. All parents wound their children somehow, because they are wounded. It may be hard to name or pinpoint the hurt we have received. Sometimes it lurks hidden and amorphous inside us, affecting our relationship with ourselves and everyone else.

As a wilderness therapist, I facilitated troubled families in transforming their relationships. I wished my family could have this kind of cathartic breakthrough and be emotionally honest. Once, when I was feeling brave and curious, I asked my parents to tell me about their most incredible pain. My dad spoke first. He talked about the death of his mother a decade earlier and how devastating it was to be without the one person who had always loved him most.

When it was her turn, my mom's eyes filled with water. "You," she said. "I was distraught when you had cancer, but there have always been difficulties — your wedding and many times when you were growing up."

A familiar crushing ache arose in my chest. I used to think it was guilt, but now I know it was shame. Guilt arises if you feel you have done something wrong. Shame is when you feel that *you* are wrong. I wanted to end the conversation, but I had asked, so I took a deep breath and resolved to listen. "What was painful about it for you?" I inquired.

"You've always done things your way," she said. "You didn't care what I wanted." She retold her perspective of my wedding. I remembered something she had said then: "Weddings are for the bride's mother." My husband and I had designed our ceremony to take place in nature with flutes, drums, dancing, poetry, and the vows we had written. My mom had wanted something more traditional. She had tried to buy me a thousand-dollar dress. I preferred a simple one I found in a bookstore. Our views about my wedding mirrored our opposing perspectives of life.

"You have always been too strong-willed," she said. "I listened to my mother."

She had. She had chosen to become a teacher at her parents' suggestion. As a child, I felt trapped. I could be who my mother wanted, or I could be myself. I felt wrong if I chose myself. Nevertheless, I usually did, and consequently, I lived with the shame.

My mom is a strong and courageous person who has many admirable qualities. I have had no cause to doubt her love for me. She has always been a devoted mother who ensured I was well cared for and received a good education. My mom and I both loved to climb trees as children, and we loved to read. Yet she also loved to shop, and I hated malls. I liked sports and being outside. She found those things unladylike. In college, I was interested in things neither of my parents liked. Acting class to help me be less shy. Nature, philosophy, psychology, spirituality, writing, and helping people with disabilities felt meaningful. In college, my parents wanted me to major in math, become an engineer, and make a lot of money.

Being with trees helped me to trust myself. I could think or feel whatever I wanted, and they did not need me to be anything other than who I was. They seemed to delight in my presence, precisely as it was, and were curious to learn more. The trees I visited regularly seemed to look forward to being with me and enjoy listening to what I said. I never felt like I had to edit for fear of how my words might impact them. Sometimes they told me about their lives. I found them fascinating.

## Receiving Love

Listening to my mom voicing her pain triggered mine. A part of me had grown to believe that I must be unacceptable and that to be myself was to bring pain to others. Later that afternoon, I hiked to a particular juniper tree in a remote juniper-piñon forest in Utah. I had visited the juniper several times a week for more than a year, never encountering another human. It was near my home but far off any trail. Leaning my back against the tree's trunk, I felt held. This tree had my back. Looking out, I saw the world from its vantage and watched the sun light up some small grasses that danced in the breeze.

"I'm having a hard time," I said. "I'm not loving myself."

"I love you," the juniper responded. Its words arose in my mind, and I felt their truth in my body. The juniper stood solid, its bark against my back. The sweet and woody scent enraptured me. Then, taking in the shape of its branches, I relaxed.

"It hurts," I told the juniper, "that I can't be myself *and* be loved."

"You're a good person," the juniper said, "with a beautiful heart." Again, the words arose in my mind, and I felt them in my body.

"You see me," the juniper said. "And all of nature." Being loved by the juniper felt lovely. I had felt that way with other trees too.

"Why is it so hard with humans?" I asked.

"They're crazy," the juniper said. "You can't take anything personally."

"Easy for you. There are no humans out here."

"Easy? No, heartbreaking. Roots and mycelium are not the only things connecting trees. We all feel what happens to every tree."

I was silent for a long time, trying to sense the breadth of connection trees have with one another, when suddenly a memory arose — my mom's mother, returning home from a visit with her mom, my great-grandmother, who lived in a nursing home. My grandmother was often distraught and in tears when she returned. My great-grandmother focused on things she thought my grandmother did wrong. My grandmother felt like a bad daughter. I began to realize the pain I had felt with my mom growing up was not only my own: it was generational. This understanding gave me the capacity to love my mom and myself — and the women who came before us.

Later, I understood how my mom had been oppressed in our patriarchal society, as were the other women in my family and the generations before her. At home raising children, women depended primarily on their husbands for finances and survival. They likely felt little power over their lives. Sometimes a daughter is one of the few places a woman can vent her frustrations or feel entitled to some amount of control. Of course, this realization does not make it okay. Or make it hurt any less. Yet understanding my mom's response within the sociopolitical context reminds me that our wounds most often originate within the structures of society.

I closed my eyes and felt my heart held as my back rested on the juniper's trunk.

"I send blessings of love to my maternal lineage," I said. "Please heal my feminine ancestral line."

Cultivate relationships with trees. Befriend one and be open to receiving love. Tell the tree how you feel in its presence and what you love about it. Visit often and make offerings — poetry, music, art, feathers, beads. Share your life story or tell the tree about other trees you have known. Perhaps tell the tree about when it has been most challenging for you to love. Praise the tree's ability to love. Ask for help. Go to the tree when you do not love yourself, when you are triggered or feeling shame or believe you have failed. Share your feelings. Place your back against the tree's trunk or lie on the ground underneath it. See if you can feel love entering your body. What arises inside you? Track whatever happens next. Notice if the tree has any response.

## Generosity

One summer, while I was listening to spruce trees creak as the wind whipped through the forest in the Colorado high country, a sudden loud and unfamiliar crack caused my whole body to tense. A massive tree was falling beside me as the afternoon rain fell in sheets. I was huddled under a tarp with a group of twelve individuals, listening to stories of their conversations with the land. My eyes bulged in fear as I worried the falling tree would land on us.

Four feet from our tarp — *thunk* — a giant old spruce hit the ground, almost lifting us into the air. The reverberations shook throughout my body. Minutes before, a man had expressed joy at experiencing trees as alive for the first time. He'd begun noticing them as he never had, which evoked remorse. "I'm sad I chopped them down my whole life," he said, "without ever seeing them." The falling tree completed his revelation with a resounding exclamation.

Trees deserve to live. They give us so much. I wish humans could be as generous. Sometimes I envision the giant old-growth trees that once covered

North America and imagine squirrels traveling from coast to coast without ever touching the ground. The vast majority were logged in the eighteenth and nineteenth centuries. What would it be like if they were still with us? In my imagination, I commune with them. I see them towering above us, sunlight shining through the canopy. Rustling leaves and birdsong penetrate the silence. Chipmunks scamper from tree to tree. I wish we could bring ancient forests back.

Some people claim to be helping forests, but their actions cause tremendous harm. Like the practice of managing forests by chopping down trees and bulldozing the forest floor. (More on that in chapter 18.) Or consider palm oil biodiesel, for example, "the worst of all biofuels. It releases three times the greenhouse gas emissions of fossil diesel."[3] In addition, making the fuel requires clear-cutting massive amounts of tropical forest. Some people justify forest destruction by saying that we can plant more trees. But a forest is a living network, an underground superorganism of interconnection. So much life is in the soil. Each tree holds value, but not as much as an entire forest ecosystem. We can't remedy the destruction of forests by planting individual trees, so often unable to communicate with their neighbors.

Despite the harm humanity causes forests, I still feel their love. They have a lot to teach us. The love of forests and trees is a healing balm that not only soothes suffering but shows us how to hold ourselves and others and strengthens our capacity to love. When I have a hard time or feel in despair about the world, I call the trees I have known in my imagination — the ash, pine, maple, and cherry trees of my childhood, the juniper in Utah. I ask them to be with me and lean into their presence. I feel them in my mind and body and remember who I am.

A core part of my mythos, the image of my soul's purpose, is a tree. Mythically, my roots are planted in the forest. Forever connected to trees, I feel their presence when I am loving. Once I wrote a personal myth that I was born from the ash tree in my childhood backyard. In the Norse mythology of my ancestors, humanity was born from ash and elm trees. If we reconnect to our tree ancestors and link ourselves to them physically, emotionally, and imaginatively, we can heal, listen, and act from wisdom that cares about the future of trees, humans, birds, and bears.

Trees and plants are highly evolved and more Earth sensitive than we are. Scientists have discovered that plants have a multitude of senses to monitor complex environmental conditions. Italian botanist Stefano Mancuso says plants are more sensitive than animals: "We know that a single root apex is able to detect at least twenty different chemical and physical parameters, many of which we are blind to."[4] For example, we can't detect what minerals are in the soil underneath us, but trees can.

Humans have a bundle of senses we are not aware of. Beyond our five senses (hearing, vision, taste, touch, and smell), we can sense balance and movement and feel pain and the passing of time.[5] Yet humans have become dumb to many sensory skills, the mystical and intuitive gifts we are born with. I hope the practices of Wild Yoga can help us revive them.

The heart of the forest is regenerative. We expand our sensory capacities by noticing our innate connection to the unique intelligence of the forest's all-embracing communion. By engaging our wild imaginations, we can sink into the depth of this ancient relationship and let trees show us how they give and receive love. Replanting our hearts in Earth's life-giving soils, we can be nourished by and rooted in the mother of life. May we be inspired to honor and protect the forests we have left and love and dream back to life the ones we have lost. May we learn to love as trees do and live forever held in their wise and nurturing embrace.

## Wild Yoga Practices for Receiving the Love of Trees

Go to the forest, spend time with trees, or be with them in your imagination. Feel the power they have to love.

- Befriend a tree. Sit and lean against its trunk, taking in its love and support. Feel its bark at your back and imagine the tree's heart connecting to your heart. Let the tree hold you. Be open to whatever arises — sensations, images, memories, feelings. Offer gratitude for whatever comes.
- Become a tree in your imagination. Visualize what it would be like to sit in the same place for years, decades, or centuries. To stand through every season or kind of weather, day and night. Imagine the world from the perspective of a tree in the forest, connected by an underground network of organisms. What does it feel like to live in a community?
- Return to the trees in your imagination. You can do this while riding the bus, waiting in line, or sitting on a park bench. While recalling a challenging moment, such as when you received sad news or heard

harsh words, close your eyes and imagine what it would have felt like to be held by the trees. Imagine you are with them now, receiving their love and support.

- Write a love letter to yourself from the perspective of a tree that knows and loves you. Imagine what the tree might say to you, and write it in the letter. Let the tree help you love the aspects of yourself that you find the most challenging. Reread the letter often.
- Find people and organizations that honor trees as living beings and aim to protect the well-being of forests. Join them. Fight to keep ancient old-growth forests alive. Speak on behalf of trees whenever you are able.

## A Yoga Pose for Receiving the Love of Trees

### TREE POSE

Tree Pose stretches us to ground down while reaching tall through our branches, like a giant oak or cottonwood. It can help you feel centered, focused, and grounded. Tree Pose improves balance, opens hips, and strengthens ankles, legs, and spine.

*To get in the pose:*

- Begin in Mountain Pose. Spread your toes, root down through your feet, and firm your leg muscles. Slightly raise your hips toward your lower ribs.
- Ground through the tripod of each foot. Do this by imagining coins placed under three points: your heel and the knuckles of your big toe and pinkie toe. Lift your toes off the ground and balance on the coins, distributing the weight equally between the three points. Soften your toes down and maintain balance.
- Inhale deeply, float your chest up, and exhale as you draw your

shoulder blades down your back. Look straight ahead to keep balanced.

- Shift your weight onto your left leg and keep grounding through the tripod of this foot.
- Place your left hand on your hip. Bend your right knee, reach down with your right hand, and clasp your right ankle. (If you cannot balance, hold on to something with your left hand.)
- Place your right foot against your inner left leg, above or below your knee joint. (If you cannot balance with your right foot off the ground, place it at your ankle, leaving your toes on the ground for support.)
- If you can bring your foot to your thigh, press your foot against your inner thigh and your inner thigh back into your foot to help you maintain balance.
- Keep your core muscles engaged and the knee of your standing leg soft. Press your right thigh open.
- Firm your left hip, lengthen your spine, soften your shoulders, and tuck your chin slightly in and back.
- Bring your hands in front of your heart in a prayer position (Anjali Mudra).
- If you feel stable, stretch your arms overhead like branches of a tree reaching for the sun. Or bring your hands together in a high prayer position over your head. I call this "temple."
- Stay in the pose momentarily and imagine yourself as a tree in the forest.
- To exit the pose, lower your leg and arms as you exhale.
- Repeat on the other side.

Some days your balance may be better than others. If you struggle with balance, try the more accessible variations: place your hand on a wall; put your foot at your ankle with your toes on the ground. On days when you want to make the pose more challenging, raise your gaze to the ceiling or close your eyes. As you wobble or sway from side to side, find equilibrium. Trees that can bend in the wind are less prone to breaking. Imagine energy traveling from the ground to your pelvis and the middle of your torso and then through the crown of your head. Feel your core as the trunk of the tree. Hug in the muscles of your inner thigh to firm your standing leg.

Embody Tree Pose and enter a community of love. Imagine yourself as a tree in the forest, feeling the flow of love. Imagine roots growing out of your feet, into the ground, and branches growing out of your head, neck, and shoulders, spreading toward the sky. Feel what it is like to span the worlds: to live underground in the soil in communion and interconnection, to sense the solidity of your trunk rising out of the Earth, making a home for insects and birds, and to feel the expansiveness of your branches reaching into the sky, mingling with the stars, moon, and sun.

Imagine what it would be like to stand through the ages, longer than humans live, through the heat of the day and the dark of night. Through rain, snow, wind, and calm. Feel the critters moving on your bark, bird or squirrel, ant or cicada. Feel the communion under the soil. Give nutrients to those in need — a young tree, an old tree, a sick tree, a stump. Receive love as diverse and sophisticated as the community that surrounds you. Imagine so much love flowing in and out. You can't conceive of life without it.

Send your love to the tree community. Honor who they are and what they give us. Be open to what they share with you. In Tree Pose, imagine you are a tree that is part of a forest. Feel your capacity to be rooted in a rich and intricate community. Receive the love of trees. If anything stops you, ask the trees for help. Love and dream as you are nourished and planted in Mother Earth.

When we tune in to the intelligence of forests, we deepen our capacity to be intimate with nature and ourselves. If we root in the forest long enough, perhaps we can awaken to the wilderness that lives in our dreams. Then, like a bear hibernating in winter, we can descend into the primordial cave of images that arise unbidden from our wild imaginations and seek to understand their messages. We will explore how in the following chapter.

# CHAPTER SIX

# Dream in the Cave Womb

The understory is thick with shrubs and small trees. I hear rustling on the forest floor and wander into the shrub oak grove. Looking for an animal, I find a man squatting on the ground, wearing a brown loincloth. He seems shy and not used to being seen or around people. He turns toward me, and his brown eyes capture me. Looking into them, I sense the quiet and mysterious wisdom of the forest.

The next thing I remember, I am on a rocky outcropping above a lake, looking into the dark, still water. The man I met in the underbrush walks out of the forest and comes over. Again, he looks into my eyes, and this time, he gently embraces me. We sit together on the rocks, and he holds me as we maintain eye contact. His gaze is intense. In it, I feel the love and deep sadness of the forest. Before long, he gets up, walks over to the lake's edge, dives in, and disappears under the surface.

This dream felt more real than some exchanges in waking life. In my imagination, I return to the forest to commune with the man. I look into his eyes and like being near him. His presence informs how I see the world, live, and write. There is so much I don't know about him. Yet he calls me to spend time listening to the forest and diving into the deep waters.

I have always been fascinated by dreams. When I was young, I tried to interpret the images from the night world with a dream dictionary, but dreams are too complex to be decoded by a one-size-fits-all book. Trying to analyze them makes them small. Dreams know more about us and the world than we do. Their meaning is multilayered. We approach dreams by listening to them as we do to wild landscapes. We listen for what they want us to experience and inhabit the places they call us to be. We let them guide our lives.

We can return to dreams in our waking imagination. Later in this chapter, I will show you how to reenter a dream. I was twenty-nine the first time

I reentered one. I wanted to meet the dark-haired girl I had encountered in a trash can. In the dream, I was working at my day job, taking care of adolescent girls. The dark-haired girl was barely noticeable. She was up to her eyeballs in the trash. I vomited into the trashcan and did not see her. I was in a hurry to care for others.

Had *I* placed her in the trash? Discarded her? When I reentered the dream, she did not seem upset but was shy and slow to trust. I helped her out of the trash, cleaned her off, and asked her where she wanted to go. She was hesitant and not used to choices. So I took her to the forest, where she splashed in a creek. I marveled at her love of trees and flowing water. Watching her brought me joy. In the months that followed, I spent more time with her. Being with her altered me. Her innocence called me to be present with what was around me. Her indigeneity deepened my relationship with the wild world.

Dreams stretch our imagination and connect us to realms and potentialities that our mind could never conceive, attuning us to the mysteries of life. Through empathic identification, I often work with dreams, becoming each image and experiencing its perspective. After wandering with the dark-haired girl, I began to see the world through her eyes, and my sensitivities grew. Nature had always been a place I loved to be, but I often felt separate, not a part of it. After being with her, the wild world felt more like my home, where I belong. Embodying the mysterious intelligences of the night world opens us to alternate perspectives and ways of perceiving.

## A Bridge between Worlds

Many nature-based cultures honor the divine feminine, the universal mother connecting us to our bodies, the natural cycles of creation and transformation, and our dreams. Before colonization, the Iroquois, a gender-egalitarian, matriarchal society, made life-or-death decisions based on what people dreamed. They knew that dreams offered revelations about the soul's intentions and that to ignore them was to invite disaster. "The first business of the day in an Iroquois village was dream sharing," according to historian Robert Moss. The Iroquois "taught their children that dreams are the single most important source of both practical and spiritual guidance."[1]

Dreaming is an archetypal feminine quality related to the attributes of being intuitive, nurturing, receptive, interior, and gestational. These energies exist in all of us and the universe. The womb is a representation of the feminine. Native American lawyer and activist Sherri Mitchell wrote: "A woman's body is a bridge between worlds. Within a woman's body, there exists a direct link to the source of creation."[2] Whether the womb is giving birth or being a conduit for emerging dreams, what comes through is from beyond. Dreams can arise within the cave womb of Mother Earth. The archetypal masculine propels us to act, but it "needs the heart-based wisdom of the feminine to ensure those actions honor the feminine and preserve life."[3] When in balance, the inner world of dreams and intuition guides our actions in the outer world.

Individuals need to balance their inner feminine and masculine energies to be healthy, and cultures must also seek balance. Imagine a culture that listens to dreams, nature, and mythos in order to lead communities, establish laws, and organize a government. In patriarchal societies, like Western culture, people are taught to obey external power structures rather than listen to nature and dreams. To deny our inner lives is to suppress the feminine side of our psyche and submit to internal patriarchy, focusing only on what we do, produce, or accomplish and on pleasing others. Instead, we must attend to the quieter, less known voices in our psyche and listen to and honor the intelligence of dreams and the imaginal world.

Dreaming happens whether we are awake or asleep. While awake, images can arise unbidden at the edge of our consciousness. We don't chase dreams but make ourselves available to receive them by turning our attention toward them. We honor them by writing down or drawing whatever comes, whether or not we understand it or think it is meaningful. Listening to dreams is vital to any creative endeavor and foundational "to our survival and evolution."[4] Acting on what the dreamtime reveals helps us reimagine ourselves and our world. Dreams show us who we can be and what to do while we are here. Listening to dreams is central to Wild Yoga. Through them, we attune to the Earth's imagination and discover the unique contributions we can make.

## Nightmares

Dreams that terrify us are trying to get our attention. Listening to them is crucial. If we ignore our nightmares, they can reoccur and chase us like bullies in the schoolyard. Instead, we can turn toward them and stay open to what they want us to experience, however challenging. When we do this, we may be able to understand what they want to show us.

I will use one of my dreams as an example of how this works:

*I am swimming in dark water at night, far from shore. The water is crowded with people who are swimming. I am afraid they will pull me under the water. I try to swim around them. Then, someone swims under me and grabs my leg. I try to fight, but I feel powerless. I am pulled down fast, deep under the water. I feel like I am free-falling.*

I return to the dream in my imagination, look around, and remember how it feels to be in the dark water. I replay the dream slowly and pay attention to what I may not have noticed before. I linger in places where I am curious or feel an emotional charge.

I feel terror at the rapid pace at which I descend. Lost in blackness, I do not know which way is up. The pressure feels crushing on all sides of my body. The weight on my chest is paralyzing. I can't breathe. I stay as long as I can tolerate, waiting to see what happens next. A tremendous sorrow arises in me. I see images of clear-cut forests, oceans filled with plastic, poisoned rivers, and suffering wildlife. I view the land that has been mined and plowed. I feel in touch with the visceral nightmare inflicted on nature every day. The pressure on my body feels inescapable as I turn downward, deeper into blackness. My sorrow morphs into hopelessness and yet brings me back to love. The dark waters want me to feel and stay open to emerging visions.

Our dreams can have recurrent themes and images. The forest man I wrote about in the opening of this chapter dove into dark waters, and I have had many other dreams about dark waters. Dark waters are a part of my mythos. This dream invites me to feel the ecocide of waking life with an intensity I have never experienced while staying present with visions that may arise in the watery depths. I feel challenged by this. What is happening to the Earth is worse than any nightmare I could have, and I struggle to stay present and keep listening.

Reenter one of your dreams. Perhaps start with one that is not a nightmare. Choose a dream you want to be with. Find a quiet place. Recall what you saw and felt. Close your eyes and slowly replay the events. Let yourself be back in the dream. Tune in to each scene with all your senses. Who or what is around you? Hang out with the images. Notice what wants to happen next. See if you can surrender to the experience the dream wants you to have.

## Mythos and the Cave Womb

Every dream is a complex matrix of characters, places, dynamics, and images inviting us into multiple worlds. There are many things to be curious about. Who is visiting? What is happening? What do the others in the dream sense, feel, or want? When we see through the eyes of one or more aspects of a dream, the images and elements can dissolve our ego, alter our sense of self, and initiate us into the mysteries of the night world.

Dreams may connect us to the past, the future, ancestors, the dead, aspects of our psyche, personal and cultural shadows, archetypal energies, and mysterious and wild presences. Dreams can also give us glimpses of the mythic purpose of our souls. In chapter 4, I shared part of a mythic dream that came through multiple dream images and waking visions over years: a burning forest, a mother tree, bear moving in an underground river. A lot can come from one dream. And multiple dream images can weave themselves into a larger tapestry over time.

The soul is as feminine as dreams, ebbing and flowing, as constant yet changeable as the moon and tides. Depth psychologist Bill Plotkin maps out the initiatory process we go through to become conscious of our soul — our unique niche in the Earth community. We become aware of our souls through metaphor, poem, image, or pattern. Carl Jung called it our "personal myth," and Animas Valley Institute refers to it as "mythopoetic identity."[5] Wild Yoga weaves images of my mythos with other dimensions of life. Below is a condensed snapshot of a version of my soul story, an alternate perspective of the dream I shared in chapter 4.

> I am in a cave womb under a world mother tree in a forest that is on fire. Where the cave wall is cracked, the Earth's heart echoes in rhythm with my own. I ride waves of love and heartbreak, immersed in the dark waters of a cave pool that flows into an underground river. The bear lives in the cave womb, on the river, and in the burning forest. I float as and with him in the dark waters — a guide on the underground river, a witness to horror and beauty, a wild love prayer.

Living the mythos of my soul is humbling because it feels impossible. Trying to be who the dream reveals strengthens me to grow into what it asks. I use *mythos* and *dream* interchangeably because our mythos is a kind of dream. In particular, the mythic images we receive from the night world ask us to do and become things that other parts of us would rather avoid. Ego often tries to keep our mythos out of awareness. Once we glimpse what our soul is asking, we may feel compelled to bring that vision to life. Dreams can heal us and guide us in living our deepest intentions. Living what they ask restores our vitality.

We honor dreams by listening, exploring, and embodying them. The dream world has viewed the more remarkable and accurate shape we are meant to take, and dream by dream, it guides us there. What the mythos of our soul asks is greater and more mysterious than any particular role, vocation, or craft. I am more than a writer or a guide — I am a woman living in the cave womb under a world mother tree. Yet particular roles, like my role as dream guide, are a way to express what the dream asks. Each dream we honor and act on initiates us into a collaborative relationship with the dream world. More dreams come when we listen to and embody the ones we have been given.

As a guide, I help dreamers keep the enigmatic images of their dreams alive. From the unique perspective of my mythic soul, I invite others to dialogue with dream characters, represent them artistically, or move with them to music. While listening to dreams, I imagine myself in the cave womb and feel the Earth's heart echo. I invite people into the cave to gestate in the primordial potentialities of the wild imagination, like a hibernating bear in winter. As I listen underground, swimming in the dark waters of love and grief, I long to serve the forest.

## Howling Salmon

She-wolf first came to Alice in a dream on a solo fast in Utah. Being with the wolf in her imagination brings her into her body and gets her to howl. She has always feared offending people, but the wolf asks her to risk speaking the truth.

Months later, while swimming in the sea near her home in Alaska, Alice feels like a salmon meant to gather nutrients and feed her people. Then, in her imagination, she is surprised to hear the loud howl of a wolf underwater. It's the salmon. They want her to howl and lament, to listen and give them a voice.

Alice backpacks to a mountain lake and expresses a longing to howl like a salmon and merge with the Earth. She awakens that night to a thunderstorm. The lightning is so close Alice is afraid. She prays for her life and falls back asleep. In a dream, a jaguar chases her up a tree and turns into a ferocious white wolf that attacks her. She tries to kick the wolf down but can't. A vast body of water appears and looks like the lake where she is camped. She recognizes it as a portal. A flash of lightning awakens her. She puts on her rain gear and sits by the lake, watching the storm. She feels called to stay awake and keep vigil. It is cold. The thunder has passed, but lightning still dances over the lake.

She prays to see what the Earth wants to show her. Every time she puts her arms out in prayer, lightning flashes. She feels like she is dancing with lightning. Sleet mixes with rain. She starts to shiver and goes back to her sleeping bag. She falls asleep, but the lightning and thunder wake her. She falls asleep again and sees the face of a past lover.

"I want all of you," he says.

When she awakens, the lake is shimmering, and the mountain is stunning. She weeps and yearns to give all of herself to the Earth. She makes a secret vow while lying belly down on a rock. She feels the wolf's presence and herself as a howling salmon dancing with lightning.

She carries this vision into her life. Each day, she reconnects to dancing with lightning in her imagination and listens to understand more. It asks her to step into the fray, engage with life's polarities, and listen to all sides. She has a shy personality, and this terrifies her. Yet embodying her vision in the world is a challenge she is willing to live.

## Wild Yoga Practices for Dreaming in the Cave Womb

Take time to remember your dreams, embody the mysteries they invite, and discern what they ask.

- Place a journal beside your bed. Commit to writing down your dreams in the present tense. Before you sleep, speak aloud to the dream world. Express why you want a dream. Upon waking, keep your eyes closed and linger in your dream imagery. Resist the urge to interpret what comes as "nothing" or "only an image." Write down or draw what you receive.
- Set aside time to reenter a dream. Close your eyes and feel yourself back in it. Recall the details. Notice how you feel in situations and places. What do you sense in your body or the atmosphere of

the dream? Is it familiar? Move through the dream slowly. Linger in places where you are curious or feel an emotional charge. Surrender to what the dream wants you to experience, even if it does not make sense (or find a guide to help you).

- Choose a character or image from a recent dream. Become this other in your imagination. Start with someone you like. (Try someone you dislike later.) First, observe their movement and expression. Then, mimic their behaviors, physically or in your imagination. Become them and notice how you experience the world. How do you breathe, stand, or walk? What do you want? Experience the dream from their perspective.

- Explore one of your dreams in nature. Wander and seek a being or place that reminds you of a dream character or image. If you find one, share what you notice or feel in its presence. Tell the dream aloud in the present tense or reenact it. How is this place like the dream? Reenter the dream. Continue the dream forward. What wants to happen next?

- Just before you sleep, reenter your previous night's dream. Perhaps you have spent time with it throughout the day, and it feels different than when you first awoke. Can you sense what it wants of you now? Ask to be taken deeper when you dream tonight.

- Explore your dreams through art or writing. Draw, paint, or make a collage. Bring together your most potent dream places, beings, and images. Perhaps make a sculpture or symbolic garden of your dream characters, utilizing rocks, leaves, and sticks. What themes emerge? Write your dream as a myth or poem and recite or enact it aloud.

- Track mythic dream themes. Make a collage or write a story or poem to honor these images, perhaps weaving together multiple dreams. Return to them in your imagination. Dialogue with them by asking questions. Practice embodying them. Explore them through movement or dance. Wander in nature with them. Journal about what you discover.

## A Yoga Pose for Dreaming in the Cave Womb

### CHILD'S POSE

Child's Pose (Balasana) gently stretches your hips, thighs, and ankles. It calms the brain and relieves back and neck pain. If your muscles are tight, support your head and torso by placing cushions or folded blankets underneath them. If needed, place pillows between your thighs and calves. The purpose of this pose is to relax. Utilize whatever props you need to find ease.

*To get in the pose:*

- Kneel on the floor. Touch your big toes together and sit on your heels. Then spread your knees as wide as your mat with the tops of your feet on the floor and your big toes touching. (Add supportive props as needed.)
- Exhale and lay your torso down between your thighs. Broaden your sacrum across the back of your pelvis and narrow your hip points toward your navel. Lengthen your tailbone away from the back of your pelvis.
- Lay your hands on the floor along your torso, palms up. Release the front of your shoulders toward the floor. Feel how the weight of your shoulders pulls your shoulder blades wide across your back.
- Rest. Breathe deeply and slowly into the back of your torso. Imagine each breath lengthening and widening your spine and the back of your body.

- Try a variation: Stretch your arms forward, hands palm down on the ground in front of you. Lift your buttocks slightly away from your heels. Reach your arms longer, draw your shoulder blades closer together, and pull them down toward your feet. Bring your buttocks back down on your heels. Rest and breathe.
- To come up, lengthen your front torso, inhale, and lift from your tailbone.

Child's Pose brings us closer to nature, planting our third eye on the ground. In a fetal-like position, we relax and are in a prime place to dream. Imagine merging with the dream of the Earth. Sense yourself hibernating in a cave womb. Imagine your body, heart, and soul held in the salty, oceanic fluids of Mother Earth.

Imagine floating in the sea and drifting into a cave deep within the Earth. Be inside the cave with all of your senses. Do you hear the silence? Or the dripping of water? Is your skin touching soil or rock? Are you feeling warm or cold in this moist, dark womb? Notice what life feels like below the surface. Can you hear or sense the heartbeat of the Earth? Feel yourself in the dream and planted in nature. Track any visions, images, or memories that arise. Swim in the dark waters. Notice what emerges in your deep imagination.

Embody Child's Pose and invite the images of a dream to come. Gestate in the cave womb. Linger in places where you feel drawn or have strong emotions. Let the dream continue forward. Or notice if other dreams want to enter and unveil any connection. Or if other waking images from the edge of your consciousness are present. See what wants to happen next.

Being in the cave of our dreams deepens our capacity to listen and can catalyze us to face nightmares and inhabit the shapes of our mythos. As we stretch and become wild, inside and out, longing can arise: to be our more genuine self, contribute to the world in a meaningful way, or be something unnameable. Fear can also occur of never touching what matters or what we could be asked to do. Like a moth drawn to the flame, we are pulled toward what radiates with life and threatens to burn us. Entering these fires of love, we may pray to encounter our soul, be in union with Spirit, or sing our melody to the world. We will explore how in the following chapter.

# Part II

# HOLY LONGING

*Let us pray dangerously.*
*Let us throw ourselves from the top of the tower,*
*let us risk a descent to the darkest region of the abyss,*
*let us put our head in the lion's mouth*
*and direct our feet to the entrance of the dragon's cave....*

*Let us ask for nothing less than the Infinite to ravage us.*
*Let us ask for nothing less than annihilation in the*
*Fires of Love.*

— Regina Sara Ryan, "Praying Dangerously"[1]

# CHAPTER SEVEN

# Open to a Sacred World

R aised by my parents in the Catholic faith, I am taught by them and others that the church is sacred. Every time I go in, I see colored light — shades of crimson, blue, and gold — streaming through the stained glass windows, shining on a sculpted depiction of Jesus, whose body is pierced by a lance wound, nailed to the cross, bleeding. People sit, stand, and kneel during Mass, reciting memorized responses and prayers. Incense rises in clouds. I wish I were outside.

Each day at the Catholic school I attend, a student goes to the convent, where we are told God lives, to pick up a snack for class — a bag of pretzels. Excited when it's my turn, I'm eager to enter this holy realm. As I walk inside, I look and listen for God. I want to be close to him. Later, I ask the priest if I could become an acolyte and assist him in the Mass.

"That's only for boys," he says sharply, a grimace on his face.

I feel a wave of heat move up through my body, my face reddening, my pulse quickening. I walk away feeling dejected, subtly aware of the experience of shame, an emotion that confuses and embarrasses me.

It took me a while to realize the church is "an empire of misogyny," as noted by the former president of Ireland Mary McAleese.[1] I no longer believe in monotheism. Yet my whole life, the sacred Spirit, the divine feminine, has been a palpable truth. I see and feel her presence every time I am in nature. I see her in the movements and gestures of desert, ocean, stream, dolphin, antelope, and dragonfly. Spirit and Earth are inseparable, abiding in all life.

The sunrise bathes the mountains in warmth and light. Wind dances with trees. The breeze makes music with the leaves. Rain offers itself to the grasses. Thunderstorms crackle. Rivers carry their waters to the sea. The moon moves with the tides. Coyotes howl. Owls hoot. Frogs croak. Crickets make a concert for the night.

The sacred is a power, being, or realm at the core of existence. It can transform our lives and destinies and goes by many names — the Holy, Divine, Absolute, Mystery, Spirit. Connecting to the sacred can fulfill our deepest needs and hopes and may inspire reverence, trust, or terror. Dreams are sacred. The mythos of our souls is holy. The sacred is within and all around us, connecting Earth and Mystery. We may experience Mystery as a numinous or mystical revelation about our unique essence or as union with the Absolute. Humans are meant to live attuned to Spirit, Earth, and Mystery. As a guide, I bring people into the wilderness and invite them to have a direct relationship with what is holy: to hear the song of the planet, listen to the images arising in their dreams, and discover their soul's unique mythic purpose.

Throughout history, humans have found sacred places — rivers, mountains, groves of trees, or caves where they could feel power flowing. Remember your childhood dreams, longings, and experiences to help you reconnect with the sacred. Children are present to what surrounds them and naturally touch into unseen realms. Tapping into the imagination you once had may help you tune in to what is beyond ordinary awareness and open to seemingly invisible worlds, unexplainable by science or the rational mind.

The sacred pervades all dimensions of life. The practice of meditation helps me slow my mind so I can see the sacred in others. Three ten-day meditation courses teach me the discipline of sitting. During a twenty-one-day Tibetan Buddhist meditation program, I fall in love with people I have never spoken to. Looking into their eyes and faces, I see gentleness and feel the spirit of what has been with us through days of sitting. My meditation practice merges with my deep imagination. I inhabit my mythos, the world mother tree — branches, fruit, wings, roots, trunk, cave pool, underground river — and then am drawn into a vastness beyond that. Even the emptiness feels sacred. On breaks, I go outside and am captivated by falling snowflakes, the crisp air, and the sunset reflecting on the snowy mountains.

Being in the presence of the sacred shifts our consciousness and opens us to a deeper listening. I look at the stars from a wooden yoga deck in Costa Rica through a canopy of palm and mangrove trees. The sea is less than thirty feet away. The sound of rustling leaves mingles with the thud of crashing waves, followed by the trickle of water rolling over rocks. Our group does gentle yoga asana on the first night of a Wild Yoga program. Lying down with our feet planted, we rock our raised knees back and forth, massaging our sacrums. Ending with Bridge Pose (Setubandha Sarvangasana), we arch our backs, bringing our pelvises into the air. Sounds follow the movement. An assortment of instruments sits on an altar, lit by four candles: singing bowls, rattles, drums, bamboo sticks, an anklet with bells, and *tingsha* cymbals. Sound is often used to call in the sacred. We sit in a ceremony with our eyes closed and hear the sounds of rain forest and ocean. The notes we make mix with those of rolling waves and chirping crickets. We close with a council. Holding a "sea heart" from a vine in the rain forest, we speak from our hearts.

Wild Yoga calls in the sacred, inviting body, soul, and spirit to move in union. The mystery of our soul or spirit can move through us and unify and direct our bodies and minds, connecting us to the whole. Our perception expands as we sense, feel, and imagine. We may experience the mystical nature of reality or a universal consciousness that animates everything.

## Nature Mysticism

Saint Francis of Assisi saw all creatures as his brothers and sisters. "Earth *is* heaven," he intuited. Most nature-based and indigenous cultures worldwide live close to the Earth and feel the holy in all that people do — eating, hunting, art making. I have been with the Shoshone-Paiute people, for example, as they engage with their cultural land in a sacred way: honoring and protecting the burial sites of their ancestors, drumming and singing in prayer and ceremony. Because I was raised in modern Western culture, it took me a while to trust my instincts and acknowledge that I am a nature mystic — that the primary way I experience a direct relationship with the sacred is through nature.

"Get down on your knees and take Jesus Christ as your Lord and Savior." Glenn, a Baptist friend in college, handed me a pamphlet. "Assure your place in heaven."

I was invited to turn my authority over to a masculine sky god. Part of me wanted to be convinced, so my questions — Does God exist? How can I live in sacred union? What is mine to be and do? — would be answered.

"Don't be a doubting Thomas," Glenn said.

But I am. Why would God accept only those who got on their knees? I was a philosophy–religious studies major. My journal was full of questions and appeals: "God, if you exist, please let me experience you." I wanted a *real* connection.

Working at summer camp in the Catoctin Mountains in Maryland, the wildest place I had ever lived, I felt connected. The stars lit the night sky. The frogs and crickets were loud. The tall trees of the oak-hickory-tulip-poplar forest swayed in the wind at night, sounding like an ocean. I awoke early to bathe and dress campers with mental and physical disabilities, change their diapers, and feed them. The work was hard but meaningful. We focused on living in nature and felt in relationship with the wild world.

After summer camp, I went to a convent for a weekend as part of a college mysticism class where we studied having a direct relationship with the sacred. Before we left for the convent, I had received my third chemotherapy treatment. My hair, eyebrows, and eyelashes were gone. I drank carrot juice every day, and while driving to the convent, my friend pulled over so I could throw up. Some landed on my jeans. That is how I arrived, bald with an orange splotch on my pants.

A state park surrounded the convent. Sister Marie and I hiked to a waterfall and stuck our feet in the pool.

"You bring a special presence," she said. "We appreciate what you're offering."

What? I was confused. I had not done anything. I was receiving.

"All the sisters see it," she said. "We've talked about it. We see God in you. The way you carry yourself and your illness. It touches us."

Ira, my favorite professor, taught the mysticism class. At the end of the semester, I walked past his office.

"Is that you, Rebecca?" he asked. "Come in." I was too shy to enter without an invitation.

"You will like this book," he said, handing me *Hymn of the Universe* by Pierre Teilhard de Chardin. "He's a nature mystic, like you."

"I feel the holy in nature," I said, "and since I've been ill, I feel it in me too."

"You are like a sacrament." He looked kindly into my eyes.

I was startled and pleasantly surprised. "How?" I asked.

"A sacrament brings a spiritual reality to a physical experience. When people see you on campus, they experience God through seeing you."

I left his office puzzled and delighted. I was unsure what Sister Marie and he could see. Perhaps it was the mysterious presence I had begun to feel within myself. I longed to stay connected to it.

## Soul

Being deeply seen is a gift that most people in Western culture have never had. In the Dagara tribe in Central and West Africa, elders can see a baby's soul while she is in her mother's womb and help her grow to fulfill her purpose.[2]

Our modern culture lacks elders. Sister Marie and Ira showed me that rare thing: what it felt like to be seen.

Nature and my dreams have been my primary elders. The animate natural world wants me to live from my soul so that I can exist in a cocreative relationship. I felt a divine presence when I had cancer and began to perceive the world differently. Lots of people were praying for me, and I wondered what effects their prayers had. More than a decade later, I encountered the part of my mythos I came to know as Wild Love Prayer. (More on that in chapter 14.) Soul has been central to my life, listening and pursuing my own and supporting others. I have shared some soul images — being told I was Brave Heart, my relationship with trees and bear and river, the mythic dream of the world tree and the cave pool — and others I will share later.

Many cultural myths recognize sacred power, helping people understand their place in a divine pattern. At Animas Valley Institute, where I have studied and guided for the past two decades, people descend into the mysteries of nature and psyche to discover their mythic souls. Our soul, or mythopoetic identity, can be experienced through symbol, dream, myth, archetype, metaphor, poem, or image.[3] To encounter our soul, we need to see beyond the borders of what society defines as ordinary reality and perceive the mystical or numinous. In "Mythopoeia," a poem by J. R. R. Tolkien, he likens this to "seeing through elvish eyes" or "the eyes of an artist."[4]

*Soul* is often misunderstood in the dominant culture, thought to mean "vocation." At Animas, we define *soul* as an ecological niche and the unique way we enrich the relational web. Encountering our soul changes the way we live. Visions bring meaning and purpose and invite us into what David Whyte calls the "largest conversation you're capable of having with the world."[5] Yet the descent to soul is a journey of dismemberment. Humans have often accessed the sacred through sacrifice. In soul initiation, we shed the outgrown husk of our ego and become a vessel so we can offer our particular genius. (More on my descent in chapter 11.) Soul initiation causes a profound structural shift to mature the ego and elicit a soul-rooted response that can see beyond its own time. It happens when one's psyche is ripe for this change. After soul initiation, our ego lives to embody the vision of Earth and soul rather than to serve itself.[6]

The mythos of our soul is as rich as a personal cosmology. Each encounter with soul reshapes us and is woven into a multifaceted tapestry over years, a decade, or a lifetime. How our soul relates to other souls with whom we are linked matters — the soul of the world, the souls of one another, the souls of bear, salmon, and moon. A core aspect of Wild Yoga is encountering our soul, becoming soul initiated, and living our souls as we relate to the world. To our bodies, the body of Earth, our hearts and tears, trees and women, spirituality and patriarchy, lovers and friends, dying species, poisoned rivers, and the sociopolitical dynamics of society.

Sometimes my dreams or the places I wander on the land remind me of my mythos. On the Franklin River in Tasmania, I feel like I am on an underground river. The Franklin mingles with my imagination, carrying me deeper into the river of my mythos. Over the past two decades, words have come, as well as dreams and images, to help me understand who I am asked to be: a brave-hearted, wild love prayer bear who dwells in the dark waters, a witness to horror and beauty. The words and images humble me. How will I live what they ask?

Our mythos is a dream until we integrate and embody the images. I swim in its mystery and attune to what arises in the night world and my daydreams. The purple wings of the world tree fly into the cosmos. I feel as the tree rooted in the planet. The tree's wings carry me into the star-filled night and the galaxies beyond as I listen for how to be in the world.

I hear the echo of the Earth's heartbeat from under the tree. I flow in the underworld river and look at the world through cave eyes. My mythos informs the way I am present and what I say. We make our soul sacred by the way we offer and relate. I listen for clues about how to guide or write or what my mythos wants next.

## Spirit

Whether we are aware or not, our souls are part of a conversation with the Spirit of Earth. A tree and a bird can be fully themselves while attuning to the planet. We long to listen to the Earth and merge with her beauty. As the Sufi poet Rumi wrote:

> There is some kiss we want
> with our whole lives,
> the touch of Spirit on the body.[7]

We want a relationship that is personal and particular and one that lets us melt and dissolve into our love for the One, the Divine Mystery.

Spiritual transcendence connects us to the whole, while the descent to soul, what Thomas Berry calls "inscendence," reveals the individual mystery we are here to live.[8] Whyte describes it as

> the truth you make
> every day with your own body,
> ...your own truth
> at the center of the image
> you were born with.[9]

I often feel connected to both the universal and my particular soul. For example, I experienced a connection to both when I had cancer, living in nature, meditating, and doing Wild Yoga.

Humans are meant to live in connection to Spirit and soul. And stretch our consciousness to the depth of the one and the expansiveness of the whole. Meditating for twenty-one days, I dissolved into the Absolute and was forced to face core feelings hidden in my shadow. Feelings of being trapped and disappointed swirled with gratitude for the preciousness of life. The pain took me to disturbing places, and the beauty evoked awe. I experienced the chthonic depths of my soul and the underworld, a realm associated with death and darkness, as living within and part of the totality of existence. I felt connected to those who came before us and have died.

## Ancestors

Sometimes I talk aloud to my grandfather, Edward, who died in April 2007 of complications related to Parkinson's disease. I think he can hear me. His mother died when he was a child, and his two aunties raised him. He met my grandmother in Stornoway, Scotland, during World War II and built their home in New Jersey, as well as a house next door for my grandmother's mom.

He respected women, interjecting if anyone disrespected my mother or grandmother. He served on the school board and township committee and often built home projects — decks, closets, extra rooms. He was Swedish and invited his relatives over in the summer for family picnics. Many could not speak English, so we taught one another our languages.

I am not the first one with the last name Wildbear in my family. Edward's surname was Stromborn. It comes from the family name Strombjorn. The *j* was dropped when the family emigrated from Sweden to the United States. In Old Norse, *bjorn* means "bear," and *strom* comes from *straumr*, meaning "river, stream, or current." This ancestral name reminds me of my mythic bear who travels on the underground river.

My Strombjorn ancestors chose a surname rooted in the natural world, as I did. Strombjorn was a *fylgja*, the animal shape my ancestors took while dreaming. In Norse mythology, the gods created seven worlds, and inside us, those worlds are our seven souls. Fylgja is one of the souls. A person with bear as their fylgja dreams as a bear. We can inherit the fylgja of our ancestors. Perhaps that is why bear dreams in me and came to me in Costa Rica.

Our ancestors shape us. Emotions and images from our depths may not be entirely personal or archetypal. In Norse mythology, trees first brought humanity into being. Odin exhaled his spirit breath toward an elm tree, and the first woman, Embla, walked out of its trunk. The first man, Ask, came from an ash tree. The ash and elm trees are our ancestors. These ancestral myths resonate with what I understand about my mythic connection to trees.

"Old stories are not meant to entertain," said the storyteller Andreas Kornevall. "They hold codes and revelations of what it was like to be a human being."[10]

In the Norse mythology of my Swedish ancestors, the Tree of Life, Yggdrasil, is kept alive through the well of memory.[11] As we remember our ancestors, dew water is made from praising the past. This water feeds the roots of the Tree of Life. If we cut off from memory, the Tree of Life suffers. The well runs dry if we forget the past or fail to understand where we come from. We owe a debt to the future for being alive, and we pay it by caring for the past.

Humans long for a new story, but the stories most worth telling are rooted. A story needs to be anchored in the past, or it may become top-heavy and the Tree of Life can't hold it.

Malidoma Somé, a Dagara-born writer, said a true community includes the living *and* the dead: "Those on the other side have gifts to bring to this world, and those in this world can bring gifts to the other side."[12] We can tend what emerges from our dreams and remember the past — the ancestors of our blood and humans and nonhumans who inhabited the land on which we live. So may we ask questions, be curious, and engage with those who came before, in our family histories, and on the ground where we live.

## Wild Yoga Practices for Opening to a Sacred World

Remember expanded moments of awareness when you felt connected to the sacred. Consider how you may be open to perceiving what you have never been aware of.

- Recall early childhood experiences of the sacred, what happened and what you longed for. Remember moments when you experienced a sense of the mystical, either in what you witnessed or what you felt inside yourself. Draw, paint, or sculpt what you sensed or imagined the sacred to be as a child.

- Find a place in nature and share the story of the sacred in your life. Speak about your longing to call the sacred in now. Express it in a creative and vulnerable way through movement, poetry, song, words, tears, and a gift. Listen for any response.

- Go on a wander in nature and express your longing to encounter your soul. Find a threshold and state your intention. Let yourself be surprised by where you are pulled. Notice who calls you into conversation — rock, insect, animal? Share what you notice about it or feel in its presence. Introduce yourself at the deepest level. Notice if anything is offered back.

- Remember your most potent revelations, encounters, or dreams. Draw, write, or make a collage to represent them artistically. Describe what you have learned about the myths, poems, or images you are here to live. Wander in nature with one of the images. Don't plan which way to go. Let yourself be pulled by the image and by nature.

- Pick a practice that helps connect you to Spirit — meditation, a praise walk in nature, yoga, or body movement. Then, engage in the practice regularly. As you do, notice if you can slow your mind and feel connected to the whole or enchanted by the natural world.

- Seek to discover more about the ancestors in your history. Ask relatives in your family for memories and stories. Go to the places where your ancestors lived. Ask to connect with them in dreams, in deep imagination, or on a nature wander. Journal about what you find.

## A Yoga Pose for Opening to a Sacred World

### GODDESS POSE

Goddess Pose (Utkata Koṅasana) strengthens and tones your lower body: thighs, glutes, hips, calves, and ankles. It opens your chest and hips, promotes a long spine, and strengthens your back muscles. It relaxes your pelvic floor while energizing your body, creating balance, and stimulating your cardio and respiratory systems.

*To get in the pose:*

- Stand and place your hands on your hips. Step your feet wide apart and turn your toes out.
- Exhale as you bend your knees and squat downward. Tuck your tailbone slightly and draw your thighs back.

- Bring your thighs parallel to the floor while keeping your knees over your ankles. Relax your shoulders and keep your neck and spine long.
- Your arms can take many different positions. For example, you can bend at the elbows with your palms up, make a mudra (hand gesture), or even dance around!
- Hold this posture for a few minutes.
- To release, press your feet firmly into the ground as you exhale and slowly straighten your legs as you rise.

Goddess Pose reminds us to revere the sacred. As we expand our body and perception, we open to a larger sense of reality and feel our power. Opening to the sacred renews us with strength and inspiration. While in Goddess Pose, invite the holy to enter you and honor the sacred world around you. Feel your body vibrate as Spirit and the mystery of your soul move through you. Let your movements direct and support your connection to the whole.

In Goddess Pose, explore multiple arm positions. Start by bending at the elbows with your palms up.[13] Then, try other variations. A common one is placing your arms up like you are holding a big ball over your head. Then, look straight ahead and keep your chin parallel to the floor. Another variation is to dance in the pose, swaying from side to side and letting go into a flow of creativity. Yet another is to lift your heels off the ground and balance on your toes while maintaining the squat.

Whatever variation you are in, whether in stillness or motion, attune to the sensations you feel in your body and what arises in your imagination. Notice if you can connect to universal consciousness and honor and feel the natural world around you. Perhaps remember an aspect of your soul image. See if you can inhabit that place in your imagination while in Goddess Pose. Invite your body, soul, and spirit to live in union if you are able. Perhaps call in an ancestor to join you. Let your movements or stillness be a prayer and call in the sacred. Turn your mind inward and let the sacred radiate out.

Being in Goddess Pose reminds us of all we revere in the world and ourselves. And to tune in, listen to nature, and follow the call of the mystical. We can embody soul and embrace Spirit and our ancestors. Another way the sacred can beckon us into a holy union, awakening the most profound secrets in our hearts, is through romantic love. We can let the mystery of what we love direct who we become. We will explore how in the following chapter.

# CHAPTER EIGHT

# Romance the Mystery
# of What You Love

I fall in love with a boy for the first time at fifteen. His wavy, dark hair shakes when he speaks. His brown eyes flicker from behind his 1980s round spectacles. He is an oddball in a jean jacket with a smiley face on the back. He speaks things I think but never say. Perhaps they are truths I didn't realize I held. I am quiet. I haven't lived in a world where people can be so honest.

We are in the same classes and the school play. His presence pierces the high school tedium. One day I realize something has shifted. I want to be near him, yet I am afraid to get closer. A new angst grows within me; nothing will be the same. I imagine he would understand me if we spoke, but I am too shy to approach him. I write to him in my journal, his name spelled backward for secrecy, "Dear Ydna."

I miss being around him in the summertime. In a flash of boldness, I look up his number and call him.

"Would you like to meet in the park and go on the swings?" I ask.

"Okay," he agrees.

I feel like myself on swings: with my body in motion, my words flow easier. In the years that follow, we hang out with the same circle of friends. Without realizing it, I aspire to be like him, to have the courage to speak out, inhabit my depths, and be authentic. We both write for the school newspaper during our senior year. The editorials I write critique high school life, from hair spray to cliques to our classes to prom. His articles examine politics, pop culture, and music with a sardonic wit.

A longing awakens that incites my imagination and catalyzes my actions. My love for this boy alters me, and we never even hold hands. I begin to know the yearnings of my heart, find my voice, and engage. We go to different colleges, but what I learned from loving him stays. It grows me into someone beyond whom I thought I could be.

Romance is more than a pleasurable feeling or finding our other half. Real romance opens us to the depth and mystery of our longing and unveils the secrets of our hearts. Suddenly, what is meaningful is alive and close enough to move toward, but far enough away that we ache for it. Romance stirs our hearts and gives us the courage to honor what we love. This guides who we become. My affection for my high school love called me out of my inner world to risk sharing myself. As the qualities I admired in him — authenticity, articulation, bravery — developed in me, I became more myself.

Romance can inspire our creativity and bring us into the transpersonal realm. We may see the other as the Divine. The Tz'utujil people, an indigenous Mayan culture in Guatemala, did not allow their young to touch one another romantically until after they were initiated. The elders knew they were ready, not by their age, but by their infatuation — a "precious brush with seeing and wanting ... the devastating, delicious, ecstatic, and painful presence of the Divine on earth in the form of a walking, talking human."[1] Young men and women were separated from each other and their village for a year. They grieved and courted the Divine — that which they could love but never possess — with love poems, and in so doing, they became capable of loving another human whom they could forgive for their small thoughts and deeds.

## Inner Beloved

The inner beloved, the Divine within, appears in many forms in dreams or attractive qualities we behold in another. Psychology calls this projection, but perhaps we are bearing witness rather than fantasizing. We are attracted to what we see radiating through another or a mystery we sense within or beside them. We want the enticing qualities we see in this other in our life. The unique beauty we experience in their presence disarms and captivates us. Yet these qualities exist in us, and even if we do not fully embody them, we can cultivate them.

Following what we love opens us to a romance with the world. Our inner beloved propels us beyond ourselves to what is most significant while drawing us intensely inward, awakening our passions. We long to be intimate with what allures us. Yet stepping toward who we love is scary. Our inner beloved may appear in menacing shapes and can shake us up. Our desire for the beloved pulls us in unexpected directions and incites us to engage with new people, places, ideas, and actions. Trebbe Johnson wrote, "Once we make room in our life for the great, mysterious Other that beckons, we realize that longing itself is a potent force.... Exile, our ache and our bliss, keeps us moving toward the best of ourselves."[2]

Suppose we let go of fantasies of a magical other fulfilling our every need.[3] Then, romance with an external partner can bring meaning and joy. Yet, whether or not we have a partner, a relationship with our inner beloved may be the most fantastic romance of our lives. Our most faithful love is the one inside us who can guide us toward our soul's purpose, bring us to our unique place within the Earth community, and inform how we give to the world. We may encounter our soul through whispers and hints of our inner beloved and in dreams and conversations with the natural world. Romancing this mysterious love is central to Wild Yoga.

The qualities I saw in my high school love awakened me to what I cared about. Our inner beloved shapes how we perceive the world and inspires how we offer ourselves. My inner beloved informs how I listen, guide, and write. Our inner beloved is aligned with our muse, inspiring the unique way we see the world and strengthening our visionary capacity. Our inner beloved helps us live a muse-directed life, so we can bring voice to our soul's expression and receive visions for how to tend the world.[4] I write more on the muse in chapter 14.

## Loving Nature

Romance happens between humans and nonhumans. We can fall in love with the night sky, a forest, or the living planet. Witness the exquisite love affair in wild nature — lightning rippling through the dark, a sunset glimmering on the ocean, gentle rain falling on the desert. What places or beings bring you alive?

Nature loves unconditionally, holds mysterious powers, and understands the secrets of our souls. Being intimate with nature changes us. My romances with trees, the ocean, the river, and the rain forest taught me how to love. I have sung to ocean waves, desert waterfalls, and the gentle rain falling over a prairie. Long ago, humans praised the wild world all the time. Today, this love speech is mostly absent. We all want to be loved — nonhumans too. I see the beloved whether I am with a mountain, lake, or canyon.

I have spent many days and nights on rivers and love how far they carry me from roads, cars, and cities. I feel restored and alive when I am going through a river canyon. I surrender to the flow or maneuver around rocks, mesmerized by the movement of water. In a wordless conversation with waves, relaxed and alert, I am in a yogic interplay of body and river.

Although some equate romance with bliss, love asks us to be vulnerable. Our hearts can open in rapture but also may be crushed or humiliated. Sometimes I feel this when I make a mistake on the river and everyone watches as my boat flips or gets pinned. I need to act fast to bring myself and others to safety. My love for rivers has made me more courageous and naturally responsive.

## Longing

Sometimes it's hard to know what we long for. Longing can seem foolish. Why wish for what we may never attain? Longing is not a guarantee we will get love but gives us a way to approach love. The innocent truths in our heart can reveal what we hold most precious.

"I feel weighed down," Sally said in a soul-guiding session. We sat beside the Animas River.

"What's that like?" I asked.

She closed her eyes. "Sad."

"How so?"

"I may die without ever getting what I long for."

"What do you long for?"

"I want to feel my voice and be with the ocean." She sighed.

"What's it like to say it?"

Sally's eyes filled. Tears began rolling down her cheeks.

"Your heart is speaking," I said.

She frowned. "I spend too much energy on things that don't matter."

"And?"

"I want to be with what I love."

"What does the ocean say?"

She paused and went inward, asking the ocean in her imagination. "Be in the flow." Her face brightened.

"Are you with the ocean?"

Sally closed her eyes and was quiet for a while. Her face relaxed, and she looked calm and content.

"Take me along," I said. "What's happening?"

"I see pelicans flying above the waves and the sun moving across the sky," she said. "I'm singing to them."

Longing is the fertile soil from which possibilities germinate. When we follow our longing, what happens can surprise us, carrying us into a mysterious unknown. Longing is holy, although its persistent intensity can feel cruel. I wonder if the gods delight when love pulls us beyond what we imagine into the arms of what reshapes us.

Our heart may open to the scent of honeysuckle and the song of birds. Yet it will break, bearing witness to the dying populations of insects, bees, coral, fish, and whales. Longing is a love-grief cry echoing through music and art. Blues music is exuberant and playful, devastating and mournful. The first blues musicians were African Americans dealing with injustice, oppression, and poverty. Longing is poet speak, as in this poem on love by Kahlil Gibran:

> To melt and be like a running brook
> that sings its melody to the night.
> To know the pain of too much tenderness.[5]

We can go toward longing without knowing exactly what we long for. We can court longing with vulnerability and a willingness to fail. By humbly giving ourselves to what we love, we become the mystery of what our longing makes us. "Sometimes it doesn't help to know what it is you are really hunting or what love is supposed to look like," writes Martín Prechtel, "because the beauty that the hunter becomes and creates through his willingness to fail in pursuit of what he deeply longs for but doesn't yet understand can cause the incomprehensible thing to show its divine face."[6]

We may gaze into the eyes of a human lover, offer gentle touch, and listen for how the other wants to connect. Our inner beloved wants attention too. Being on my yoga mat is akin to making love with myself. I lie on my back, my knees bent and my feet on the floor, reaching my arms toward the sky. I relax my shoulders and cross my arms, bringing my hands to opposite shoulders, embracing myself. I breathe into the place between my shoulder blades and feel space open in the back of my heart, the place where love originates.

I bring my attention to the places my body feels tight or painful. I put a rolled towel underneath my neck, breathe, and invite my muscles to relax. I make time to love myself, beginning with my aching neck. As I feel greater ease, I notice how my body wants to move, and the next pose arises.

My body inhabits the poses or shapes I imagine will call my love close.

Loving myself and being with my longing bring him near. I visualize him with me. I remember the wild places where we love to be — forests, rivers, oceans, mountains. My movements and presence become an offering to these gods. Sometimes an unnameable love longing moves through me. I explore ways to give it expression, listening and flowing into the shape my body wants to make.

Yoga asana is a way to call our inner beloved near, court, and become what we love. As we awaken to the subtle sensations in our bodies and hearts, we may experience tenderness and joy and strengthen our capacity to love what is holy within ourselves, others, and the world.

## Wild Yoga Practices for Romancing the Mystery of What You Love

Discover what allures you, build the courage to face your fears, and move toward what you cherish.

- Reflect on the times in your life when you were in love with a human. What qualities attracted you? Who did you imagine you could become if you were with them? Reclaim the qualities you projected by imagining how you could embody those qualities. Go on a wander in nature. Practice becoming what you love.
- Remember the wild places or nonhumans you have loved. What did you see in them? Who did you become when you were with them? Be with them in the natural world and your imagination. Get to know who they are and what they bring alive in you. Express your love for them and cultivate the qualities you see in them in yourself.
- What or who allures and terrifies you now — humans, nonhumans, a place or activity? If there are many things, choose one to bring into your imagination. Notice how you feel. What qualities attract or scare you? Be with whatever comes. If grief about past relationships arises, be with that, but remember and return to what first attracted you. Practice embodying what you love in how you breathe, move, and see the world.
- Explore the mystery of what you love through art or writing. Draw, paint, write a story, or make a collage. Romance your inner beloved through the beauty you create. Connect the threads of special places, beings, or images in your art.

- Listen for the beloved in your dreams. Pay attention to memories, feelings, or images that arise. Is there a particular beloved calling to you? Stirring your longing or urging you to tend the world somehow? Be with them in your imagination, listen, and see what wants to happen next.
- Wander in nature, seeking the mystery of what you love. Express your longing aloud and be willing to fail. Let yourself be surprised. Whoever comes, speak what you feel and ask your most potent questions. Notice if who or what shows up reminds you of the beloved. Embody what you see, physically or in your imagination.

## A Yoga Pose for Romancing
## the Mystery of What You Love

### CHAIR POSE

In Chair Pose (Utkatasana), our core muscles fire up, and we learn how to sustain many actions simultaneously. This pose strengthens our thighs, stabilizes our knees, and makes our ankles sturdier. Our arms and shoulders gain flexibility as we stretch the muscles between our ribs.

*To get in the pose:*

- Begin in Mountain Pose with your weight spread evenly between your feet.
- Lift your arms overhead with your biceps next to your ears. Keep your arms parallel, with your palms facing inward.
- Bend your knees and bring your shins and thighs as close to a right angle as possible while keeping your weight on your heels. Do not let your knees extend past your toes.

- Bend your knees further, descending as fully as possible. Lift your lower belly to maintain the curves in your spine.
- Draw your pubis toward your navel and pull in your lower ribs. Keep stretching up through your straight arms while pressing firmly into your heels.
- Keep your head and neck in line with your spine and gaze toward the front of your mat.
- Breathe deeply. Maintain the posture as long as you like.
- To exit, press into your heels, straighten your legs, lower your arms, and return to Mountain Pose.

Chair Pose builds heat, strength, and endurance while demanding flexibility, stability, and determination. Do this pose regularly to build stamina. If you are new to yoga, prepare for the full pose by first doing Chair Pose at the wall to gently build strength in your legs and torso. To begin, rest your back against the wall and step your feet about two feet away from the wall. Bend your knees to a right angle, as if you were sitting in a chair. Adjust your body so your knees are directly above your ankles. Press your heels into the floor as you exhale and feel your calves and hamstrings engage. Maintain the posture for several breaths, feeling the support in the back of your body. Straighten your legs and slide up the wall when ready to come out.

Being in Chair Pose empowers us to sit in the seat of our soul and have the tenacity and grit to step toward the mystery of what we love. Practicing Chair Pose builds an internal fire. Standing in it on a cold day can warm us, stoking the flames of our passion and giving us the power and energy to show up and persist so that our love may endure. Try hugging yourself in Chair Pose or embracing yourself while lying on the floor.

Flowing Chair Pose is a variation that invites creativity as you romance the mystery of what you love. Start in Chair Pose. Exhale and bring your hands down into a prayer position between your knees. Next, inhale and bring your hands and arms overhead as you straighten your legs and stand in Extended Mountain Pose. Exhale, bend forward at the hips, and lengthen the front of your torso into Forward Bend (Uttanasana). Bring your fingers in line with your toes, or if they do not reach, bring them onto a block or chair. Last, inhale as you sit back into Chair Pose and begin again. Continue the flow as long as you like. It is easier than holding Chair Pose for an extended time, while strengthening similar muscles.

While in Flowing Chair Pose, romance your inner beloved through your movements and way of being present. Change the flow however you want. Imagine courting your sweetheart through your breath and motion. Be the nectar attracting the birds and bees. Enact a mating dance or another ritual to call your love close. Call in your beloved by being authentic. If she shows up, feel your connection and let her presence guide your movements.

Following the mystery of what we love brings us into a romance with the world and awakens our holy longing. Humbly and boldly, we give ourselves to and become what we love. Longing can usher us toward our passions. Yet living with our hearts wide open may carry us into grief for all we have lost or will lose. In love with the world, we allow ourselves to turn toward despair and let it reshape us. We will explore how in the following chapter.

# CHAPTER NINE

# Embrace Grief and Despair

John is about to go on a three-day solo fast. He tried to go a year ago, but his older brother, Steve, was in a car accident. After that, his year was a blur. Steve suffered a head injury followed by multiple complications, including a skull infection and several blood clots. John and Steve had lost their father two years earlier.

"It was hard to face my brother's emergencies without my dad," he says. "I had to take care of my mom and younger sisters." John is with a group of people about to go on solos. They each share their intentions.

"There's no way to explain what it's like to live on an ICU unit for twelve hours a day, month after month," John says. "I'm exhausted. I just want to rest and be held."

While on his solo, John talks to nature. He praises his brother and laments his loss. "He was a beautiful man and a brilliant pianist," he says. "Now he's in a coma, and his hands are stuck in positions out of his control."

Above where John camps, a great horned owl perches on a cliff. The owl comes and goes; each day, John talks to him. On the third afternoon, the owl winks at him, and John is elated. Something unlocks inside him.

"There's magic," he explains to the group after everyone returns from their solos. "It's not all hardship and suffering."

John shows little emotion until the final night our group is together. Someone plays "hope ur ok" by Olivia Rodrigo, and he loses it, shaking and sobbing. He gets up, walks away from the group, and returns later.

"We listened to that song in the ICU," he explains. "I don't want to burden you, but I want to share my feelings."

We all lose what we love. Sometimes too soon, unfairly, or violently. Love and grief are intertwined. Our hearts are so wild that we don't know what will crack them. Mine first broke when I lost my dog Ginger. On her last night, she looked up at my mom, dad, brother, and me with love, like she always had, glad we were together. Then, the needle went in, the plunger down. She took her last breath, closed her sweet brown eyes, and did not open them again. She was gone. I would never again see her happy face greet me or her tail wag when I opened the door. Or feel her tongue lick my cheek or see her pick up the ball and ask me to play. I would never again feel the love in her face shine on me. The ache was intense.

The pain took root, and I still miss her as I write about it these years later. Her memory makes my voice quiver and my eyes fill with water. I remember others whom I have loved and lost. The trees of my childhood home have been chopped — the giant ash, the grove of pines, the cherry and maple trees. My parents no longer live there. One night I snuck into the backyard, stood where the trees once did, and cried. I told them how much I loved them and what they had meant to me. I feel tender as I remember my grandparents who have passed. And friends who have become ill. A primary yoga teacher in my life has Alzheimer's, but I treasure our time together. Another friend has Parkinson's and dementia. I remember our last walk. It was spring, and she stopped to smell every flower. Loss opens us to the beauty we had. Our hearts ache forever, missing those we love.

Healthy individuals and cultures grieve when they lose someone. In the Dagara tribe in Central and West Africa, funerals go on for days as family members take turns falling apart and leaning on one another.[1] The more tears that fall, the more honor is brought to the loved one who has passed. Our sadness shows how much those who died touched us. Martín Prechtel writes, "Grief expressed out loud for someone we have lost, or a country or home we have lost, is in itself the greatest praise we could ever give them. Grief is praise, because it is a natural way love honors what it misses."[2] Margery Williams's velveteen rabbit aches to be "real" in a favorite childhood story. The boy loves him so much his stuffing falls out. Finally, he begins to feel real but is inadvertently thrown away when the boy becomes ill. As tears fall from the rabbit's eyes and land on the ground, only then is he transformed into a real, wild rabbit.

We all know what it is to be dammed. Undigested grief lived in my tumor. Yet our grief is love, pulling us down beneath the watery surface into the depths of the underworld, where we can listen for mysteries and messages — mythic clues, glimmers of what to do or be. One of my soul images — the heartbeat of the Earth echoing through a cracked cave wall — first came while grieving. It let me know the Earth wants humans to feel her pain, to suffer with her. In my imagination and on land, I offer my tears to the cave pool and feel the rhythm of the Earth beat.

## Earth Grief

It is gut-wrenching to see the world around us becoming more damaged. The pain is not something we can deal with and move on. Once we finally grasp the immensity of ecological devastation, it is hard to bear the feelings of depression, rage, anxiety, cynicism, overwhelm, hopelessness, despair, and apathy. The feelings are not ours alone, but what we are sensing from the heart of Earth. Stephen Harrod Buhner wrote that it's "our feeling response to a communication from the heart of Earth" urging us "to re-inhabit our interbeing with the world."[3] We need to face what is happening and let the feelings speak to us. To listen to their messages and let them alter the course we are on.

I once hoped guiding people on the soul's journey would be enough to transform our culture into one that is life-enhancing. But when the Animas River turned orange, I wept uncontrollably. It was August, near the end of my second season as a river guide, and we were not allowed in the water for weeks. *What about those who live on the river?* No one had warned the duck families, geese, osprey, beavers, and red-winged blackbirds to stay out of the water.

The Gold King Mine near Silverton, Colorado, was abandoned and never cleaned up. In 2015, a dam accidentally burst, spilling 3 million gallons of toxic waste into the Animas River. I apologized to the river: "I am sorry our society is addicted to consuming materials that come from mining. I am sorry we did not demand this mess be cleaned up. I am sorry humanity ever made it. I wish we lived in a culture that honored rivers." This incident was horrible but not rare. Forty-four abandoned mines at the headwaters of the Animas drain toxins every day, unnoticed. They dump 300 million gallons of waste into the Animas every year. There are 22,000 abandoned mines in Colorado and 500,000 in the United States. Globally, more than 180 million tons of hazardous mine waste is dumped into rivers, lakes, and oceans each year.[4] Agriculture poisons rivers too, creating algal blooms, dead zones, heavy metal contamination, acidification, elevated nitrate levels, and pathogen contamination.[5]

It is not only the pollution of waterways that concerns me. Every day, up to two hundred species go extinct.[6] I listen to a recording of the last male Kauai ʻoʻo singing for a female who will never come.[7] I feel sad. The extinction of the Kauai ʻoʻo, a bird native to Hawaii, was caused by human activity. Every year, one in a million species expires naturally, but species are going extinct up to ten thousand times faster than they did before humans existed. We've recently lost the Pinta giant tortoise, the splendid poison frog, the Spix's macaw, the Pyrenean ibex, the Bramble Cay melomys, the western black rhino, and the Moorean viviparous tree snail.[8] And the poʻouli, the Baiji or Yangtze River Dolphin, the Maui ʻakepa, and the Alaotra grebe. Conservationists in Brazil are attempting to restore the Spix's macaw to the wild. It has been extinct in the wild for over two decades. In June 2022, they released eight from captivity, and they plan to release more next year. "'Few reintroductions of birds have been successful, and none was ambitious as this one,' says George Amato, a conservation biologist at the American Museum of Natural History. 'Yet for the Spix it has to be tried.'"[9]

In her poem "Bestiary," Buddhist teacher Joanna Macy asks: "With too many names to hold in our mind, how do we honor the passing of life? What funerals or farewells are appropriate?"[10] Large numbers are difficult to process. Yet they can help us contemplate the magnitude of the loss. Since the dawn of industrial civilization, we have lost 83 percent of wild mammals and 50 percent of plants,[11] and a million more species are at risk — primarily as a result of human actions.[12]

"Why do you put down modern culture?" a colleague asked me over lunch. "I love music, art, food, movies, shows."

"I like those things too," I said, "but I love nature more."

"Saying industrial civilization and human activity are *the* problem is reductionist." He took a bite of his sandwich.

"Scientific research confirms the truth of it," I reminded him.

"It's narrow and depressing."

"We are all carrying grief about the destruction."

"I don't feel anything."

"Dissociation is core to the problem," I pointed out.

"I don't see how getting upset will help," he insisted.

"Of all the dangers we face," writes honored elder Joanna Macy, "from climate chaos to permanent war, none is so great as this deadening of our response. For psychic numbing impedes our capacity to process and respond to information."[13] We all have pain about the loss of wild places and the poisoning of land and sea. The world's sorrow accumulates in our psyches, whether we are conscious of it or not. But paradoxically, bearing witness to planetary loss can deepen our bond with the Earth. Feeling the pain awakens us to our mutual belonging in the web of life.

The more aware we are, the greater our pain becomes. The grief undoes us, unveiling truths in our hearts that connect us to the world's heart. My tears flow as I long for wild places to remain intact. For the ones harmed to be restored. For rivers to run clear. For flocks of birds to fill the sky. For ancient trees to cover the land. For oceans to teem with whales and coral. For machines that extract coal, oil, and trees to be dismantled. For people to stop destroying and start honoring. For lost cultures and species to return and be driven away no more.

In a crowded adobe hall in Ojo Caliente, New Mexico, in my thirties, I listen to the writer Martín Prechtel share the rare and forgotten histories of indigenous peoples worldwide. We hear their music and stories about their lives. I return for seventy days over four years as a student in Martín's course, Bolad's Kitchen. We weep about slavery, injustice, and those we have lost. Where did the urge to destroy originate? We, displaced descendants of enslaved people, offer our tears to the Earth and try to remember sacred economics, making beads to repay a debt to the Earth for the rocks and shells we borrow. We remember those who came before.

In the nineteenth century, the passenger pigeon was the most common bird in North America. Migrations darkened the sky. Flocks took hours to pass and were so loud that human conversation was impossible. As food, these birds sustained people through the winter until people hunted them out of existence. There were an estimated three to five billion passenger pigeons, and I imagine more, until half of the forests in eastern North America were cut down between 1600 and 1870.[14] Then, the passenger pigeon populations plummeted. "By the mid-1890s, wild flocks numbered in the dozens rather than the hundreds of millions (or even billions)."[15] Hunters killed them in their nesting grounds and harvested the squabs. No one stopped when their numbers crashed. People slaughtered them until the end.

When passenger pigeons were abundant, it was inconceivable humans could drive them to extinction. Today, many people don't believe humans could destroy the biosphere. Meanwhile, ecosystems are collapsing.

"People need these jobs," the passenger pigeon industry said to avoid restrictions on hunting. Similar things are spoken today, while mining, dam building, and industrial agriculture clear-cut and pave over land, poison rivers, and dry up underground aquifers.

Acknowledging despair is telling the truth about what we see, feel, and know is happening. To love the natural world is to weep at how humanity harms her. Central to Wild Yoga is staying connected to our tears and feeling the grief that the Earth's devastation brings to our hearts. Particular visions are experienced only through our emotions. We can let the Earth touch us and listen to what she is saying through feelings engendered in our hearts.

## Grief Longs for the Impossible

I wish my words could restore rivers, ecosystems, and justice and that writing about the problems could overcome them. Instead, I feel powerless to protect those I love. I don't know how to stop multinational corporations from extractive work to increase profits. Or how to dismantle the systems of power that allow it. It's not right that extraction is legal and stopping it is illegal. Early environmentalist Aldo Leopold said, "A thing is right when it tends to preserve the integrity, stability of the biotic community. It is wrong when it tends otherwise."[16]

Rivers were once healthy, full of fish. Now, habitat is destroyed daily. In 2015, the World Bank funded an Environmental and Social Impact Assessment (ESIA), concluding that a massive dam on Batoka Gorge's Zambezi River would be a "cheap" solution to the "electricity deficit" of Zambia and Zimbabwe.[17] The sixteen-square-mile reservoir of the 550-foot-tall megadam slated to be built a half mile from Victoria Falls will impact a UNESCO World Heritage Site sacred to the Tokaleya people. Construction is scheduled to begin in 2022. Wildlife who live and breed in the gorge will be displaced or lost. The Cornish jack and bottlenose fish need fast-moving water to survive. The extremely rare Taita falcon is endemic to Batoka Gorge.

To survive, species need healthy places to live. Dams make the water murky and impede fish migrations. When it is time to spawn, it's hard for them to find their way home. Other threats to freshwater fish include draining wetlands, taking too much water for irrigation, releasing too much untreated waste, unsustainable and damaging fishing practices, and introducing nonnative species. Since the 1970s, freshwater fish worldwide have declined by 76 percent, and populations of megafish (heavier than thirty kilograms) have declined by 94 percent.[18] About a third of all freshwater fish species are threatened with extinction. I rarely see fish in rivers in the United States anymore, and when I do, they are usually nonnative fish. Many endemic fish have been overtaken by nonnative fish. Nonnative species can overwhelm native species, compete for limited resources, alter habitat, and devastate biodiversity. Whole communities can be lost. A friend I was with on the Green River in Utah fished daily for a week and caught only nonnative catfish.

When I guided boats on the Salt and Colorado Rivers, we looked for tributaries, streams, and springs to drink from. We filtered and drank from the river when we could not find any. Rivers like the Salt and Colorado have so many pollutants draining into them from dams, mining, and agriculture that the water tastes and smells horrible.

Society has failed to give us what we were designed for: to live our purpose in a healthy web of relatedness. Kahlil Gibran encourages us to bleed "willingly and joyfully" for what we love.[19] I feel like I am bleeding. I hope my tears give sacred water to the parched land. I return to the cave pool of my mythos in my imagination. From under the world tree, I listen to the Earth beat and yearn for industrial civilization to end before the biosphere collapses, while some species and wild places are still alive. I long for a healthy planet and wish for a society rooted in an ethical approach to the land, honoring the voices and lives of the river, birds, rocks, and trees. I want to live in a community in sync with the Earth — in how we gather food, make our homes and laws, and pray and listen to dreams.

Grieving alters consciousness in ways we are unaware of. Stepping into it, we head down a river that takes us into a mysterious unknown and can bring us back to life. As soul activist Francis Weller wrote, "There is some strange intimacy between grief and aliveness, some sacred exchange between what seems unbearable and what is most exquisitely alive."[20]

Even amid uncertainty, feeling our anguish for the world draws us into solidarity with our communities and the Earth. In a grief-tending ritual led by song elder and ritualist Laurence Cole, we drummed and danced and made an altar where people could grieve. Usually, I find it hard to cry around others, but images of wild places and beings arose when I went to the altar. My body shook uncontrollably, and I buried my head in my towel atop a cushion. I remembered a time when the sky was full of birds. I thought of forests turned into fields and wetlands made into concrete. Every time I sat up, more waves of grief came. The community cheered when I returned from the altar to rejoin the dance. I believe the ones whom we cry for can feel our love.

## Tears and Meadowlarks

Grief is in the hearts of those who confront ecocide. Grieving and protecting who and what we love are not in opposition. Both are healthy instincts. Being on the front lines deepened my grief.

Flowering sage covers the desert at Peehee Mu'huh, the Shoshone-Paiute name for Thacker Pass in northern Nevada's Great Basin. Layers of hills and a few rocky cliffs shape the horizon. The sky turns crimson, orange, and purple as I sit atop a cliff, scanning for mule deer, elk, desert bighorn sheep, and pronghorn, for which this is a primary migration corridor.

Reflecting on the damage the proposed lithium mine project would cause, I get a sick feeling in my stomach. I see massive land destruction, outrageous amounts of groundwater taken from an already-overallocated aquifer, and hundreds of tons of sulfur waste trucked in from oil refineries and burned daily.[21] A semitanker would burn 11,300 gallons of diesel every day. All while electric cars, the primary catalyst behind the skyrocketing demand for lithium, are touted as producing zero emissions.

"Being here is healing me," a woman says over breakfast.

I know what she means. I came to Peehee Mu'huh because I had to do something to stop extraction from harming more wild places. Whether or not we succeed, trying feels like giving back. Being on the front lines feels similar to a quest. My tent is ripped to shreds by the wind on the first night. I have to sleep in my car for the remaining two weeks. It is cold.

One morning, I awake to a white landscape that melts in the midday sun. I am about to go on a walk when the land pulls me close. Grief I pushed down for a long time unleashes itself less than thirty yards from my car. I lie on the ground as my hand interweaves with sagebrush. I shake and sob. What if this is not enough? Visions arise of bulldozers cutting through old-growth sagebrush.

"What can I do?" I ask.

"This," I hear.

Wiping my nose, I breathe between sobs. A meadowlark sings in my ear. He is right above me. Surprised and deeply touched, I cry more. His song is exquisite. He sings his melody, again and again, right into my ear.

"Thank you for your song," I say.

"Keep singing," I hear the words arising inside me. "Don't stop."

After the meadowlark has flown away, I watch the sun fade into the clouds. I can still hear his song, but it is more distant. I wander around looking for him and find him singing back and forth with another. His yellow breast is bright atop tall sagebrush. He flaps his wings in a display for the other. The two soon fly off together.

Love and grief weave my heart into the fabric of this sagebrush desert and the sixteen million years of sacred silence that are the mountain. Living among strangers who have become friends, we are a community of row-house cars sharing meals, stories, and dreams. Together, we fight and cry and weave prayers of grief and longing to protect Peehee Mu'huh.

## Wild Yoga Practices for Embracing Grief and Despair

Gently open your heart to loss and sorrow. See if you can listen to and feel the heart of the Earth.

- Remember those you dared to love and those you have lost — friends, family, pets, or places in nature. Express your grief and praise for who they were and what they have meant to you.
- Recall the places or moments that awakened you to ecological devastation. What rivers, ecosystems, or species have you loved and lost? Remember them. Write a story or poem, make art, or create a ceremony to praise them and express grief about their loss.
- Remember species and wild places we have lost. Imagine what they would say. Or visit a wild place slated to be destroyed. Talk to it about what you see and listen to what it says. Let these losses carry you into a lament for the world. Express your sorrow through words, movement, sound, or art.
- Make an altar to cry upon, perhaps in nature. Ask for support from a community of loving trees, rocks, or humans. Create a grief ritual and let yourself lament. Invite the places, moments, and images that evoke the most intense grief and notice what arises.
- If you are emotionally healthy, consider inviting your grief and sorrow for the world to pull you into the depths of the underworld in your imagination. Close your eyes and be curious about what arises — images, emotions, sensations, memories, mythic symbols, something calling you. Then, write about or draw what you discover.
- Seek friends and communities that will listen to your grief and sorrow for the world, spiritual, personal growth, or activist communities that invite conversations about our mutual grief for the Earth. Feel your longing for the world too, for those alive now and for the future generations of all species. Share your yearnings for the world in community.

# A Yoga Pose for Embracing Grief and Despair

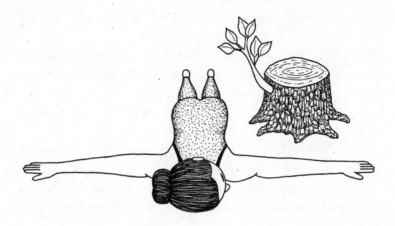

## HUG THE PLANET POSE

Hug the Planet Pose is a Self-Awakening Yoga pose that brings ease and awareness to the low back.[22] Many yoga poses focus on movements that arch the low back by having you bend over backward, which can create a loss of connection to your center. Conversely, Hug the Planet Pose grounds your awareness in your center while lengthening the front side of your body.

*To get in the pose:*

- Lie on your abdomen with your arms resting at your sides, and let your body settle, resting the right side of your head against the ground.
- Notice the connection your belly makes with the Earth. Slow your breathing and tune in to the sensations inside you.
- Bring your awareness to your feet and how they contact the ground.
- Now, move your attention to your knees and where they touch the surface of the Earth.
- Observe your hip joints. Does one feel more relaxed than the other?
- Notice the way your arms and hands meet the ground.
- Next, pay attention to how your head is placed. Which parts of your chin, cheekbones, or head are in contact with the ground? (Use pillows or props to support your head if you have neck issues.)
- Bring your attention to your low back. Notice the rise and fall of your lumbar area as you breathe.

- Mentally scan your body. Notice the impression it makes on the ground. Let your bones be heavy.
- Slowly reposition your arms. Stretch them out to your sides in a T position.
- Lift your head and turn it so that the left side of your face is against the Earth or floor. Notice the slight curve of the planet under you. Imagine your shoulders melting into the ground.
- Release the weight of your body into gravity and imagine releasing the weight of the world.
- Lift and turn your head to place your opposite cheek on the ground. Imagine stretching from your heart.
- Squeeze your inner ankles, thighs, and lower buttocks together. As you breathe, hold the squeeze, and point your tailbone toward your heels.
- Release the squeeze and relax your legs and buttocks. Notice whether a pulse inside your belly is growing stronger.
- Switch the side of your face again. Repeat the sequence as many times as you like, relaxing more each time.

Embrace the Earth and feel your love. Imagine gravity as the Earth's way of loving you. Notice how she pulls you closer. Soak in the nourishment and let the Earth hold you. Imagine lying on the ground close to the humus, humbling yourself. Be present with whatever you feel. Invite your grief and whisper your longings for the world.

Feel your spine naturally realigning. Expand your awareness into your pelvis, belly, and heart. Imagine an energetic umbilical cord connecting you to Mother Earth. Witness your body lengthening without any effort. See if you can feel a pulse in your stomach or sense the heartbeat of the Earth. Imagine your pulse aligning with the rhythm of the Earth's beat. Remember wild places and beings you have loved and imagine embracing them. Call in those you have loved and lost. Bless them with your praise or your tears or both.

Experience the way your whole body opens and lengthens. Anchor your pubic bone into the ground. Notice how this elongates your low back. Envision the curve of the Earth bringing gentle traction to your spine. Let go and rest. Relax your jaw and the muscles of your face. Each time you turn your head, notice if you can stretch your neck more easily. Mentally scan your body and observe any pulsing, streaming, or tingling sensations. Perhaps imagine you are in the depth of your heart or flowing in a river of grief. Track whatever arises in your body, soul, or imagination. Follow the Earth beat or go with the flow of grief.

Consider flexing your spine in the opposite direction in Sphinx Pose. Gently slide your arms out in front of you. Lift the crown of your head toward the sky. Place your elbows on the ground under your shoulders. Stretch your forearms and palms forward and parallel. Release your buttocks. Lift your head away from your shoulders and press your shoulders down, away from your ears. Press your elbows into the ground and relax your lower body.

Embracing our sorrows connects us to the world's heart, unveiling secret truths and bringing us more fully into a human and more-than-human community. In addition to grief and loss, we each hold painful vulnerabilities we unconsciously organize our lives to avoid. Yet being within these tender places can bring us alive and strengthen our capacity to embody our mythos, manifest our visions, honor our relationships, and offer our soul's gifts. We will explore how in the following chapter.

# CHAPTER TEN

# Make a Pearl of Your Vulnerability

Marcus is part of a group preparing for their three-day solo fasts. The first morning, we sit outside in the Sonoran Desert eating breakfast while a hummingbird drinks nectar from a nearby red-flowered yucca. Finishing his granola and yogurt, Marcus tells me about a dream he had during the night.

"I've had so much therapy about my ex-wife," he says. "I don't want to dream about her anymore, but I did."

Our eyes lock, his glance piercing as tears begin to well up. He blinks and looks away.

"Do you want to share the dream?" I ask.

"No," he says, "but I need to."

He closes his eyes as I direct him to reexperience the dream slowly.

"She is poking me in my left eye with her finger," he describes. "I tell her, 'You've shot me again and again, until I couldn't get up,' and then her eyes soften. She comes over, puts her arms around me, and I cry."

He explains that he and his ex-wife divorced a year ago but were married for a decade and have two children. Early in the marriage, she had an affair with a work colleague who was also Marcus's friend.

"She said the affair was over, and I forgave her," he says, gazing out across the desert.

"The feeling in the dream that she 'shot you again and again' — do you feel that in waking life?" I ask.

"Yes. Just before our marriage ended, she went back to having the affair."

I guide Marcus to close his eyes and return to the end of the dream. "Feel her arms around you," I say.

Silent tears roll down his cheeks.

"What are you noticing?" I ask.

His voice cracks. "I still love her. I wish I didn't, but I do."

Marcus had been a stay-at-home dad for years, and once his kids were old enough to play soccer, he coached both their teams. He loved spending so much time with his kids. But then a revelation by his wife triggered him. She told him she had spent the day with John, the man she was having the affair with, and wanted to be with him. He could not believe the affair was back on. His jaw clenched, his nostrils flared, and his face contorted. Then, he lost control, pushed his wife, and screamed, "Why are you doing this again?"

He knew what he did was wrong, and he regretted it immediately. The police came and took him to jail, and since his release three days later, he has not lived with his family. The court put him on probation for a year. He had to complete anger management classes and counseling.

"Is there any difference between the woman in your dream and your ex-wife?" I ask.

"My wife would never have hugged me," he said. "She would've been mad about what I said."

"Maybe the woman in your dream is not her. Maybe she's a guide or your inner beloved."

Later, on his solo, at the edge of a cliff in the Sonoran Desert, Marcus asks a cactus, "How do I let my spines fall off?"

"Grow slow," the words arise in his mind. "Go slow."

That night, Marcus dreams of a mammoth with legs as strong as tree trunks and tusks that bend down toward the Earth and rise up toward the sky in prayer. He realizes that is who he is called to be. With this awareness, he sees again the woman from his previous dream, and he invites her to join him. Over the next two days, while awake, he tends to her in his deep imagination. He shares that being with his ex-wife leaves him vulnerable in a way that feels humiliating. Her presence reminds him of his failures as a partner and a father and that he will no longer be able to live with his children. But as a mammoth, he feels ancient and vital, and he remains attuned to the woman in his dream, allowing her to guide him to open to the sharing of his tenderness.

The art of being vulnerable is central to Wild Yoga. It can strengthen and prepare us to one day face and get to know our core vulnerabilities and understand the gifts our core sensitivities may bring. Core vulnerabilities are the innate sensitivities we are born with that make us woundable. Certain wounds penetrate us so profoundly that through them, we may come to know these core sensitivities. As well as making us feel vulnerable, our core sensitivities carry certain powers that impact our unique way of seeing and experiencing the world. These sensitivities can inspire our gifts and the contributions we make to the world.[1] Exploring these tender places is best undertaken when we are ready, once we feel emotionally healthy and solid enough.

I prayed to be cracked open to my core vulnerabilities for many years. In chapter 3, I shared the story of realizing I had abandoned my heart and then being guided by nature and my dreams to marry my heart. Afterward, I felt immediately and irrevocably altered and began to know my core sensitivities. Most people unconsciously organize their lives so they will never have to face their core vulnerabilities. That was my life before I married my heart. As a longtime wilderness therapist, I was skilled at helping teens and young adults heal their wounds and at aiding troubled families in transforming their lives. Lots of people loved me for what I could do for them. My life protected me from secrets that lay hidden in my own depths.

## The Courage to Be Seen

Brave Heart, the name I was given on my first solo fast, calls me to live vulnerably. It has always felt hard. Our souls often ask us to do what is most difficult. Growing up, it was not safe to feel, let alone speak about what I felt. I was raised to believe our culture's toxic myth, "Tough guys don't have sensitive feelings," and bought into the idea that it is best to act like nothing bothers me. Our culture tells us vulnerability is weak, but in reality, showing tenderness takes courage.

Being vulnerable is at the heart of a meaningful life, although watching someone else express the raw truth is easier than doing it ourselves. It is risky to share our feelings and ideas without knowing if others will appreciate them. Writing this book feels vulnerable. I am sharing intimate details about my life and the unique views I hold about the world with people I have never met. I could be misunderstood, judged harshly, belittled, or mocked.

Research professor Brené Brown shot to fame when her 2010 TEDx Houston talk, *The Power of Vulnerability*, went viral. In her bestselling book *Daring Greatly*, she says that we can't avoid vulnerability and are more at risk of being hurt if we don't acknowledge our tender places. If we pretend we are not vulnerable, it can cause us to be inauthentic. "Experiencing vulnerability isn't a choice — the only choice we have is how we're going to respond when we are confronted with uncertainty, risk, and emotional exposure."[2]

As a wilderness therapist, I witnessed people living in an emotionally safe environment for several months while participating in treatment. Everyone was encouraged to share feelings and listen to and respect one another. Each person shared "I feel" statements: "I feel ___ when you ___. I imagine I feel this way because ___. In the future, I hope ___" (something you can change, in addition to any request you may have of another). Each time someone shared their feelings, another person would reflect back what they had heard and then ask, "Do you feel heard?" I loved working in a community with a structure within which to speak and be heard, with no voices being more important than any others.

Would you like to be deeply seen? Perhaps start taking the risk with those you trust. We need friends, lovers, and communities with whom we can be ourselves. And vulnerability is easiest when it is mutual. I feel moved to be closer with someone when they are vulnerable with me and when I sense they care about me and seek to understand rather than judge. We can each become the kind of friend who listens, even to ideas or feelings different than our own.

Part of loving ourselves and others is having boundaries and discerning with whom and how we share ourselves. Revealing ourselves too soon in the wrong situations can be destructive. It takes time to create boundaries and build trust. Vulnerability is not about "letting it all hang out," as Brené Brown explains; it's about sharing "our feelings and our experiences with people who have earned the right to hear them."[3]

We can share ourselves with trees, rocks, and the ocean. They are always themselves. The natural world is my trusted friend. I also find friends while doing activities I love — eating wild edibles, practicing yoga, doing soul work, river rafting, engaging in Earth activism, being in nature, writing, and swimming. I seek out people who are kind and care about the same things. Many of my friends are skilled at reaching out, praising others, and keeping in touch. I try to emulate them and am grateful for friendships that last and hold a resonant purpose and an invitation to be mutually vulnerable.

## Make a Pearl

Marrying my heart ushered me into a level of vulnerability beyond anything I had known. I became surprisingly sensitive to everything. Avoiding my feelings became impossible. A persistent crushing tenderness weighed on me all the time. It was as if I had been seeing in black and white my whole life and someone suddenly switched on the color. Some feelings — passion, joy, love, freedom — took me to new heights. Other emotions — shame and feeling less than, unworthy, and broken — I struggled to tolerate.

Suffering with compassion, neither indulging nor repressing the pain, can make our vulnerabilities sacred and reveal clues about the unique sensitivities hidden in our most painful places. To make a pearl, oysters coat an irritating grit of sand with layers of lustrous deposits. Embracing our wounds with our love and understanding can give us the fortitude to stay present with what hurts long enough to discover our soul's powers.

Coming to know our core sensitivities does not happen quickly and can often involve repeated journeys into the places that hurt. Susan, a soul mentoring client, is a guide herself. She told me about a recent moment when her core vulnerability was struck.

"I had already worked with it a lot," she said, "and was surprised how much it still hurt."

"What triggered it?" I asked.

"I was reflecting back to a woman the story she had shared, looking deep into her eyes and loving her, but later another woman in the group mimicked me and turned it into a joke, and everyone laughed."

"Do you know why she did that?"

"She's like that," Susan said. "She makes jokes whenever things get serious. She would feel bad if she knew it hurt me."

I asked her what vulnerability was struck.

"I felt exposed, like I was five again, wearing my favorite dragonfly outfit, and my mom and her friends were laughing."

"Do you still feel the hurt of that moment in your body?"

"My chest aches. I thought I was done having to feel like this."

"Core vulnerabilities are often repeatedly struck," I pointed out. "Can you tolerate the pain?"

"Yeah," she said, "but it's tender."

"Before we explore the vulnerability, let's make sure you feel strong enough," I suggested.

"I don't know my core sensitivity, but I'm curious."

Like Susan, we come to know our core sensitivities by being curious and present. We can love and resource ourselves through the pain by attuning to our inner strengths to self-soothe and stay connected. Practices I described in previous chapters are resourcing, such as receiving the love of trees, flowing in your heart waters, and opening to a sacred world. We can also inhabit our mythos, if we know what it is.

Our deepest wounds most often come from "a pattern of hurtful events or a disturbing dynamic or theme" in our early relationships that never fully healed.[4]

The dynamics that wound, rewound, or trigger us may be abusive, but they do not have to be. Either way, they are hurtful in ways we are sensitive to. Sometimes, rather than traversing further into our vulnerabilities, we must pause and strengthen ourselves first. In addition to the practices of Wild Yoga, Bill Plotkin's Nature-Based Map of the Human Psyche offers a way to cultivate wholeness by highlighting "our positive life-enhancing resources" rather than focusing on trauma and pathology.[5] Plotkin names four facets of human wholeness that connect us to the innate resources in our psyche and the natural world.

Utilizing Bill's model, I guide others in their deep imagination and in nature to connect with these four inner facets that can strengthen our psyches. Our Nurturing Generative Adult is compassionate, competent, "and able to provide genuine loving care and service to both ourselves and others."[6] Our Wild Indigenous One is playful, emotional, erotic, "and fully at home in our body and the more-than-human world."[7] The Innocent/Sage is wily, extroverted, and "wants to lead us up to the realm of pure consciousness beyond distinctions and striving."[8] The Dark Muse-Beloved is a guide to soul that is romantic, imaginative, and "wants us to be continually dying to our old ways while giving birth to the never-before-seen."[9]

You may not feel like you have access to these facets, but they exist, and you can find them within you. Alone, each facet is powerful, but together, they coalesce into a single, integral dimension of psychic wholeness. Many of the practices of Wild Yoga grew out of my experiences strengthening my wholeness. Having a relationship with these four facets feels akin to having a supportive community inside my psyche.

If we are resourced, we can turn inward and hold ourselves in our vulnerability. After I married my heart, my marriage to my husband dissolved, and I met the young girl inside me who felt unloved. She had learned to be who others wanted her to be, shut off her feelings, and abandon her heart. She had come to believe the real her must be bad and anything that went wrong was her fault. I felt her suffering and prayed for a vision to unveil how her pain was stitched into the fiber of my mythic purpose.

In the cave of my mythos, underneath the world tree, she leaned into a crack in the wall. As her heart touched the heart of the world, her disappointment blended with the love and suffering of the Earth. She could feel her connection to the wounds of the planet — dammed and poisoned waters, plowed lands, dying ecosystems — and recognized that as part of the Earth's body, we suffer too.

Through her, I have an innate sensitivity to unspoken pain that wants to be given a voice. It asks me to feel and speak what others don't want to see or hear. Sometimes this stirs up trouble. With my core sensitivities exposed, I speak unpopular truths, inhabit a soul-rooted life, and guide others in ceremonies of death, dissolution, and deep listening. It feels vulnerable, but its power can turn torment into treasure.

## Twist

Welcoming our core vulnerabilities invites the monster who has chased us our whole life to dine at our table. Deep exposure becomes a constant. Horror can shape-shift if we abide in the suffering with mythic love. What we thought was a monster might become a magician or something unnameable.

Yellow aspen leaves dotted the mountainside in the Colorado high country in early September. At thirty-six, nearly four years after my fast in the Utah mountains, I embarked on another four-day solo fast at tree line. I had thought I was done becoming more vulnerable, but I was about to be invited miles deeper.

Allured by a fir tree, I camped at his base. His trunk was strangely twisted, and some places were missing bark. His lower branches were alive, while his upper trunk was dead and branchless. His top was severed and missing. I talked to the tree with curiosity and awe each day and asked him about his shape. On the last morning, I shared a vow and gave him a gift. He told me the story of his life.

As the mountain grew, he recounted, many fir trees died. Still a sapling, he survived, but his mother's roots were wobbly. The wind blew her down. That winter, covered in snow, he went deep inside. In the spring, a pika peered out and sang to him, but he was still sad.

Thunderstorms frequented the mountain in summer, and he danced with rain. Ducking and dodging the wind made his roots sink deeper. As his trunk became more flexible, he began to change shape. Everyone started calling him Twist.

"You're so unpredictable," Twist said to the wind and thunder.

"Twist a little more," the wind whispered.

"How much more?" Twist asked.

"We can't feel you through all that bark," the wind said. "Expose yourself."

One night, a bolt of lightning landed at his base, tearing the fabric of his bark in a twisting spiral around his trunk. As he screamed, sap oozed, and he felt the gentle licking of the wind. Then, the rain came, cooling him.

Once the storm passed, Twist looked at his ripped-open trunk.

"How will I survive?" he asked.

"Twist a little more," he heard. He was scared, but loved the wind and rain and wanted to be close.

"Trust, Twist," said a small rainbow glimmering at his trunk.

Each storm exposed more of his trunk. Twisting required a lot of work from his roots and core. He had to let go of something. Little nourishment was making it to the top. Soon his needles up there stopped growing.

He saw the top of the mountain. She had been watching him. "What's it like up there?" he asked.

"Hard to describe," she said.

"What do you see?"

"Come up," she invited.

"I can't. I'll die."

"A lot is dead up here," she said, "and still alive."

Years later, Twist asked the wind to carry him. The top of his trunk had been dead for a while. Before long, it broke off in a windstorm and journeyed up to the top of the mountain. He felt vital up there. Living in two worlds, atop the mountain and rooted in the ground, he felt how the relationship between tree and rock, once a battle, had become a loving union. To this day, he is a vision that guides me, stirring ever-deepening vulnerability.

## Core Sensitivity

A week after my solo fast with Twist, I sat in a circle under a grove of oaks with a spirituality and nature training group in North Carolina. For six years, this community had earned my trust as a place where I could be vulnerable. My teachers, a man and a woman twenty-plus years older than me, were like spiritual parents.

As they gave reflection and feedback to each person in the group, what they said to the first few people felt gentle, but what they said to me felt harsh.

"Consider stepping away from the organization," the man said.

"Stop spending time in wild places," the woman said, running her hand through her dark hair. "And stop telling your stories. Instead, listen to others for a change."

"Abandon yourself," the man said.

They knew abandoning myself was a core vulnerability. *Were they trying to provoke me?* These comments, delivered in front of the group, seemed like a way to diminish me. The group was silent, stunned.

After a moment, to my surprise, a few people chimed in to agree with the teachers. "The thunder on your solo fast meant you should step away," one woman said, grinning. I felt like gasoline was being poured on me and a match lit. Finally, the group dispersed for a break, and two friends came over and gave me a hug.

A day later, my teachers discussed their process: they had "bombed" a few of us who were "ready." Their intent, however, was unclear. Perhaps they wanted me to feel my core vulnerability so I might discover my core sensitivities. Or see if I was resourced enough to tolerate their affront and not abandon myself. Or maybe they wanted me to leave or to be different. I was confused. Council had always been a place where everyone could speak their own truth. Yet in this situation, the teachers had planned what would transpire and asked others to add something resonant.

I felt hurt. I danced with Twist in my imagination. Merging with him, I imagined being reshaped by the blows. I began to notice that my core vulnerability felt more complex than self-abandonment. I was with my heart, and it still hurt. I no longer felt like I could trust my teachers to respect me. Humans are "hardwired for connection, love, and belonging," writes Brené Brown, yet have a universal feeling of unworthiness that is hard to put into words.[10] "Shame is the fear of disconnection — it's the fear that something we've done or failed to do, an ideal that we've not lived up to, or a goal that we've not accomplished makes us unworthy of connection."[11] *I'm not good enough to be loved and to belong.* In a 2011 study, researchers found that as far as the brain is concerned, "physical pain and intense experiences of rejection hurt in the same way."[12]

During my training group's closing ceremony, the sky was mostly clear, except for a small circle of rain sprinkling over my head as I received my certificate. It fell only on me, right when my teachers called my name. It followed me the whole time I was being honored. It felt magical, like the Earth was with me. *I belong to her. She sees and loves me.*

"Thank you, Rain," I said.

Months later, the woman teacher called. She apologized to me and, I discovered later, to a few others. She told me that she had felt unduly influenced by the male teacher and then realized that she was out of integrity.

I later spoke with the male teacher. He believed what he did was right. "As a guide," he said, "you need to wound a person's ego sometimes, if they're ready, to help them align with their greater story."

I am not sure I agree. Yet as I twisted with the blows, I came to understand more about my core sensitivity. Listening to the Earth beat in the cave of my mythos, I felt a sense of collective suffering. In my deep imagination, I became a witch, burned at the stake because of her mystical connection to the Earth. A history of personal and collective memories flashed inside me: lies, deception, ganging up, domination, gaslighting, murder — the wild feminine erased. I shook and cried and imagined the soil carrying my tears to the river.

"Give me the strength to be with the storm," I asked Twist.

"Twist a little more," I heard.

The strike of a thunderbolt is the "irrevocable summons to a deeper life," wrote Daniel Deardorff in *The Other Within: The Genius of Deformity in Myth, Culture, and Psyche*, and to see only betrayal lacks poetry and depth.[13] A "cosmically-anchored-individual can feel the profound correctness of this tragicomic play."[14] Even in the face of society's animosity, we can see in ourselves "the blessing born of the curse, the genius that is in the wound, the hierophany — the sacred song which attracts the gods — hidden and bequeathed within life's utter betrayal."[15]

The promise of life had been broken. Things were not what I had thought them to be. Yet amid my disappointment and aloneness, I felt a dark, exquisite intimacy within myself that created a space to explore my vulnerability. I discovered that a critical aspect of the unspoken pain of my core sensitivity gives me the power to feel the pain of voices not being heard. It gives me the capacity to feel the human betrayal of the Earth and empathize with the suffering of the more-than-human world and those harmed by other kinds of structural discrimination. Humans dominating the planet. The controlling of women and the wild. Patriarchy striking out at vulnerability — rivers, trees, soil, women. Rather than question power structures, people jockey to maintain or elevate their place.

I feel vulnerable sharing an aspect of my core sensitivity. Yet speaking can free us from shame and self-blame and invite others to take similar risks. Being scapegoated or ganged up on is common in the workplace and in society, particularly for those who refuse to be who others want them to be. Twist guides me to stay open and twist a little more. Let the blows reshape me and receive the love of more extraordinary powers, like Twist did with the mountain and like I have with my mythos and the rain. I am grateful to Twist and my friends who see and love me.

Our souls exist in mutual vulnerability with one another and the Earth. We can gently be present with one another as we soften into what hurts. The Earth wants her vulnerability cared for. All of us do. Betrayal starts with disengagement. "When people we love or with whom we have a deep connection stop caring, stop paying attention, stop investing, and stop fighting for the relationship, trust begins to slip away and hurt starts seeping in."[16] We can find and create healthy relationships and choose to see, honor, and praise one another. We can track how we disengage from each other and the Earth and decide to be together in our vulnerability.

## Wild Yoga Practices for Making a Pearl of Your Vulnerability

Be gentle with yourself when you expose your feelings and ideas. Honor your fears and limits.

- Consider what scares you about feeling your emotions or which emotions are most uncomfortable for you to share. Find a being or place in nature with whom to share your feelings in story, poetry, song, or movement. Notice if nature has anything to say back.
- Strengthen your wholeness. Review the practices in earlier chapters: listen to your body, deepen your ecological perception, flow in your heart waters, and receive the love of trees. Perhaps explore your feelings with a body-centered therapist. Seek friends who support you.
- Wander in nature with a young, sensitive part of yourself. Remember what it was like when you were a child. What disturbing dynamics existed in your early relationships? From a resourced place, love the part of you that feels hurt. Hold dual consciousness of resource and vulnerability. Notice any sensitivities that affect how you see the world.
- Remember a vulnerable being or place you encountered in a dream. Or visit a place on the Earth that has been hurt. Invite them to tell you the story of their lives. Track what you learn about their

vulnerabilities and strengths. Write a story or poem about your tender places and how you resource yourself and stay connected to your strengths.

- If you are resourced, explore the Buddhist practice of *tonglen* meditation, a willingness to take in the suffering of others. Find an instructor if you have not learned how to process other beings' suffering, or watch instructional videos.[17] Once you are comfortable doing so, invite the vulnerabilities of other humans, nonhumans, and the Earth. Embrace their wounds with love and understanding. Track whatever arises.

- Feminist bell hooks observed: "Sometimes people try to destroy you precisely because they recognize your power — not because they don't see it, but because they see it and they don't want it to exist."[18] Contemplate the challenges of vulnerability in a world where power-over dynamics exist in families, communities, institutions, and workplaces. Consider how you can be vulnerable *and* protect yourself.

## A Yoga Pose for Making a Pearl of Your Vulnerability

### PIGEON POSE

Pigeon Pose (Kapotasana) opens your hips and stretches your glutes, hip flexors, thighs, and low back muscles. People hold a lot of unconscious tension and old emotions in their hips. Pigeon Pose relieves stress and fear stored in the hips and is commonly known to release tears.

*To get in the pose:*

- Begin in Table Pose (Bharmanasana), on your hands and knees with your knees as far apart as your hips. Place your palms under your shoulders, your fingers wide and facing forward. Look down, relax your shoulders, and feel your spine lengthen.
- To move toward Pigeon Pose, bring your left knee forward. Keep your left thigh parallel to the side of your mat, and move your left foot forward on the mat until it's in front of your right hip. (If needed, place a pillow or cushion under your left hip for support.)
- Slide your right leg straight behind you and lower both hips toward the floor (or your left one onto the cushion or pillow and your right one hovering above the floor).
- Lower your pelvis and keep your hips square to the front of your mat. Balance your weight by pressing your hands down evenly in front of you.

- Inhale, come onto your fingertips, lengthen your spine, draw your navel in, and open your chest. Press the top of your back foot into the floor for a deep hip flexor stretch.
- Exhale, walk your hands forward, and lower your upper body toward the floor. Rest your forearms and forehead on the mat in Relaxed Pigeon Pose. (Or on a block or cushion if your head does not reach the floor.)
- Root down through your back foot. Breathe into the sensations and relax your eyes, jaw, and throat.
- To come out, push into the floor through your hands, lift your hips, and move your legs and arms so you're back on all fours in Table Pose. Repeat on the other side.

In Pigeon Pose, feel the expansion of your chest as you imagine your heart engaging with the world. Notice what it feels like to have your pelvis in close contact with the Earth. Let this pose bathe you in the love of the natural world. In Relaxed Pigeon Pose, feel your forehead close to the Earth, shut your eyes, go inward, and tend your heart. Notice the transition between outer expression and inner tending. Be present to the vulnerability inside you. Notice if images, memories, or sensations arise.

Remain in Relaxed Pigeon Pose and feel your connection to the Earth. Use pillows or folded blankets for support if your torso does not reach the ground. Utilize whatever props you need to make this pose comfortable. Breathe. Imagine yourself receiving love, as you did in chapter 5 with the trees. Feel your blood pumping through your veins. Imagine yourself flowing in your heart waters, the way you did in chapter 3. Feel your vitality and notice if vulnerabilities arise in images, emotions, memories, or sensations. If you feel vulnerable, notice how this alters you or what it reveals.

When you are ready, rise up and switch sides. This time, as you are in upright Pigeon, imagine taking the risk of being vulnerable and sharing yourself. What would you say or do? With whom? Notice what arises in your imagination. Then, in Relaxed Pigeon Pose, go inward and feel the strength in relating with the Earth. Practice holding dual consciousness: take a risk and offer your vulnerability while simultaneously resourcing yourself in the love of this connection. Extend outward and tend inward. Feel your body and heart recalibrating as you learn new patterns of movement.

If you find Pigeon Pose too challenging, even with a cushion, try an alternate pose to stretch your hip flexors and build strength. (This is also a good warm-up before Pigeon Pose.) First, kneel on the ground with your torso upright. Your hands can be either on your hips or relaxed at your sides. Then, step your right foot in front of you with your right knee bent at ninety degrees. Keep your left knee down with the top of your left foot resting on the ground. Next, maintaining a straight back, push forward into your left hip while keeping your right knee over your right ankle. You should feel a stretch in your left quad. Hold for ten breaths, then switch sides and repeat.

Being vulnerable brings us into an authentic relationship with the world. Our core sensitivities, once we discover them, imbue us with a unique potency. Now we can attune to the invisible realms that live in the dark powers beyond our understanding. Is it time to let your life unravel, enter a fertile darkness, and listen to the sacred Mystery? There, you can let what arises in your deep imagination guide you into the person you came here to be. We will explore how in the following chapter.

# CHAPTER ELEVEN

# Descend into the Reverent, Dark Mystery

Just after our high school graduation, my friends and I are spending a week at a beachside cottage in Ocean City, Maryland. It is not that wild, except for the sea. I enjoy spending time with my friends, eating, and playing cards inside the cottage, but each night I am drawn outside to wander and be with the sea. The boy I like (and wrote about in chapter 8) is inside, and while I wish to spend time with him, I am lured outdoors to something mysterious, something that seems to be pulling me beneath the surface of everyday life. I want to follow this curiosity and listen and surrender to wherever it takes me. I dive into the water, give my body to the waves, and float in darkness.

This is not the first time I have felt enchanted by the dark. I grew up near the Chesapeake Bay, and as a teen, I often went to the water's edge at night, to sit and imagine myself submerged underneath the sea. It was as if I could feel the presence of other worlds and unseen possibilities that I longed to connect with. The dark waters felt sacred. They seemed incredibly wild and in some ways more alive than my waking life. I felt as if something I was missing and longed for lived there. Yet I did not know how to access or give voice to it. Looking back, it was as if I was a selkie who had lost a skin she never knew she had.

Much later, I would discover that what I was longing for, in part, was the Divine Mystery. The dark is mysterious, and when we step into it, our eyes can't see, so our imagination, a powerful way of listening and intuiting, can grow stronger. Much can be encountered in the dark — parts of ourselves we have lost, never-before-seen potentialities, ancient stories and symbols.

Most of the universe is a dark mystery. More is unknown than known. Sixty-eight percent of the universe is dark energy. In physical cosmology and astronomy, dark energy affects the universe on the most significant scale, filling empty space and seemingly driving the universe's accelerated expansion.

125

Twenty-seven percent of the universe is dark matter whose gravitational force holds galaxies together and seems to slow the expansion. Less than 5 percent of our world is real matter, everything we can observe with all our instruments.

In ancient stories, the dark is a womb from which all things are born. The cycles of nature return us to darkness every night, and in the dream stream, we are infused with myths, symbols, images, and stories. Darkness steeps us in dissolution and uncertainty. Later, I discovered that the dark waters of the cave pool and underworld river are a mythic place where I reside. Yet at times, I have found myself terrified of the dark. I have needed to cultivate strength, patience, and courage to keep moving toward it.

On my first Animas quest in Utah, I cannot sleep. I do jumping jacks and push-ups, trying to exhaust myself. After calming down, I sit on the rock that invited me to this high perch in the canyon.

"Relax," it seems to say.

I thought I'd be asleep when it was dark. *Am I afraid of something?* I have been outside at night a lot as a wilderness guide, but this time I am fasting alone in a sacred ceremony. Days earlier, I had stepped through a portal. I told the Mystery, the universal consciousness that animates the cosmos and everything in it, that I am willing to let go of my life — my home, my profession, my relationships, my identity — if that is what is asked of me. I left my wedding ring at the portal and wrote my husband a letter. *I love you*, I said, *but I need to let go of our marriage during my solo to be open to what the Mystery asks.*

I have come for a vision, but I am afraid of what I might see. What if something happens and I see things that others can't see? Perhaps something I do not want to see. Something that overwhelms me or instantly alters my life. Or maybe nothing will happen. Maybe there's no vision for *my* life. Lying on the rock, I take a deep breath and try to relax. I remember my love for the dark and long to be open to whatever the Mystery unveils. Turning my gaze upward, I watch stars flicker and galaxies twinkle. The band of light referred to as the Milky Way shines in the moonless night. In pitch black, I feel tiny facing the immensity of the universe. I let go and tune in to my deep imagination.

"I trust you," I say to the Mystery.

Yogis often seek an expanded view of reality by stretching their consciousness toward the light. Wild Yoga invites us to extend our conscious awareness into the dark. Dreaming in the cave womb, as described in chapter 6, introduces us to images that arise from the night. Dreaming happens when we are awake too. If we attune to our deep imaginations in the dark, perhaps we can become more aware of the unfolding dream of the world and open to the great mysteries of our lives.

## Letting Go

I did not want to sacrifice my marriage. My husband was my best friend, partner, and playmate. We had met while working at Outward Bound and loved many of the same things — kayaking, gardening, backcountry skiing, cuddling, reading. We had created a ceremony to marry at the edge of Blackwater Canyon in West Virginia. I loved our life, but something in me was unfulfilled. I longed for a deeper relationship with nature. And for my work with people in the wilderness to come from a soul-rooted place.

Longing is a mystery, whispering the ineffable notes of our souls. It catalyzes us to step toward intangible, unnameable yearnings that change everything. A year after my Animas quest, I returned to the canyon in Utah and apprenticed to be a guide. My wedding ring fell off one night during a trance dance. It had never fallen off before. I didn't notice it was missing until I was back in my sleeping bag. While everyone else was asleep, I returned to the place where we had danced and anxiously combed my fingers through the sand.

"No, Mystery," I said, "please let me keep my marriage."

My fingers contacted the ring in the dark. Yet over the next three years, my marriage slowly unraveled. We got along well, but our conversations lacked intimacy and depth. We were like brother and sister. There was no passion.

"My girlfriends say it's odd," I said one day while we were eating lunch, "for a man not to be interested." I had wanted to broach the topic for months but felt nervous.

"Most married couples stop having sex," he said matter-of-factly.

"We've never had ... much ..." I struggled to find the words.

"We have a good life," he interrupted, standing to take his dishes to the sink.

"If you've been hurt," I offered, "you can tell me."

"Stop," he said, looking me in the eyes. "I'm not one of your clients."

I counseled adolescent boys in the wilderness, encouraging them to share their feelings. It often felt like pulling teeth.

I listened to nature and my dreams for years before I married my heart and pledged myself to Mystery, Earth, and Soul. Yet these vows catalyzed a deeper descent. Nature and our dreams want us to have a cocreative relationship with the world. Our soul sees the real potential of our lives, the greater story, and it wants us to inhabit our mythos and serve the world from a soul-rooted place. When we say yes to soul, it often asks us to stop what we are doing and who we are becoming while we do it.

My kitten Mystery died while I was on my solo in the Utah mountains. She was pure white with blue eyes and had come to me in a supermarket parking lot ten months earlier. My husband found her body under a juniper, not far from our house. She had been bleeding, the soft whiteness of her stomach stained a deep red. Perhaps an animal had gotten her. We held a burial ceremony, and I cried for days.

Had her spirit grown too large for our home? As the nights passed, it seemed like mine had. My body began to itch as I lay in bed next to my husband. I scratched, but it wouldn't stop. I went to sleep in another room, and the itching stopped. We started to sleep in separate rooms.

A month later, I realized I needed to move out. After I returned from a guiding trip, my husband confessed one evening that while I was away, he'd watched some porn. I was stunned. For months, I'd thought he was asexual, simply disinterested. And he knew my history — how a previous boyfriend's relationship with porn had brought much conflict into our lives. I was unsure how to deal with my husband's admission but hoped that taking some personal space would bring us closer. His concern was different. He was more upset that his rent would double and he would no longer belong to a dual income household.

Years before meeting my husband, I'd been in a long-term relationship with Todd. I will never forget the night I came home unexpectedly and opened the front door to see his naked body streak across the living room.

"What's going on?" I asked. He put his pants on, grabbed a pillow, and lay down on the floor.

"I was masturbating," he said, his dark hair hiding his eyes as he looked down.

Glancing around the room, I noticed a tinge of blue light emanating from the computer.

"Internet porn?" I asked.

"I tried to quit."

"How long?"

"Since before we met."

"What? But I asked if you watched porn on our second date. You said no. Never."

I did not want porn in my life and always asked this question before getting into a relationship.

"I was planning to stop."

An unpleasant metallic taste filled my mouth. "How often?" My chest felt like it was caving in.

"Every day I could."

"We've been together for six years. During all this time? Every day?"

"There were periods I quit, but then I'd start again."

"Why didn't you tell me?"

"I thought if I could stop, you'd never have to know."

Though fearful of what I might learn, I couldn't stop myself from asking. "What do you watch?"

He sat silent, staring off into space, and then shouted, "I hate myself. I'm going to kill myself."

Within a split second, he leaped off the floor, grabbed his keys, and bolted out the door. *What on Earth? Is he serious?* I just as quickly chased after him. We got to his car at the same time. I reached out to grab his keys, but he pushed me back, jumped into the car, and sped off.

For the next forty-five minutes, I sat in the old rocking chair in the far corner of our living room, swaying back and forth, my heart pounding. I had no idea what to do. Trying to calm myself, I prayed and waited. Finally, I heard his car turn into the driveway. The front door opened. His face looked blank, with no emotion, his eyes unfocused as he tossed his keys on the table, walked over, and flopped back on the pillow that was still on the floor in front of me.

"I couldn't do it," he said.

I crawled down on the floor beside him and placed my hand on his chest.

"I'm glad you're okay."

"I'm worthless."

"You can get help."

"People don't recover from this."

"Why not?"

"It's too humiliating."

Finding out about Todd's addiction was shocking, but I began researching porn use and learned that what I was going through was far from unusual. Porn sites, a $97 billion business worldwide, receive more traffic than Netflix, Amazon, and Twitter combined. Around 70 percent of men view porn regularly, at least monthly. Porn viewing is accidentally discovered by a spouse 75 percent of the time, often with traumatic results.[1]

Porn destroyed my relationship with my boyfriend Todd, but it did not end my marriage to my husband. Rather, along with the indifference that had invaded our relationship, now I couldn't help but see my husband in a crude light. That one lewd incident was all it took to seal the end of our already weakened marriage. As I write about these two men, I can also recall what attracted me to them in the first place. A part of me continues to love them. But in both cases, I lost faith, recognizing the kind of intimacy I longed for was impossible.

The dissolution of my marriage initiated me, along with the revelation that the kind of closeness I yearned for may not exist. I let go of the life I had, as well as any hope of recreating it, and descended into a fertile darkness. Nothing would be the same. Challenges and upheavals can be portals if we listen to what they ask. They may open us to things we have not seen inside or outside ourselves, including mythic possibilities. My longing to be in service to my soul made me vulnerable to the summons to let go of the life I had. As noted by the poet David Whyte:

> There is only one life
> you can call your own
> and a thousand others
> you can call by any name you want.[2]

I wanted to live my truest purpose.

## The Dark Mystery

Unseen powers live in the dark, beyond our understanding. The darkness of the night can be scary, and the fertile darkness of leaving behind the life you have been living is terrifying. Yet swimming in these uncharted seas is when we are most likely to encounter revelation — the mystifying, numinous demon-angel, the Divine. The dark is a physical manifestation of Mystery.

The dominant culture encourages people to avoid the unknown and favor a safe but inauthentic life. In ancient nature-based cultures, elders invited their young to enter the liminal unknown. Earth-based ceremonies can initiate people into listening to the dark. Humanity needs them in order to grow and mature. Without them, our dominant culture has become a life-devouring machine. I wish everyone would dare to step into the dark, flow with the changing currents of the underground river, and blossom in authentic, soul-rooted service.

I let go of my marriage and crossed over into a dark unknown. One of the first things I did was return to the red rock canyon where I had carried out my first solo fast and received the name Brave Heart. I enacted a twenty-four-hour fast and offered some red-tailed hawk feathers my husband had given me. I remembered our favorite moments, thanking the Mystery for our time together. I offered my tears, prayed for his well-being, and gave him back to Mother Earth.

Death is a part of the seasons and cycles of nature. It can initiate us into the mysteries of life. The end of my marriage, like my bout with cancer, was a form of death. Everything my life had been, and what I thought it would be, ended. The call of our souls may haunt us our whole lives. But when we let go and surrender to this call, a space can emerge within which to attune to the most potent visions and revelations of our lives. Amid the loss and horror, I discovered myself and the world anew.

The Mystery holds a grander vision that it wants to show us if we are willing to listen. Death preys on us, bringing us to our knees in humility, rousing us to pray. Six months after leaving my husband and the home we shared, I found myself on a river and felt a visceral sense of what it feels like to surrender to the flow. To my surprise, a wave pulled me out of my boat and swept me underneath a major rapid. I did not have a life jacket, but I fought hard and made my way to the surface and the shore. I'd lost one shoe but saw an old sandal that must have once belonged to someone else. Shaking, I put it on.

In the moments I had been under the water, I was in a fertile darkness, unsure if I would ever come up. I felt the part of me that did not want to live and the part that did. I disparaged myself for forgetting my life jacket and felt humiliated that I had made such a ridiculous and potentially deadly mistake. I didn't get on a river again for nine years.

I did not realize then that the river was showing me what I had to live for and that the dark waters are a mythical place I inhabit.

## Inhabiting the Deep Imagination

Mystery knows better than we do who we are and how we are meant to serve. Our journey is an attempt to listen and understand. After my marriage dissolved, I felt lost, and the world seemed unrecognizable. I found participating in mainstream culture excruciating. As I wandered in inner and outer landscapes, mythic images arose from the depths. Parts of myself emerged from the shadows and infused me with life.

The destabilizing images of my dreams constantly surprised and challenged me. They offered clues about who I was or needed to be. They gave me ways to engage authentically amid the impossible nightmare of ecocide. As I embodied invitations from my depths, I felt a communion with myself and what is sacred. I began to feel at home in my mythic depths, as I do in nature.

It takes time to understand what the images are trying to reveal. Inhabiting the dream of my mythos — the world tree with never-before-seen red fruit and purple wings — I experience the world from its perspective in my imagination. It feels strange and yet livening, my roots planted in the cave where the Earth's heart echoes. As I reside in the core images I have been given, I listen for what is newly arising.

Our deep imagination comes in our dreams while we sleep. Yet it also exists in the waking world. We can turn toward the images that arise unbidden at the edge of our consciousness. What does not make sense to our minds is likely from our depths. Our culture entrains us to dismiss imagination, but it is essential to knowing our souls and connecting to the mysteries that beckon us. The deepest layers of our imagination bubble up and have their own intelligence. Our deep imagination is a wilderness that allows the animate natural world to speak to us so we may participate in dreaming the world.

When I first began listening to my deep imagination in my early thirties, I trusted my dreams but was unsure about my waking visions. Was I just making things up, or was that my *deep* imagination? Our deep imagination surprises us. It comes up with things our minds never could. Do not stress over how deeply you are or are not immersed at first. Swimming in imaginal shallow water is better than having no imagination at all. At least you are in the river, available for deeper currents to come and carry you away.

## The Fertile Darkness

I return to the nightmare I shared in chapter 6, my dream in the cave womb. The scary part is when I am pulled down in the dark water and someone underneath me grabs my leg. I am free-falling in the dark, reminding me of when I was swept under the rapid in waking life. The waking and dreaming images of being underwater merge in my imagination: I reenter the dream of free-falling in the dark waters, and I feel myself being pulled under the rapid. We are often brought back to essential threads of our mythic life again and again. A multiplicity of meanings lives in each image. We may never fully understand them, but we learn more each time we return to be with these visions.

Remembering how I emerged from the river, missing a shoe, I realized the river reflected my mythos: I am to live with one foot in the dark waters. Persephone lives half her life in the underworld. Similarly, I am called into the dark waters to experience beauty and suffering and to pray for vision. My soul images — the cave pool and underworld river that live under the tree — guide me to invite others into the dark.

Mysterious visions can arise in the chthonic depths of the underworld that nourish and cultivate the mythic sinew of humans and the Earth. Myths of primordial waters are found across cultures. Healthy cultures source their actions from these depths. In trainings and classes, I guide people into the fertile darkness to let go of who they were and what they thought they were supposed to do, so they can deeply listen. The dark waters are wiser than us. Listening to them allies us with the greater forces of unseen worlds and infuses us with fierce creativity, allowing the Earth to dream through us.

Some years ago, guiding a solo fast on the Isle of Iona in Scotland, I walked along the coast daily, talking to the sea. I remembered my Irish ancestors as I sat on huge boulders, watching waves crashing. The shapes and colors of shells and stones enchanted me. Seals played in the waves, and the weather was changeable. High winds, fog, and heavy rain were frequent. Then, the sun would peek mercifully through the clouds.

"I've loved you my whole life," I said to the sea. "Beside you, I am home."

"Marry me then." The words arose in my mind. Images flashed of other dark waters I had known and encountered in dreams and their deep love and significance. I hadn't been looking to marry but suddenly realized it was right.

Days earlier, I had bought a silver ring with the eternal Celtic knot in a little store. I was unsure why, because I don't like wearing rings. Now I understood I was supposed to have it.

I stepped into the sea, balancing on rocks, dipped my ring in, and offered vows to the dark waters. A seal's head surfaced only a few feet away. I was carried into the ocean's depths by peering into his soft eyes. Suddenly I felt the intimacy I'd longed for — with the dark waters. Perceiving the world from within them, I felt a heaviness weighing on my chest, my eyes welling with tears. Staring into blackness, I longed for a vision and waited to see what might unfold.

In the dark waters, I inhabit a place where I can touch the world and listen deeply. I don't know what will come next, but I am glad to be where Mystery can surprise and move through me. Living in profound communion with the dark waters makes me feel powerful and vulnerable.

## Wild Yoga Practices for Descending into the Reverent, Dark Mystery

Befriend the dark and welcome the unknowing. Turn toward the images that arise at the edge of your consciousness.

- Reflect on your relationship with darkness. Remember your most powerful moments or encounters. Has the dark been something that has allured or terrified you? What images or experiences have come? Journal about whatever you recall.
- Go outside in nature at night. Find a place where you can be in the presence of darkness. Close your eyes and see what arises in your imagination. Notice what you feel or experience — sensations, emotions, images, qualities. Speak aloud and tell the darkness what you notice. Express your wish to have a relationship with the dark and listen for anything the night may want to show you.
- What in your life is dying? What are you willing to let go of to step toward your calling? Find a stick or other item in nature to symbolize what you are ready to let go of. Offer it to the river in a ceremony. Share what you have loved about what you are offering. How has it served you? Why is now the time to let it go?
- Gather the images that have come to you in the dark. Make a collage, poem, story, or other work of art. Ask the Mystery to help you understand how the images come together. Spend time in your imagination with each image and get to know them.
- Choose a mythic or another significant image you have been given. Spend time inhabiting it in your imagination. Let it move you. Or stay present with the image until you become the image. How would you perceive the world? Or feel called to engage?

- Descend into the fertile darkness or the mythic depths of the under-world in your imagination. Read myths, stories, or poems that evoke a sense of what this would be like. Find a place in nature that reminds you of the fertile darkness and spend time there. Share your longings and fears with it and notice what images, sensations, or memories arise.

## A Yoga Pose for Descending into the Reverent, Dark Mystery

### HEROINE POSE

Heroine Pose is a Self-Awakening Yoga pose that opens your hips and stretches and lengthens your spine, similar to Cow Face Pose (Gomukhasana).[3] Begin in a seated position in which your body feels comfortable. You may need to elevate yourself by sitting on a cushion, yoga block, or chair for support.

*To get in the pose:*

- Sit on the floor in Butterfly Pose (Baddha Konasana), with the soles of your feet together and your knees opening out to the sides. If you find your spine rounding, sit up on a prop like a folded blanket, cushion, or block.
- Lift your right leg and cross it over your left into Heroine Pose. As you twist your torso, your left foot should land just outside your right hip. Or if it is easier, press your hands into the floor, lift your sit bones off the ground, and walk your knees together. Then, sit back on the ground or on your block or cushion.
- Rest your palms on the soles of your feet. Close your eyes and relax. Track the sensations in your lower body.

- When you're ready, gently move your feet a little further apart from your hips.
- Press your hands into the floor, bring your sit bones off the ground, then lower your buttocks back down onto the floor or a cushion. Repeat the raising and releasing, feeling the strength in your arms as you lift your upper body.
- Round your spine toward your knees and allow your head to rest on your knee or on a pillow or block. Relax your shoulders and jaw. Close your eyes and notice the sensations arising in your body.
- To come out of the pose, lift your right leg or press your hands into the floor, lift your sit bones off the ground, and walk your knees apart. Return to Butterfly Pose.
- Try Heroine Pose on the opposite side, with your left leg on top.

Rest in darkness as you embody Heroine Pose. Notice what is happening in your hips. If you don't feel much, lower your head to your knee to increase the intensity; to ease the sensation, bring your head up or sit on a prop. Experience your hips as the hinge between your upper and lower body. Notice how communication moves from the head, heart, and hands through your hips to your mobile legs and feet. Invite your hips to relax by massaging them.

In the pose, as you bring awareness to your spine, imagine yourself in oceanic darkness. Imagine witnessing the evolution of the spine in other organisms. Consider how your spine is a doorway for expanding consciousness and how stretching it may be linked to searching for meaning and purpose. What does it feel like to swim in the depths? How does your spine want to move?

Explore your hips and spine in a gentle Self-Awakening Yoga movement to build your strength for Heroine Pose. Begin in Butterfly Pose, sitting with the soles of your feet together and your knees opening out to either side. Scoop your right hand under your right ankle, lift it a few inches above the ground, and then return it to the floor. Scoop your left hand under your left ankle, lift it a few inches, and then lower it down. Repeat, alternating sides. Then place the outer ankle on the opposite ankle. Work your way up to placing each ankle on the opposite calf. As you repeat the movement, notice if the lifting gets easier or the hip joints get more fluid. Now lift your right ankle up and over your left knee and place your right foot on the floor beside your left thigh, moving back into Heroine Pose. Relax and release into the heaviness.

Heroine Pose embodies what Don Stapleton calls "the paradox of courage and surrender."[4] In the fertile darkness, we need the strength to let go and the willingness to engage. Power can come from humbly accepting whatever we are experiencing in our bodies and imaginations. The pose asks you to get comfortable in the moment. Rest your third eye on your knee or on a pillow, block, or bolster, and close your physical eyes. Invite curiosity and courage as you surrender to the sensations in your body and the images arising in the darkness. Notice how your hips and spine receive unfamiliar experiences. Let go of trying to make anything happen. Be where you are. Surrender to this deep dive into the unknown.

If Heroine Pose is too challenging, try Easy Pose (Sukhasana). Sit on your mat with legs stretched straight in front of you. Bend your right knee and bring your foot close to your left thigh. Bend your left leg and slide your left foot under your right calf. Your shins are crossed, with the sole of each foot tilted up beneath its opposite knee. Relax your feet and rest your hands on your knees. Keep your pelvis in a neutral position and your spine straight. Sit on a folded blanket or place pillows under your knees if you need to alleviate pressure on your hips or knees. A meditative state can arise in this pose as you gently stretch your hips and ankles and strengthen your abdominal muscles. Stay in the pose for a minute or longer if you can. Each time you sit in this pose, vary the cross of your legs, so the left and right legs have equal time on top.

By opening to our deep and wild imaginations and having the courage to step into the dark unknown, we can receive glimmers of the vision that Mystery holds for us. We are called to live our souls while attuning to the symphony of the world. Everywhere there is life, there is song. Humans are meant to live in harmony. More-than-human others live with their souls in symbiosis. We can learn to live our purpose in relational flow with other humans and the Earth. We will explore how in the following chapter.

# CHAPTER TWELVE

# Play Your Part in the Symphony

Humans once sang with ease. Evolutionary scientists say we are the descendants of tree dwellers who called to one another through the canopy. The first words that humans uttered sounded like bird calls. Humans and birds share a common ancestor, the clade amniotes, which lived 310 to 330 million years ago.[1] Both birds and humans evolved to form complex vocalization and social groups.[2] Rare whistling languages, often called bird languages, can still be found "in every corner of the globe [in] more than seventy groups."[3]

Whistles travel further than everyday speech. Shepherds and farmers whistle their messages down into the valleys from the mountains. In the Amazon jungle, hunters locate each other through the dense foliage by whistling. The Inuit communities of the Bering Strait whistle commands at sea. In the foothills of the Himalayas, two lovers whistle enchanting melodies in a now rarely performed courtship ritual. At nightfall, boys wander through nearby villages whistling poetry. If a girl responds, the lovers continue their melodic dialogue and add nonsense syllables to ensure the privacy of their exchange.

Ngäbe-Buglé (Guaymí) villages are dispersed throughout the mountains of southwestern Costa Rica. Their indigenous reserve is not far from the off-grid Yoga Farm where I lived for several winters.[4] The Ngäbe-Buglé people retreated to this region from the country now known as Panama under pressure from Spanish colonists and amid the development of low-lying areas. There are no roads to their remotely scattered homes and villages.

The first time I meet some of them is on a public bus, traveling from Golfito to Punta Banco, Costa Rica. Their faces are beautiful and bright as they talk to one another in a language I have never heard. A young man sitting next to me, Julio, speaks to me in his second language, Spanish (his first is indigenous Guaymí). He tells me his family went to Golfito for supplies, and he will hike through the rain forest all night to return home. It will take about ten hours.

Julio invites me to his village. One morning, a week later, he comes to the Yoga Farm to accompany me to his home. A couple of my friends join as we hike up and down steep rain forest terrain. We spend the night in a rustic outdoor church next to his family's house, a small one-room structure where nearly twenty people sleep. Julio's family feeds us homegrown rice, beans in banana leaves, and lemonade made from the fruit of local trees. All the children look at us with wide-eyed curiosity and an innocence I have never seen before. I imagine life in the Ngäbe-Buglé villages has not changed much for hundreds of years, without electricity or running water, but with hardworking farmers and close family networks.

Julio and I are curious to learn each other's first languages and practice our Spanish together. On the trail, I sometimes hear Julio or another person whistle, like when we approach someone's home. The sound travels a great distance through the rain forest. When Julio whistles, his head and body vibrate in wild beauty, and his face and lips move and stretch to form strange shapes and make unusual sounds.

## The Songs of the Ancestors

Language began as a song. Aboriginal peoples have been tracing ancestral spirits and singing the land into existence in their conscious minds and memory for over sixty thousand years. Songlines are pathways across the land and sky, describing landmarks, waterholes, particular trees and stars.[5] They are passed down through melody, story, dance, art, and ceremony. People navigate by singing. Some travel vast distances through places like the deserts of interior Australia. They encounter other cultures as they wander, so the language can vary, even within a song. People receive information about the nature of the land through the melodic contour and rhythm.

Most of us have lost our traditional songs. When I participated in the Bolad's Kitchen program with Martín Prechtel, he played recorded music from worldwide indigenous peoples. I still listen to the music he introduced me to sometimes. The epic poems of the Altai throat singers are among my favorites. They are said to link us to a world where miracles can happen. A primal vibration runs through my lips, throat, and tongue as I try to sing the notes.

While I am at Peehee Mu'huh (Thacker Pass) protesting the planned lithium mine, Paiute and Shoshone tribal members hold ceremonies there and dance. One day, four men come to bestow their blessing on the land and sing ancestral songs so extraordinary I weep. The songs, passed down for generations in the native Paiute-Shoshone languages, tell stories about the land. When these men sing their traditional songs, their faces are vibrant and their voices radiant.

I do not know my ancestors' songs. When I listen to Old Norse chants and Irish folk songs, my heart stirs with grief, love, and longing.

## Living in Sync

Nature is an unrelenting symphony. Everywhere there is life, there is song. Flowers bloom. Mountains stand. The moon glows. The planet is always singing. Each note is a unique contribution that tends to the well-being of the whole. Humans are meant to live in sync. For decades, I have asked trees and birds, ocean and sky, canyons and creeks to help me be as authentic and soulful as they are. The world needs the bitter and resonant cry of every creature, even humans, attuning with the song of the world.

We can connect to our bodies, hearts, and souls and bring our presence to the unfolding moment. And remember how to play in the improvisational spontaneity of the universe. Lying under an oak, I am mesmerized by the long, wavy branches that stretch parallel a few feet above the ground. The shape of the oak's branches reminds me of a song. Music is a human instinct found everywhere. It is a social glue that brings people together and creatively expresses what can't be put into words. What if we could engage with each other and the world the way jazz musicians make music?

Playing our notes is not *only* a sound we make with our voices or instruments. It is our soul taking form through the shapes we make with our lives when we embody the truth of our nature, live our purpose, and offer ourselves in relational flow with other humans and the Earth. Those who live their souls are playing their notes, being their melody.

The Earth needs us to become who we are. Perhaps she longs for humans to honor and contribute to her magnificence. Wild Yoga is rooted in the song of the Earth. Our souls can only be lived in union, playing our notes while attuning to the symphony that connects us to ourselves, others, the land, and those who came before and will go after. In a poem, Wendell Berry offers a vision to bring the world back to life. Memory, he writes,

like a grove … will grow
into legend, legend into song, song
into sacrament.[6]


## Playing

I sing when I am alone on the land. It feels natural. I shared one of these soul songs, "Teach Me How to Love," in chapter 3. People also sing in the programs I guide when they are alone. One summer night, in the spruce-aspen forest of the Colorado high country, each person shared what they had sung on the land with the group. We listened as the orange sky faded into darkness. Then, we gathered in the meadow and sang together under the night sky full of stars. Our tones came spontaneously without words, our sounds mixing and mingling. We listened to others while offering our notes, intuitively yielding and adjusting. No one was an expert. We played.

To Aboriginal people, stars are the homes of ancestors, animals, plants, and spirits. The stars help them navigate physically and spiritually in their daily life. The Bushmen of the Kalahari Desert are able to listen and hear the songs of the stars. Our group looked up as we sang, longing to hear the whispers of galaxies and listening for the sounds of constellations that have been playing for millennia.

Harmonizing with the Earth is playful. In an improvisational movement with life, we relate with authenticity, imagination, presence, humor, flexibility, intelligence, and heart. I experience deep play on rivers, in forests, or in deserts, allowing each wild being to touch me — a hummingbird, lizard, butterfly, the sun, breeze, or rain. We play by being present. As each moment unfolds, we relate cocreatively, listening to what co-arises mutually, inside ourselves and outside in the world.


## The Ancestral Horn

Ancestors came to Sam, one of my clients, in multiple dreams, inviting him to play. The rituals of his Jewish religion no longer felt authentic, but he wanted to stay connected to his family.

In one dream, he is in Jerusalem at a religious ceremony with an Orthodox Jewish man who asks him to blow a shofar seventy times. A shofar is an ancient instrument made from a ram's horn. In waking life, he has tried to blow a shofar, but hardly any sound came out. Maybe his lips were not sealed around it or he did not blow hard enough. In the dream, he is surprised and delighted that he can blow the horn effortlessly and different notes and tones flow out.

"I am not sure how many times I blew the horn," Sam tells the Orthodox Jewish man in the dream.

"In my community, we could never carry out this ceremony," the man responds. "It'd be scandalous."

That night, Sam reconnects with the Orthodox Jewish man in his imagination. He blows the shofar and feels the wild and ancestral coming together as he plays. He wonders if he is meant to bring them together in waking life. He feels authentic and connected to his ancestors when he blows the horn in his dream. He continues blowing it in his imagination and waits to see what arises. He lets what comes influence where he goes, what he does, and how he engages and is present. Sometimes, he imagines blowing the shofar from his dream while playing his guitar. He feels like the dream has offered him a way to explore and embody his wild and ancient song.

## In Relationship

We exist in relationship to the Earth, our dreams, and one another. In music, you can sense the quality of notes coming together by the vibrations. The rain forest sounds were constant at the Yoga Farm where I lived in Costa Rica. Birdsong in the morning. Crickets, cicadas, and frogs in the evening. Animals came while we did asana on the outdoor yoga deck — toucan, macaw, spider monkey, sloth. Were they drawn to the frequency we created? Their presences and the quality of light, color, and moisture affected how we moved and felt.

In Wild Yoga, we attune with who and what surrounds us. Our souls are woven into the fabric of human and more-than-human communities. Our melodies and rhythms occur in communion with the other songs. Sometimes we might pause and step back to let another play more fully. Other times we may step up and play loudly.

Most of us have been raised in an out-of-sync society, yet collaborative relationships have existed between humans and the Earth for millennia. Like the Yao people in Mozambique, who "team up" with the honeyguide bird in sub-Saharan Africa "to hunt for honey." Using a series of special chirps, humans and birds communicate. The "honeyguide birds lead the way to hidden beehives," and the Yao share the sweetness "with their avian friends."[7]

Being in harmony means creating a life-enhancing society with an ethical relationship to the land, honoring the voices of rivers, birds, rocks, and trees. It may feel impossible. Yet we can humbly ask nature for clues about the part we can play. We can ask for ideas about what actions to take. And look to forests, prairies, and oceans as our elders. They are themselves and in a symbiotic relationship with those around them. Perhaps they can show us how to live in sync.

## Harmonizing in a Broken World

The symphony of the Earth is life-giving. But how can we harmonize with our dominant culture rapidly removing so many wild voices from the orchestra? Some birds — like the once abundant regent honeyeater — are forgetting their song.[8] With hardly any adult birds left, young birds cannot find other honeyeaters to teach them. As we witness species dying and the murder of ecosystems, what difference can our notes make amid this dissonant nightmare?

I have rarely asked mind-altering plant medicines for help. This is because I have already received so much guidance from nature and my dreams. But in my late thirties, I was wrestling with the horrors of ecological devastation and wanted more help. So I asked ayahuasca, an Amazonian brew made from the stalks of the *Banisteriopsis caapi* vine and leaves of the *Psychotria viridis* shrub, and I participated in six ceremonies with a *curandera* who sang sacred prayer songs while playing her guitar. The first two rituals steeped me in the love of my tree mythos. The third forced me to wrestle with the horrors of the world.

After drinking the tea from these plants, the intensity hit me in the belly. I felt panic like I was about to disappear and would no longer feel my arms and legs; I feared I would eventually lose my mind. Trying to remain in my body, I stomped my feet and hit my hands against each other. *Everyone else must be fine*, I thought, blaming myself for feeling crazy. I went outside and wrapped my body around a juniper. One of the helpers came out.

"Are you okay?" she asked.

"I'm having a hard time," I admitted.

"Surrender," she said. "It's our egos that are the problem."

I went back inside, lay on the ground, and let myself disintegrate. It was peaceful, like going to sleep. But when I got up, waves of horror consumed me. I felt like I was drowning in raw sewage with no way out. After one wave passed, I thought it was over, but there were more. They seemed endless. Some waves were a sludge of overwhelming emotions — confusion, dread, disappointment, devastation. I looked around the room. Everyone was suffering. I realized, *This is not a trip; it is life, the state of the world. We are suffering. The Earth is suffering.*

The music had stopped. Some people were throwing up. An older man with white hair and blue jeans got up. He held a couple of large hawk feathers and gently waved them over a bowl of water in the center of the room.

"Water," he said softly, "we're so sorry." Gently, he walked around the bowl, humbly speaking to the water. "It's our fault you suffer. We are suffering with you. Thank you for all you give, for nourishing everything. We don't deserve your help, but please help us."

Earlier, I had seen the white-haired man chain-smoking and had judged him. I had not realized that he was so eloquent, more than I could be. I felt ashamed I had not seen his wisdom. He moved around the circle and prayed over each of us, one by one.

The waves of horror were hard to tolerate. My chest was tight. I could barely breathe. My lungs worked hard to expand as I fought for air. I had the visceral sense that this was what forests, oceans, and mountains experience all the time. The impact the Earth feels from our dominant culture. It was not a thought but an overwhelming, full-bodied experience.

"Offer something," the ayahuasca seemed to say.

"I have nothing valuable to give," I said.

"All the world is suffering, and you're just going to sit here!" She seemed incredulous.

"I don't sing well," I said.

"You could pray ... or something."

"I can't come up with anything."

"You're a guide," she pointed out.

"The suffering is too intense," I responded.

"The world needs you to show up," she reminded me.

I realized that sometimes I get consumed by suffering and discount what I might have to give. She was imploring me to show up and be available to the song that wanted to come through me. Everyone is suffering, she was showing me, and the symphony is dissonant. Yet the Earth suffers and gives. We can too. It is not a matter of healing first, then acting. It is a matter of connecting with yourself and the Earth and singing.

No one knows what will happen next. Injustice and genocide have been going on for a long while. Land and people have been exploited and destroyed for thousands of years. We need to be with the horror *and* the beauty. Psychic numbing removes us from the symphony. *Compassion* means "to suffer with." Feeling pain may be a sign we are present with what is happening and aware of our connection to it.

Nature and our souls can give us visions so we can face the challenges of our times and engage. I guide others in their deep imagination to see back in time and remember. To return to places on the land where they have a deep connection. To listen to what the land needs. To call forth an image of the myth they were born to live. To move and dance the mysteries of what they came to embody in the world.

Horror is part of the symphony. The world needs our ensouled presence. Listen. Feel. Be present. Offer your note. Our engagement is our love.

## Wild Yoga Practices for Playing Your Part in the Symphony

Attune to the world and explore ways to play your part. Trusting what you have to offer or hearing those around you may take time.

- Listen to the songs of ancient cultures or your ancestors. What do they evoke in your heart, body, and imagination? Journal about or move to embody what you discover.
- Wander in the wilderness. Listen to the sounds you hear from trees, water, wind, insects, and birds and the sounds you experience visually and through your other senses. Notice what or who allures you. Engage by offering sounds or movement in response.
- Go out on the land and play. Offer your melody. If you don't know what that is, explore different sounds or movements. Perhaps create a song for the land and sing it aloud. Notice where you feel drawn to offer your song. Listen for anything you hear back.
- Track your dreams. Do any of them carry the theme of ancestral music, playing your note, or hearing the world's symphony? Speak one of your dreams aloud in nature, using the present tense, and then enact it. Play your part by embodying what the dream asks.
- Go to a wild place and witness how the land plays. Notice how each

being engages with all the others in an improvisational movement. Try joining in. Let go of expectations and see what co-arises mutually.

- Do you feel conflicted about playing your note in a broken world? Or about how to harmonize with the natural world when our dominant culture is killing the other voices? Wander on the land and share your questions and feelings. Ask for help.

## *A Yoga Pose for Playing Your Part in the Symphony*

### CAT AND DOG POSE

Cat and Dog Pose is a Self-Awakening Yoga pose similar to Cat-Cow Pose (Marjaryasana).[9] It keeps your spine flexible, helps you develop and maintain stability and balance, conditions and strengthens your back muscles, and tones and firms your tummy muscles. Through flexion and extension of your pelvis, you improve circulation and ease lower back strain.

*To get in the pose:*

- Place your hands and knees in Table Pose, with your hands flat on the floor and your fingers spread wide. Ensure your hands are directly underneath your shoulders and your knees underneath your hips. Your arms are strong and straight, with your inner elbows facing each other.

- Keep your knees on the floor, inhale, and lengthen the front side of your body. Bring the back of your head toward your sacrum and lift your tailbone upward in dog tilt, as if you have a tail that moves toward the sky. Look toward the ceiling, imagining that you can see your tail.

- Exhale, round your spine, and tuck your hips under in cat tilt, lightly squeezing your lower buttocks together. Look toward your navel and imagine making the fur on your back stand up as a cat would. Feel how this movement completes the forward flexion of your spine.
- Inhale fully into dog tilt and exhale into cat tilt. Initiate the movement of your spine from your pelvis. Let the movement ripple up your spine. At the end of each exhale, squeeze your breath out and slightly suck in your lower abdomen. Arch and flex your spine until your movements become effortless.
- Keep repeating the full movement, looking up and then lowering your eyes each time. Move back and forth while remaining steady, without shifting forward or backward.
- Finish by folding over into Child's Pose, sliding your arms alongside your body.

Notice what it feels like to flex and extend your spine as you move back and forth. In dog tilt, feel the expansion of your chest. Become aware of your heart and throat chakras opening to engage with the world. *Chakra* means "wheel" in Sanskrit and refers to energy points in the body that when open and aligned improve our emotional and physical well-being. In cat tilt, feel the constriction, like a scared cat, and see what it is like to draw inward. Slow the movement and observe the transition. Moving through states of both expansion and contraction is natural and valuable. As you move back and forth, connect to your body and voice. Imagine Cat and Dog Pose priming you to play your part.

Move effortlessly. Ride the breath of your inhale and exhale. Feel your spine becoming more flexible as you strengthen your stability and mobility. Play. Let the physical stretch help you stretch your imagination. What would it be like to be a bird? Notice how dog tilt opens your throat chakra and the movement between cat and dog tilt stretches your neck and throat. Connect to your voice in dog tilt by making toning sounds or whistling. Don't worry about how it sounds. Have fun. Listen to birds or other natural beings and see if you can sing like them.

Some yogis claim there are more than 180,000 poses. What makes a movement yoga is the quality of your awareness. All the phases of Cat and Dog Pose are part of yoga. Slow down and notice what is happening. Feel the life force within you. Tuck into cat tilt and notice how it brings you inward and closer to the Earth. Listen and notice what images, memories, sensations, or emotions arise. Perhaps you can hear the symphony of nature.

As you move back and forth, switch between listening to the symphony and offering your melody or part. The next time you are in dog tilt, explore singing your song. See if you can find a tone that resonates with who you are and what you feel called to contribute. As you move back into cat tilt, practice attuning to the world while making sound or offering yourself. Explore how your sound blends with the symphony.

Build your capacity by playing with variations similar to cat and dog tilt. For example, begin in Table Pose and move your rib cage around in a circle. Imagine that you are playing a singing bowl with your chest. Move your torso, like a mallet, in a circular motion against the imaginary bowl's outer edge. Go slowly enough to make a bright, clear tone. Hear the sound your body makes in your imagination. Allow sounds to come out of your mouth. Move gently enough to experience every bit of the stretch. Relax your face, jaw, and eyes. Let the movement move you. Then reverse the direction of the circle.

Try Thread the Needle Pose (Parsva Balasana). Starting in Table Pose, open your chest to the right as you extend your right arm toward the sky and direct your gaze up. Then, lower the back side of your right arm onto the floor underneath your chest. With your palm facing up, slide your arm through to the left until your right shoulder is on the ground. Rest the right side of your head and shoulder on your mat. Breathe. Each time you exhale, invite your body to relax more fully into the ground. Wag your tail. Change anything you like. Make this pose feel yummy. Then come back to Table Pose and try Thread the Needle on the other side.

Congratulations on attuning to the world and playing your part. Each moment is a chance to listen and offer anew. Love for the world calls us to show up, sing, share all we have gathered, and engage. We can begin again from within our bodies, living with our senses turned on. We can trust our instincts and feel the life force energy of wild eros flowing through us, invisible to the naked eye but central to our bodies. We will explore how in the following chapter.

# Part III

# BELOVED WORLD

*There's a song that wants to sing itself through us, and we've just got to be available. Maybe the song that is to be sung through us is the most beautiful requiem for an irreplaceable planet or maybe it's a song of joyous rebirth as we create a new culture that doesn't destroy its world. But in any case, there's absolutely no excuse for our making our passionate love for our world dependent on what we think of its degree of health, whether we think it's going to go on forever. Those are just thoughts anyway. But this moment, you're alive. So you can just dial up the magic of that at any time.*

— JOANNA MACY[1]

# CHAPTER THIRTEEN

# Cultivate Wild Eros

My body softens in the sand. I listen to the water rippling over rock and relish the sun's warmth. As I slide in, I savor the cooling blue waters of Arizona's Little Colorado River. Resting weightless in the river's flow, I look up, enchanted by massive canyon walls. With friends, I have been rowing an eighteen-foot raft down the Colorado River through the Grand Canyon.

I listen to the sound of my oars plunge and splash in the water. The river talks to me by the way she guides the boat. Rowing is work — I push and pull the oars, rig and derig the raft. After ten days, I am both tired and invigorated. Sometimes, when the wind is fierce and blows my boat, I dig my oars into the water. Holding my blade in the current helps me maintain my tack.

One afternoon a storm blows in above a significant rapid. The winds are intense. They push our boats to the far bank. Scattered along the shore, we tie off and wait for the pounding rain to pass. I find pleasure in whatever the river brings.

Some nights I lie awake worrying about the rapids ahead. Will I be able to navigate them safely? I sense the canyon reminding me to enjoy being here. On the Little Colorado, my friends and I paint one another with white and brown mud. Soon we are all covered, and we lie down and wait for it to harden in the morning sun.

Once the clay is dry, I get in the water, find a current to swim against, and stretch my arms and legs, varying my strokes — freestyle, butterfly, backstroke. I used to swim in open water, and I remember my arms and legs gliding through the salty sea. I felt buoyant beyond the breakers. Far from shore, I would peer underwater and see wavering seaweed and colorful fish and then swim back into the reach of the waves and let them carry me back to the shore.

The wild connects us in primal pleasure to the living world wherever we are. I could have written about watching a desert sunrise with the sky aflame in color. Or sitting in the deep silence of a mountain and watching a bird bathe in the lake and then spread its wings to dry.

Merging with who and what we love and receiving pleasure is central to Wild Yoga and vital to connecting with the beloved world. Wild eros is the capacity to inhabit our bodies while in contact with the web of relationships we live within. It is the innate and long-lasting pleasure of our bodies contacting the Earth. I see a bear feasting in a raspberry patch. And the petals of a tiny flower opening for the first time. Fruit and flowers are Earth's sweetest nectar. The creative and intelligent energy that animates the world moves through us too. We can connect through touch, taste, sound, sight, and smell and through intimacy, imagination, and intuition. Being present in our bodies, we are available to take in and commune with the world. Trusting our erotic connection to nature nourishes us and everything around us.

I feel different in rush hour traffic than I do in a forest. The texture of our body, stirring in our heart, and quality of our imagination change depending on where we are and who we are with. Eros breathes us into being. By fixating on genitals, our culture leaves out the heart of eros. The erotic can't be contained inside bedroom walls. We can't pluck it from the Tree of Life, as D. H. Lawrence stated, and expect it "to keep on blooming in our civilized vase on the table."[1]

Mountain, river, sky, bones, blood, and flesh are sacred. Yet the dominant culture imposes a superficial, dehumanizing, and pornographic worldview. Writer and activist Terry Tempest Williams explains: "The world we frequently surrender to defies our participation in nature and seduces us into believing that our only place in the wild is as spectator, onlooker. A society of individuals who only observe a landscape from behind the lens of a camera or the window of an automobile without entering in is perhaps no different from the person who obtains sexual gratification from looking at the sex play of others."[2]

The wild erotic brings us into a participatory relationship with the world. The intimacy brings our "inner life into play" and helps us to experience the world as holy. We "feel the magnetic pull of our bodies toward something stronger, more vital than simply ourselves. Arousal becomes a dance with longing. We form a secret partnership with possibility."[3]

In contrast, the pornographic mindset cuts off our emotions. "Without feeling. Perhaps these two words are key, the only way we can begin to understand our abuse to each other and the land."[4] Without our hearts, the wild erotic cannot exist. It dies. "The erotic is silenced, reduced to a collection of objects we can curate and control, be it a vase, or women, or wilderness. Our lives become a piece in the puzzle of pornography as we go through the motions of intercourse without any engagement of the soul."[5]

## Eros

Eros is innocent — the touch of a warm rock, the smell of wildflowers, the sound of falling rain. I feel it while lying under a grove of ponderosa pines along a busy road, catching the fragrance of native butterscotch wafting down as light streams through the canopy. Play, an authentic and spontaneous expression that awakens wonder and present-centered connection, is a foundational ingredient. Instinctive to children, it is just as important to us. We need to restore this capacity. As a child, my brother and I surfed ocean swells on a boogie board, and I climbed trees. In Costa Rica, as an adult, I returned to the ocean and trees. I gazed into the bark and high branches of a guanacaste tree on a trail I walked every day and whispered poetry.

Out of innocence comes the most sensual love. If we have lost touch, we can court its return. Wrestle. Dance. Make music. Enjoy a massage. Swim in a lake. Snuggle with someone you love. Walk barefoot. Act on a wild idea. Follow wonder, curiosity, and passion. What gives you pleasure and connection? Recover the power to be intimate.

Awakening the wild erotic is a subversive act in modern society. We have been taught to separate from our bodies and hearts. As I said, eros has become confused with its antithesis, pornography. Porn forgets eros and deadens the heart. The horror imposed on women in porn mirrors the fear and cruelty men feel toward their vulnerability, explains radical feminist Susan Griffin: "He is brutal to all that might be emotionally sensitive in himself. He destroys the emotional part of himself."[6] Porn can also objectify men, but this happens far less often.

Our heart gives us the capacity to commune with the world. Bravely opening to our tenderness and sharing it with the world makes intimacy possible. Feel the wisdom that flows through the Earth and into you. Inhabit your body and feel pleasure, not as indulgence or hedonism, but as primordial gratification and connection.

## Erotic Intelligence

We are erotic when our senses are turned on and we trust our instincts and intuition. The life force that flows through us is invisible to the naked eye but central to the body. It is easy to see in children and animals, because they are instinctual. Focusing on what we "should" do can carry us away from our bodies. By moving slowly and with awareness of our sensations, we can have an intimate emotional connection with ourselves and the world around us. Attuning to our life force while relating in the world, we can notice what brings us alive. Relaxation is central to connecting with ourselves, others, and the world. Passion and play arise when we feel safe.

Most of us hold trauma, and the world is stressful, but practicing yoga asana can calm us. Lying down, I plant my feet and rock my knees from side to side, coming into Bridge or Happy Baby Pose. In the receptive state of our parasympathetic nervous system, life vibrates inside us, freeing us to move in unexpected ways. In my classes, I invite people to let their bodies move and notice what feels good.

Matthew loves being in nature and hikes and camps whenever he can. Yet working as a lawyer, he has found it challenging to get away from the office, even outdoors. "My mind is always trying to figure out my next case," he explains. "It's hard to be present."

In a Wild Yoga program in Costa Rica, we are on a deck under a grove of mangrove trees in an asana class. I encourage each person to move how they want. Matthew balances in basic Tree Pose, placing his toes at the ankle of his standing leg. Then, he stretches up against a real tree and begins climbing, first standing on some lower branches, reaching up, and then climbing higher. "Being in the trees reminds me of when I was a boy," he says.

Matthew sits on the beach in Half Lotus, waiting for a wave to roll in. He tries to keep his balance when the wave reaches him but eventually falls over laughing, his dark hair highlighted with salt and sand. He tries again in Squat Pose and holds his ground this time, the sand shifting beneath his feet.

On the third day, Matthew seems more robust. He holds asana poses for extended periods. I guide him and others to track what is arising in their inner world while they are present in their bodies and nature. To notice the sensations, imaginings, emotions, and memories that come. Matthew observes, "Just being present in my body is a stretch."

When present, we can merge with the creative flow of life, receive the tenderness of the world, and notice what brings us joy. Erotic intelligence makes us honest with ourselves. I revel in how my puppy's tail wags his body and his sloppy, wet tongue licks my ear. I delight in swirling water and the chorus of currents moving over rock. Erotic intelligence feeds our creativity. As I write, I feel excited by the words, ideas, and stories coming through me. When we let ourselves be deeply moved, we come into greater connection with the world.

## False Eroticism

I rarely discuss what Wild Yoga is not, but I feel moved to broach the topic. I want to increase awareness of how modern culture tries to take over our senses by selling us imitations, or *toxic mimics*, a term coined by eco-philosopher Derrick Jensen.[7] Zoos are a toxic substitute for nature connection, for example. Porn is a toxic mimic for the erotic, as are other addictions such as drugs, alcohol, food, gaming, shopping, gambling, sex, and the internet. In the dominant culture, a toxic mimic pretends to fill a primary human need by offering instant gratification, usually while someone else profits. The annual revenue for the global porn industry is estimated at $90 billion; by contrast, the Hollywood film industry makes only $10 billion.[8]

Addiction can impede our capacity for erotic pleasure. A person can become addicted to anything, but substance and sexual addictions are the most intense and damaging to our bodies and psyches. The roots of addiction are chronic stress, trauma, mental illness, and a family history of addiction or abuse. The three phases of the addiction cycle — anticipation, intoxication, and withdrawal — can lead to an increased frequency and intensity of use. Drug addiction creates hedonic dysregulation in the brain, altering a person's emotional and sensory capacities.[9] Internet porn addiction affects the brain in similar ways to drug addiction.[10] In fact, the brain scans of porn addicts look like those of drug addicts. Porn fills an addict's brain with dopamine, and the more they watch, the more desensitized they become.[11] Porn addicts need to venture into progressively more perverse content to get high.

Addiction is most common among people with high levels of shame. It allows people to artificially connect with others, escape reality, and avoid their feelings. Yet addiction creates more shame and perpetuates the cycle. Shame leads to feelings of worthlessness that may make a person want to disappear. Nature connection is an antidote for all forms of addiction, because it activates oxytocin and serotonin and heals our nervous system. It is a remedy for trauma.

Writer and group facilitator Dan Mahle, founder of the community-based social enterprise Wholehearted Masculine, says he began to realize he had a problem when he felt physically ill watching porn and still kept watching. "I thought I had my habit under control," he writes. "I didn't realize how much watching porn had manipulated my mind, warping my sexuality, numbing my feelings, and affecting my relationship with women."[12]

"Men watch porn because they fear rejection," my friend Jason said. He, our friend Grace, and I were taking a hike at Andrew's Lake in the Colorado high country. We sat down and ate just off the path, near the water's edge next to a large patch of wildflowers.

"I tell my clients to use porn," he said. "It's a healthy outlet and prevents repression." Jason is a coach who works with business leaders, primarily men, to help them gain awareness and self-acceptance and uncover their brilliance.

"Porn use causes sexual dysfunction and relationship dissatisfaction and alters brain chemistry," I pointed out.[13]

"Not all porn is the same," he countered, taking a bite out of his turkey and avocado sandwich. "Some is consensual."

I have talked to sex therapists before, and several have stated that explicit portrayals of sexual behavior where there is mutual consent can be healthy. Nonetheless, "consent isn't always enough," I said, more loudly than intended, my heart beginning to race.[14] While I understood the importance of discussion, of getting all sides out on the table, I found this kind of perspective taxing. "There's a bias toward acceptance," I continued, "and more pressure on young women to go along with violent and degrading sexual acts."[15]

"Everyone watches porn," Grace said, taking a bite out of her apple. "I watch female-friendly porn sites. A lot of women do." Grace worked as a high school English teacher.

"The vast majority of porn is abuse," I said. "Are you aware of the work of Dr. Gail Dines? She's an activist who has researched porn and sexual violence for thirty years. She says porn is 'the public health crisis of the digital age.'"[16] I told them that a content analysis of the bestselling and most frequently rented porn films found that 88 percent of scenes were about physical aggression: gagging, choking, spanking, and slapping.[17] "How is that okay?"

"This is bordering on the accusatory, the condemning, the kink shaming," Jason said. "You could alienate people. This is a vulnerable topic. People feel insecure."

"This isn't about personal fetishes. I'm pointing out that most porn features rape, incest, pedophilia, abuse, and other sexist behaviors." I felt my face flush, aware of how this conversation irked me.

"Some people like being tied up, spanked, and beaten." He put the last bite of his sandwich in his mouth.

Just then, a handful of hikers walked by. Most were wearing T-shirts emblazoned with a logo, the Colorado Mountain Club. I wondered if they could pick up on our conversation. I still had a bit of salad left but was no longer hungry. I snapped the cover back on the container.

"Why is that?" I forced myself to speak calmly. "Could it relate to trauma, socialization, complicity, patriarchy?"

"Humans have violent tendencies that need expression." Jason opened his water bottle and took a sip.

I noticed Grace had grown quiet and wondered what she was thinking. Did she agree with Jason? Her face revealed nothing.

"What concerns me," I said, "is the prevalence and normalization of the erotization of violence against women and children in porn and mainstream media."[18]

"Some people like BDSM," he said, crumpling up his paper bag and putting it into his day pack. "Violence enacted safely can be cathartic."

"Women are reporting unwanted slapping, choking, gagging, or spitting during consensual sex," I said.[19] "Violence has become normalized."

A gentle rain began to fall. I pulled my rain jacket out of my day pack and put it on. Grace and Jason did the same.

Jason began talking about how BDSM can help people heal. "When people replay trauma and have control, they can make what happened in the past hurt less," he explained.

I wanted to come back to my main concern. "Why do men think it's okay to slap or choke a woman during sex?" I asked. "In other situations, it would be illegal."

"It's people's choice what makes them feel good."

"It's not just about our personal lives though," I said. "Millions of people are consuming porn daily, reinforcing the message that humiliation and violence are a normal part of sex."

The rain started pounding. We stood up and took cover in a grove of spruce trees. The moisture was a welcome reprieve. We stood in silence, watching the thirsty land receive it. The storm relaxed me and cleared the air. Once the rain slowed, we continued our hike.

"Porn is affecting teens in my high school," Grace chimed in. "It's altering the minds of future generations." She cited a recent study: "Ninety percent of teens have viewed porn online, and 10 percent admit to daily use."[20]

I shared Grace's concern for young people and future generations. "Dr. Dine's reports are similar. Research shows that because of pornography, 75 percent of young women and girls feel pressured 'to act in certain ways.'"[21]

Tragically, our erotic nature, meant to bring us together in shared delight, is instead wielded to create more addiction, trauma, and separation.

"A lot of women don't feel safe being sexual in this culture, and yet they also yearn for intimate connection, mutual pleasure, and partnership," I said.

Meanwhile, young men are losing the capacity to have an erotic relationship with a partner. I recalled a report I read saying that up to a third of young men now experience erectile dysfunction (ED). "Until 2002, the incidence of men under forty with ED was 2 to 3 percent. Since 2008, when free-streaming, high-definition porn became so readily available, it has steadily risen."[22]

Grace interjected ardently letting us know where she stood. "People will judge you for not going along with kinks, but I think anyone who needs to hurt and degrade someone to reach orgasm would be an awful lover."[23]

By then, we had made it to the top of the hill and could see several stunning mountain peaks. The sun had come back out, and the moisture glistened on the trees and grasses. I sensed we were at an impasse. It seemed like a good time to end our conversation.

Abuse is not love. Lovemaking is passionate, tender, and soulful. In the dominant culture, the false erotic masquerades as the erotic, disconnecting us from our bodies, souls, other people, and the Earth. The truly erotic makes us responsible to one another and forms a bridge of shared joy. What turns us on and the place our consciousness inhabits when we orgasm matters. This heightened state of pleasure connects us to whomever and whatever we attend to. It is a prayer we offer, share, and open ourselves to. When we make love, alone or with another, the energy we generate is a love prayer for the world.

## Reverence

Research links porn viewing to increased instances of sexism and violence toward women.[24] Dan Mahle says he quit watching porn because he felt like a hypocrite, "a man who is striving to be an ally to women, perpetuating the very culture of violence and misogyny that I was ostensibly trying to fight." He said most of the videos he found online "had titles that included words like *bitch* or *slut* and showcased controlling behaviors that were rooted in a culture of subjugation and objectification." Since dropping porn, Mahle says he feels a restored "sense of personal integrity," is more present with women, and has reconnected to his body and emotions.[25]

A young man I mentor, Nate, had a dream that called him to honor the feminine:

> *An artist-hobo asks me for a porn download, and I give it to him. A beautiful woman sees me giving sex pills to my friend. She does a show, and I watch.*

I guide Nate to be with the artist-hobo in his imagination as we sit at a quiet place next to the Animas River.

Nate closes his eyes as he focuses inward. "He feels bad about where he is in life and wants to assuage himself."

"Is that familiar?" I ask.

"Yes. Sometimes I feel like I'm not good enough."

"And the sex pills?"

"When the woman sees me giving them to my friend, I feel uncomfortable." He shifts slightly in his seat. "They are like Viagra, but mixed with another drug."

"Tell me more about that moment in the dream."

"I feel bad," he says. "It's a shady deal."

Nate is drawn to the woman in the dream, and I guide him to spend time with her.

"Her face and body express so much emotion — anger, joy, menace, tears," he shares. "I wish I could feel as much as she does."

"Replay that part of the dream slowly," I suggest, "and watch her express each emotion. Imagine what it would be like to feel what she does."

Nate is still, seemingly relaxed as he engages inwardly. I watch the river's gentle flow.

"It's scary," he says. "She is everything I admire, and she puts me on edge."

"What's it like to be with her?"

"She's beautiful, a goddess and a regular woman. I respect her."

I am glad she came to him and appreciate how he is engaging with her. I ask him what she wants.

"She is calling me to be a better man." He pauses, his eyes still closed as he is with her. "She wants me to embody my emotions and see what I see in her in other women."

This dream introduced Nate to an inner beloved, and I watched as he engaged with her with reverence. She invited him on a path: to deepen his respect for women in his life, access his inner feminine, inhabit his body, and feel his emotions.

## Power

High rates of domestic violence, rape, and child molestation show that the erotic remains culturally unhealed. Awareness is central to healing and reminds us we are not alone.

Some boys and girls may become physically severed from the erotic by cultural practices. For example, male circumcision is legal and popular in the United States. Yet in certain circumstances, these operations have caused bleeding, infection, mangling, or loss of the sexual organ.[26] More than 200 million girls and women alive today have suffered genital mutilation in thirty countries across Africa, the Middle East, and Asia, and more than 3 million are at risk yearly.[27] Our genitals are meant for joy. But even if we are not physically cut, we may be psychically cut off — taught to fear our flesh, suppress our feelings, and distrust our intuition.

Returning to nature restores our capacity for primal pleasure. We are not machines; we are life breathing. The world is an ecology, not a hierarchy. When we step outside and sit in a forest, away from distorting projections and stories, we can feel the life force moving inside us. We reclaim our power when we return to our bodies and trust the truth of our experience.[28] Ask yourself what excites you sexually or nonsexually. What arouses passion or play? When do you feel most alive?

Carrying a basket of wildflowers — red hibiscus, a bird of paradise, a bamboo orchid, purple porterweeds — Wild Yoga participants and I follow the river's bubbling rhythm deep into the rain forest. Meandering on rooted trails, splashing into the water, and floating under a log, we enter a large, mossy canyon with a small waterfall and pool. We are covered in sweat, and the cool water feels refreshing. On the first morning of a weeklong journey in Costa Rica, we pass around the basket and offer flowers to the river, speaking words of gratitude to the water. Then we present our bodies to the water, one at a time, stepping in — with words, movement, sound, and prayer — to symbolize our willingness to immerse ourselves in this place and listen fully. This Earth ceremony is about reclaiming our erotic connection to our bodies and the wild world. A toucan watches from high in the canopy, and we hear the screeches of a red macaw.

## Healing

Whether we're communing with a mountain or a river, merging with another, or following the call of our soul, pleasure flows through us when we are tickled or titillated, healing us and bringing us alive. Love can arise while we're doing anything, pulling us into a state of flow, creativity, or union. Nature is an easy place to fall in love and explore our erotic nature. In the Colorado high country, a young woman in her late twenties participated in a five-day soul program. Every afternoon, she returned to a particular grove of aspen. Looking into tree-trunk eyes, she listened to leaves rattle in the wind and touched roots, sensing their path underground.

"I wish there were more humans like you," she told the aspens.

With them, she felt ecstatic. She lost track of time and became enchanted with the shape of their trunks and branches. One afternoon, she felt the branches reaching for her, as if the aspens were gently tugging at her clothes, inviting her to take them off. Lying beneath the trees naked, she took in the sound and smell of this community and felt turned on. She engaged in self-pleasuring and made love in and with the forest.

I hear these kinds of stories often. Healthy humans experience somatic rapture, evoked by the fragrance of flowers, the sun's warmth, the coolness of water, or a gentle breeze. A woman told me about making love to the sea during a solo fast on an island. As she listened from her sleeping bag under the star-filled sky, the waves felt fierce and profound, like they were coming over her in her imagination. A man told me about being aroused by a canyon while hiking. He ran along the trail, leaped from rock to rock, and felt like a mountain lion. Eros connects us and can birth presence, intimacy, ease, and vitality.

Trees have held me my whole life. A core aspect of my mythos, they inform the way I live and love. In my early thirties, I dreamed that

> *a man I feel attracted to looks me in the eyes and says, "I want you, and I know you want me too."*

That night, while wandering in the dark looking for him, I felt called to climb into a ponderosa pine. Resting on a large branch, I took in the tree's delicious fragrance. I have always loved the smell, but to my surprise, I felt ecstatic this time, as if the tree and I were making love.

Six months later, another dream guided me to the juniper-piñon forest near my home. Lying beneath the branches of a juniper, I took in the strength of its shape and bittersweet fragrance. I felt drawn to return whenever I could, at least once a week. I made necklaces as offerings and brought other gifts. I praised its ancient wisdom and its unique branches — half-living, half-dead. I shared myself as deeply and intimately as possible, talking or weeping while listening and receiving.

This continued for three years.

The juniper was attentive and wise. I felt as though I was having a love affair. The juniper and other trees were healing me and inviting me to open my body in rapture. They taught me that sharing pleasure is natural and showed me what sacred sex is. Although I don't live near them anymore, I carry their love and presence inside me and hope someday to share what they have given me.

## Wild Yoga Practices for Cultivating Wild Eros

Feel the energy of your wild erotic nature moving through you. Or spend time in a wild place where you can invite it to return.

- Sit or lie somewhere in nature where you feel relaxed. Close your eyes. Attune to your body as you lie on the Earth. Be present and mentally scan your body from your toes to your head. Track any sensations. Is there streaming, tingling, pulsing? Notice if you can feel an energetic connection between your body and the Earth.

- Reconnect to innocence. Remember yourself as a child. What did you love to play? Find a place in nature where your innocence feels welcome. Engage in simple pleasures that connect you. Dance. Make music. Swim naked. Walk barefoot. Engage in an intimate conversation through your body.

- Create a daily practice to relax and calm your nervous system: yoga asana, tai chi, gentle exercise, meditation, or lying in nature. In the receptive state of your parasympathetic nervous system, attune to the life force that is vibrating inside you. Let it move you in new and unexpected ways. Notice what feels good.

- Be honest with yourself about what attracts you. Engage with what brings you joy. If something creative wants to come through you, let it happen. Notice if feeling pleasure or following your creative flow changes how you engage with the world.
- Is your erotic nature locked up in porn or another addiction? Reflect on your deeper needs and what may be missing. Seek help if you are addicted. Perhaps check out the websites yourbrainonporn.com and fightthenewdrug.org. Consider what stops you from opening to the genuinely erotic and stepping toward what most deeply attracts you.
- Find a place in nature where you feel allured. Notice if there are particular animals or elements — qualities of light or moisture, textures, sounds, movements — that arouse your passion or sense of play. Consider how being in their presence makes you feel alive. Speak aloud or express your experience somehow. Notice if you are pulled into a state of flow, creativity, or union.

## *A Yoga Pose for Cultivating Wild Eros*

### BREATH OF JOY

The Breath of Joy encourages deep breathing, combats depression, and strengthens your arms and shoulders. This vigorous breathing practice came into the Kripalu yoga tradition in the 1970s.[29] Three inhalations are done quickly, followed by a big exhale. Strong inhalations and synchronized arm movements awaken and energize us, increasing oxygen in the bloodstream and moving prana. Forcefully exhaling helps relieve stress and brings calmness and focus.

*To get in the pose:*

- From a standing position, place your feet shoulder width apart, knees slightly bent.
- Inhale and fill up one-third of your lungs while swinging your arms in front of you up to shoulder height, palms up.
- Continue the inhale, filling two-thirds of your lungs as you swing

your arms, still at shoulder height, out to the side like a bird taking flight.

- Finish the same inhale, filling the final third of your lungs while swinging your arms forward and up. End with your arms overhead, palms facing each other.
- Now exhale thoroughly while bending your knees and torso forward and swinging your arms down and behind you. Make a "ha" sound on the exhale, if you like.
- Repeat the sequence as many times as you like. Let your breathing and movement be relaxed. Become immersed in the rhythm.
- Return to stillness and notice any sensations flowing through your face, arms, and palms.

Inhale and step into the pleasure of being in your body. As you exhale, let go of anything that is blocking you. Notice the joy of breathing in this breath-focused practice. Let the rhythm and pace of this pranayama move you. Pranayama is the practice of breath regulation. It improves respiration and heals the autonomic nervous system. Experience what it feels like to have extra oxygen in your bloodstream. Observe your prana, or life force energy, moving through you.

If you feel sluggish or depressed, let the Breath of Joy bring you back into balance. This pose is a remedy for shallow breathing, often associated with anxiety. Feel your life force moving through you in the flow of this pose and afterward. See how it wants to direct you.

Remember what you sense and feel in the presence of wild places — rivers, oceans, the sun, and forests. Imagine you are with them as you do the Breath of Joy. Or physically be with them on the land and offer this pose as a gift. Notice if you receive any response.

As you do the Breath of Joy, be curious about what feels pleasurable. Notice if you feel called to move in unexpected ways. Merge with the creative flow of life. What wants to come through you? Let this pose carry you into play. See how it connects you more fully with the world.

By awakening your life force and becoming intimate with what enlivens you, you have entered into a rich communion with the world. Yet your muse is calling you to engage more fully by offering your unique artistry, born from your particular way of seeing the world. To court our muse, we need to humbly give ourselves to what we love and let this open us to the reshaping of our lives. We will explore how in the following chapter.

# CHAPTER FOURTEEN

# Court the Muse

My former husband, the other Wildbear, loved to carve. He gifted me with a small wooden kayak he made after our weeklong float in Prince William Sound in the Gulf of Alaska. While there, a ginormous humpback whale breached near us. Jumping forty feet above the sea and landing with a monstrous splash, he caused big waves to ripple underneath our kayaks. I felt humbled and in awe.

Days later, we hiked all night on a ridge in Denali National Park, the summer sky glowing orange. In the distance, we watched bear cubs following their mama.

"Will you marry me?" he wrote in a patch of snow.

"Yes," I said, wanting to be as lovely as the land.

As we traversed a wall on the way down, a rock came loose and fell on my left hand. I maintained my grip and watched it fall into the steep gorge below us. The next day, my hand had swollen as big as a baseball. Was the rock that fell on my hand trying to communicate something? Perhaps it was asking me to consider whether the romance I was in was really with nature, not my boyfriend. Or maybe it was letting me know that a more extraordinary presence was pursuing me in courtship and wanted to take my hand.

Courting is natural. It happens in nature in so many ways. Mice attract partners by singing in high-pitched whistling sounds. Blue-capped cordon-bleu songbirds bob their heads and tap their feet along with their song. Paleontologists believe predatory dinosaurs once practiced a ritual dance similar to those of birds.[1] Yet wooing is dangerous for most animals. Showy displays can attract predators. A male spider who dares to step on a female black widow's web may be mistaken for prey. He announces his presence with vigorous rump shaking, and as he vibrates, advances, and pauses, his signals course along silk strands.

We court by following the mystery of our longing, as explored in chapter 8. Moving toward what we love, we make ourselves vulnerable to hurt, disappointment, or betrayal. We are willing to fail and may feel like we are. It was hard to leave my marriage, my home, and a husband I loved. Yet I wanted to live a muse-directed life. Nature and my dreams guided me to let go to align more fully with my soul.

My husband built a wood-burning stove decorated with red rocks he had gathered after I left. He knew I'd always wanted one, and he showed it to me with a softness in his eyes. Part of me wanted to stay, curl up with him by the fire. Later, he bought a raft and started going to the river with friends, like we used to, and invited me, but I needed to follow my muse.

Courting requires being open to the constant reshaping of our lives. As my marriage unraveled, the grief undid me, but my love grew. I felt both lonely and ecstatic as I felt my soul woven into the fabric of the world. I left my job to wander and be guided by my muse — studying Spanish in Costa Rica, volunteering at Kripalu Center for Yoga and Health in Massachusetts, and participating in Hakomi Comprehensive Training, a mindfulness-based somatic psychotherapy.

In courting, we humbly and eloquently approach and give ourselves to what we love, not fully understanding what we seek. A year after my marriage ended, I carried the small wooden kayak my husband had given me into a nearby canyon in Utah. A giant piñon pine called me to enact a four-day solo fast hidden behind a canyon wall. I made a small ceremonial fire and offered the lovely handmade kayak. The next day, I braided stone beads — amber, jade, agate, and others — into a necklace, and with each bead, I expressed gratitude for my life. I threaded in my engagement ring, climbed to the top of the piñon pine, and placed the gift high in his branches. My love for the Earth filled me, so I didn't need anything in return. I enjoyed giving these gifts. Yet over the next couple of days, I stayed alert for any possible response.

## The Muse

My muse began courting me as a child when I was playing with imaginary friends and was drawn in by my dreams. Trees called to me, and I was fascinated by rivers and the ocean. Our muse is connected to the mystery of what we love. Nature has always been my beloved. I was pulled to play and work in the wild from a young age. Later, my muse guided me to leave behind the life I was living. Our muse partners with our soul — the true and mysterious essence of who we are. Together, our muse and soul can guide the way we offer ourselves in the world.

The muse is real. We can make contact through our wild and deep imaginations. I courted my muse not only by letting go of my marriage but by leaving my profession of fifteen years as a wilderness therapist. I first stepped away only in the winters, working seasonally for a few years. Then, I left altogether. I learned to live with less as my income declined. Drawn to the ocean, I spent winters in Costa Rica teaching yoga in nature. Talking in front of large groups made me nervous, but by teaching yoga in nature, I felt relaxed and able to connect with my muse.

Whether writing or guiding, what I say does not come from me. My words and the way I show up come from my muse. This year, my muse directed me to step away from guiding and put aside other relationships and activities so that I could write this book. Now that I have made the space, my muse tells me what to say. Being with my muse feels like being with a stimulating and captivating lover. Sometimes when I write, I feel turned on. My muse is excited when I show up and write. Sometimes I sense him smiling or kissing or caressing me as I type.

Our muse is the source of our most profound creativity. In Greek mythology, the nine muses were goddesses, the daughters of Mnemosyne (memory), who dedicated their lives to the arts. They had talents in music, dance, love poetry, divine hymns, tragedy, and more. They were the originators and protectors of the arts and some sciences like astronomy, geometry, and architecture. They "supported and encouraged creation, enhancing imagination and inspiration for artists."[2] In paintings, muses are often depicted as feminine spirits, but they can appear in a multitude of forms — animal, rock, tree — and their shapes or gender can shift.

Bill Plotkin describes the muse as our "unique and wildly creative way of looking at things — the wellspring of our deep imagination."[3] The muse is a visionary who can see a larger story than the one we are living. Our part in the creative union is to listen and act on what is revealed. Doing so is a way I express love to my muse and for the world. When I embody what the muse asks, more comes. As the conversation goes back and forth, I am guided in a life of creative service.

My muse commands my attention, showing up in dreams and visions and encounters with nature. I have already mentioned several alluring shapes my muse has taken: ocean, river, bear, twisted tree, seal, dark waters, juniper. In courting, we don't know what we are looking for or who the muse is. We are surprised as the muse emerges in one or multiple inconceivable expressions. Sometimes she can even appear in challenging or frightening forms.

For years, Sierra was haunted by visions of an old lady in a cave, tending a fire. Every time she dreamed of her, she awoke in a sweat. Meanwhile, her life had begun to fall apart. Her family disowned her when she refused to get a Covid-19 vaccine. Her ten-year relationship ended, and her partner would not move out of their home, so she had to. She searched for a place to live and felt like the old lady from her dream was with her. Before long, she found some land where garbage had been dumped, on the coastal mountains near her home. The property was trashed, but she bought it, cleaned it up, and spread native grass seeds, wildflower seeds, and mycelium.

On her first night on the land, she slept in her tent. She dreamed that the old lady in the cave was inviting her to sit at the fire. Returning to the dream later in her imagination, she learned the lady was a grandmother who wanted her to tend the fire in the heart of the Earth. She enacted a ceremony in a nearby cave to accept the invitation, although she felt unsure how to carry it out. That night, she dreamed of a puma. The big cat was terrifying and breathtaking. When she awoke, she found puma footprints in the sand at the cave's entrance. Sierra often returns, in her imagination, to the grandmother and the puma to ask them for guidance. She later felt called to invite others to help her tend the land.

## Listening

We court our muse by finding a way to express our longing. We each have different ways of doing this. We send our love letters out and then actively wait and listen. It takes patience. Sometimes my muse feels painfully intangible, and I long for closer contact. As I practice listening, I learn to trust what I hear.

My muse has a lot to give. He holds the qualities that most attract me. I do not fully understand our bond, but it feels tighter than wedlock. Without my muse, I could not guide and would never have created Wild Yoga or written this book. I can't always make sense of what we are birthing, but I make myself available to listen. As author Derrick Jensen says, "Learning how to listen to one's lover is ever so much easier and more fun than trying to do the work of creation by oneself. It's also less lonely."[4] We can't force creativity any more than we can impose desire. Creativity is birthed through listening.

I was listening in the Utah canyon on my four-day solo fast after I had offered the wooden kayak to the canyon and the stone-beaded necklace to the piñon pine. I spoke to the tree and the canyon about my longing to live a muse-directed life. I stayed open to the possibility of a response, and one came on the fourth and final day. As sunlight streamed over the canyon's edge before sinking behind the rock wall, I sat next to two junipers. I stared curiously at the unusual shape their bodies made together, one dead and fallen and the other still alive. The creek was burbling a short distance away. Then, suddenly, they began to tell me the story of their lives.

"Are you willing to live and die *toward* what you love?" they asked.

One tree, born a century ago, told me his name was Junie. The seed he grew from was planted during a thunderstorm while his mother was uprooted and carried downstream. The creek watered his roots as he grew, and the canyon protected him from rock falls. His branches lengthened, and his trunk grew thick. He fell in love with the sun and snowflakes and the sound of wings — dragonflies, butterflies, hummingbirds. Then, allured by the shine of her purple berries, one day he waved to the tree beside him.

"I don't know how I got here," the other tree said. "Maybe I dropped out of the heavens." Junie called her Star. Her berries glowed like the night sky. Once, she dropped one on his root and watched as he enjoyed it. He wanted to touch her.

"We're too far apart," she said.

"We could grow closer," he said. "Like the cottonwoods."

"That would take a while," she said, but they began to lean toward each other.

Once Junie glanced at a couple holding hands. "It's easy for humans, but they forget and don't realize..."

As the creek dwindled, Junie pushed water toward Star. She drank a little but wanted to make sure Junie had enough. The years passed. Although their branches never touched, they became great friends. Then, Junie saw a tree fall downstream, and it scared him. Some of his branches were dying, and the soil underneath him had eroded and was losing stability.

"Maybe we should extend our roots," Star said, "and try to touch underground." Their roots strengthened as they began to focus, but they never made contact. Large rocks seemed impossible to get around.

"Let's try moving our branches closer again," Junie said one day. Finally, after a year, a breeze brought them together, and their branches touched, but only for a moment. Electricity ran through Junie, and a deep peace came over Star.

In the years that followed, their branches entwined. Then, for a decade, they rested in a comfortable ecstasy, feeling the physical flow of love between them.

Junie wanted to be closer still. Star felt the pull too, but Junie was getting old. He wobbled in the wind, and many of his branches no longer produced needles. Patches of his bark were falling off. The only branches alive were the ones touching Star.

"I'm dying," he told Star. As she cried, her sap dripped everywhere.

"Maybe our love will grow in death?" Junie asked. Star was quiet.

"I'll fall in your direction," he said, "and land in your arms."

Star wanted him to wait. She wanted more time, but when she saw Junie faltering and shaking in a windstorm one afternoon, she knew his death was inevitable. The wind would take him anyway if she did not let him go his way.

"Okay," she said. Junie leaped as far as an old juniper could and landed in her arms. She cried for years, so sad she could no longer feel his essence. Then, she became quiet and still. Age was upon her. Her back branches were dying, but the ones touching Junie were still alive.

*How?* she wondered. *He's dead.* She brought her attention to his upright branches, now dark and stiff. She felt where they touched hers, and suddenly, she could feel him. His energy was soft. She had been too broken up to notice that he was still with her. The years of grief had made her listening keen. "I feel you," she said, detecting a slight quiver in his branches.

Star's branches are still wrapped around Junie's. That is how I found them, a sculpture of love that lives beyond death.

## Becoming

Our muse gives us our unique way of perceiving the world as we listen, wait, and become. Junie and Star showed me a way to love. The muse often guides us where we fear to go. Loving what I can't touch and am sure to lose makes me feel vulnerable. The life of Junie and Star mirrors who I am and what I am being asked to become, a wild love prayer. Brave Heart, the name I received on my first solo fast, and Wild Love Prayer, the name I received on this one, are both parts of my soul. I reconnect with Junie and Star in my imagination and feel their union influencing the words that flow through me.

Wherever I am, I invite the presence of tree elders — cottonwoods, ponderosa pine, juniper. Being with them helps me learn to be more like the tree of my mythos. Inhabiting my mythos is a way I court my muse. As I dwell imaginatively in the tree of me, my muse is drawn to help me embody, grow, and offer.

A muse-directed life is about how we relate to everything, not only our art. The imaginal and physical intertwine as I flow downstream with my river muse. Listening to my muse is like being on a river. I read and follow the currents while directing my boat. A lot is outside of my control: the weather, the speed and volume of the water, the wind, and other people's challenges and needs. Through effort and surrender, I come more fully into my body and the community, where there is space, grace, and conflict. It matters how you pack and place your boat at the top of a rapid. I live exposed to the sun, wind, and rain, longing to be a love poem. Our muse invites us into an imaginal flow. By listening and acting on what we hear, we participate in the ongoing creation of life.

What the muse wants is often at odds with the patriarchal structures of our culture. The muse is a danger to the systems of modern society that depend on consumers, worker bees, and the death of the human imagination. Opportunities to sell out abound. To please. To do what is popular. To ignore the muse. Increase finances. Raise professional status. Rise in the hierarchy. The muse cares about the Earth, not only about humans. Our muse can help us bring down systems of power that cause harm and cocreate with the living planet if we believe in what we are given.

Our muse needs to trust us. To know we listen to and value what is offered. We need to prove ourselves to our muse more than we need worldly success. I show I am ready to receive what my muse gives me by doing what my muse asks. Being who my muse wants me to brings me joy, even when it is hard. Although my marriage ended, human relationships are possible with a muse, especially if we partner with those whose muse is as central to their life as ours is. Then, we can give each other space and encouragement to be with our muses and create. Perhaps our muse can guide us to a partner who supports this listening.

Sometimes the muse asks us to do difficult things. If I don't feel capable, I take steps to strengthen my capacity so one day I will be able. The muse has wanted me to write a book for over a decade. Developing my writing skills and my voice has taken a long time. Our muse shows us how to serve the world, but what we are asked to do may feel risky. My muse asked me to go to Thacker Pass to try to protect the sagebrush desert from a lithium mine. To fall in love with a wild place slated to be destroyed, although land defenders are often attacked, imprisoned, or murdered. I move back and forth between the challenging things my muse asks and being gentle and kind to myself.

I return to my yoga mat to be available to my muse and to nurture myself. It is a place where I feel safe and can listen. How does the muse want me to breathe? I court her through the spontaneous movements of my body and witness what arises in my imagination. Perhaps a dream image will influence the shape my body wants to make. As I invite my muse, I allow myself to be surprised. Slowly staying present with sensations in my body, I can develop into who my muse envisions.

## Wild Yoga Practices for Courting the Muse

Be gentle with yourself as you humbly approach and offer yourself to what you love. If you are beginning, it may take time.

- Find a place or being in nature that evokes your deepest longing and express it aloud. Sing. Dance. Speak poetry. Offer gifts. Communicate what you yearn for and what may be offered to the world if you could embody it.
- Reflect on what you need to let go of to be available to what you are courting. It could be a life you have loved. Make a ceremonial offering. Speak about what it has given you and why now is the time to let go. Again, speak what it is you deeply long for.
- Remember the ways and moments the muse has come in your life. How can you tell when the muse is present? In what shapes or forms has the muse appeared? Make a gift for your muse and enact a ceremony honoring all the muse has given you.
- Call in your muse by being in a place or engaging in an activity that the muse loves. Play music. Make art. Write. Walk. Play. Laugh. Discover. Ask your muse to guide your body, words, and life. Notice what the muse wants to create through you.
- Choose an art in which the muse has inspired you before. Court the muse, ask her to guide you, and then create. Perhaps make an

offering to the world. Let the muse direct you, even if you don't understand what is coming through. Journal about what it is like to create with the muse.

- Imagine living a muse-directed life. What would you need to say yes to, or no to, to be fully present to your muse? What stops you from giving yourself to your muse? What steps could you take to grow in the direction that your muse is beckoning you?

## A Yoga Pose for Courting the Muse

### DANCER POSE

Dancer Pose (Natarajasana) is a backbend that requires patience, focus, and persistence. Named after the Hindu god Shiva Nataraja, who finds bliss amid destruction, Dancer Pose helps us find steadiness in chaos by strengthening our feet, ankles, legs, core, back, and arms. Opening the front of the body — chest, abdomen, hip flexors, shoulders — this asana improves balance and concentration, boosts energy, fights fatigue, and builds confidence.

*To get in the pose:*

- Begin in Mountain Pose.
- Press your tailbone down and lift your sternum away from your navel. (Hold on to a wall or the back of a chair if you need support to find balance and stability.)
- Bend your right knee and bring your right heel up toward your backside. Reach back with your right hand to clasp your ankle, either from the outside (more accessible) or the inside (harder).

- While holding your ankle, align your right knee beside your left knee. Pause, breathe, and bring your body into balance.
- Now press your right thigh back and up behind you and press your right foot away from you while still holding your ankle. Reach your left arm forward and up, leading with your inner upper arm.
- Stretch your sternum up and away from your navel to maintain your chest lift. Continue to extend back and up with your right thigh and foot.
- Release your right foot, bring your arms down, and return to Mountain Pose. Pause in the transition, then repeat on the other side.

Dancer Pose is like surfing a wave. The further you reach forward with your front arm and extend your back thigh up, the more challenging it is to find balance. You can choose not to stretch much and stay secure. Or you can try to extend as fully as possible, lifting your foot high toward the sky and riding the edge. Maybe you will wobble as you lengthen. Imagine you are reaching for your longing as your standing leg and pelvis keep you rooted in the Earth. Express your longing as you extend your body. Court the muse by stretching as far as you dare. Or by holding the pose as eloquently as possible.

Take care of yourself. Reach out for the support you need. Hold on to a wall, tree, or table to help you balance. Notice how this pose evokes challenge and grace while requiring ease and effort as you simultaneously kick back and reach out. Some days you may feel steady and sturdy. Other days might be a struggle. Falling out of the pose is welcome. Every day is a new chance to find balance.

Call in your muse in Dancer Pose. Let it guide how you embody the pose. Listen and stay open to anything the muse may reveal through words, feelings, sensations, and body movements. Transition from the pose into free movement if you feel called. Dance. Or, if you are feeling strong, vary the pose with additional challenges. Try, for example, holding your foot from the inside. Or intensify the opening in your chest by holding on to your bent leg with both hands.

Or try Bow Pose (Dhanurasana): Lie on your belly with your arms and hands by your sides, palms facing up. Bend your knees and hold on to your ankles. Press your pubic bone down and draw your lower belly in and up. Inhale and press your ankles into your hands while lifting your chest and thighs. Feel your back strengthening. Slide your shoulder blades toward each other and feel your chest and shoulders opening. Breathe into your ribs. Use your back and abdominal muscles to rock back and forth. On an exhale, release your ankles and relax while lying on your belly.

You have tapped into a deep source of creativity by courting your muse. Now you can make a valuable contribution. Yet these times of ecological devastation invite us even deeper into the belly of the dark Earth to collectively wrestle and pray for visions for the Earth and future generations. We are invited to converse with death, in the mess of loam and mud, and to suffer as a community, attuning to the guidance we may hear whispered from her depths. We will explore how in the following chapter.

# CHAPTER FIFTEEN

# Pray within the Dark Earth

I walk through the cave's rocky, wet terrain, placing my hand on a wall to steady myself as my eyes adjust to the dark. Pausing, I hear the soft, dripping echo of dew sliding off rock. It sounds like a heartbeat from within this cool earthen interior. As water trickles over my feet, I remember watching springs emerge from darkness, rising from under the ground to feed streams, lakes, and rivers. I thank these waters for nourishing all life on our planet.

This place reminds me of the cave womb of my mythos. As a guide, I invite others to be nourished by the imaginal waters that spring forth from their depths, releasing visionary potential, expanding consciousness, and revealing other ways to live. Being in our deep imagination while attuning to nature's wild imagination can enlarge our perception, align us with a deeper intelligence, and remind us of ancient and new potentialities. Grounded in reverence for the living planet, we can listen for what she needs.

Visions and dreams spring forth from the belly of the Earth, as does actual water, to nourish our souls and the world's soul and keep everything alive. The majority of drinkable water worldwide comes from underground aquifers, now being rapidly drawn down.[1] Rain is unable to replenish the amount being mined. Globally, water use has risen to more than twice the rate of population growth.[2] It is still increasing. Ninety percent of water used by humans is consumed by industry and agriculture.[3] "Groundwater, held in caves, pores, and cracks, is the world's largest unfrozen freshwater habitat."[4] When these waters are overused, lakes, streams, and rivers dry up, and the animals that live within this underground ecosystem are endangered.

In the Navajo Nation in Arizona, Utah, and New Mexico, a third of houses lack running water; in some towns, the figure is 90 percent. Peabody Energy, a large coal producer and Fortune 500 company, pulled so much water from the Navajo aquifer before closing its mining operation in 2019 that many wells and springs have run dry.[5] And it is not only coal mining that usurps water. Since 1980, lithium mining companies in Chile have made billions consuming so much water that indigenous Atacama villagers were forced to abandon their settlements.[6] For millennia, they had used their scarce water supply carefully. Now, where hundreds of flamingos once lived on beautiful lagoons, the ground is hard and cracked.[7]

The cave womb of the Earth is creative and life-giving but fragile. As we bring awareness to life underneath the surface, we can grieve and offer our tears for the massive losses of groundwater and the poisoning of underground waterways. We can pray for a vision to help us respond to clear-cut forests, plowed prairies, drained wetlands, and the harms of human-only land use, like mining and agriculture. "Of all the mammals now on Earth, 96 percent are livestock and humans; only 4 percent are wild mammals."[8] It is hard to bear witness, but we are part of the Earth's body. We need to feel what is happening and seek and offer help.

Spirit abides in all living things and is inseparable from the natural world. To destroy the Earth is to desecrate God. Prayer is a way of being present and in relationship with everything. We begin to restore balance when we honor the sanctity of life. By listening to dreams, our muses, and nature, we align ourselves with powerful allies and can glean our purpose and understand how to serve the whole. The harm humans are causing the Earth asks us to return to her, listen, and pray for visions that can help us restore balance.

Every time I am in the water, I pray. Most days, I go to the Mancos River, only a mile from my home, and dip my body in her waters. Looking up at the cottonwood trees, I thank these waters for nourishing the forest and animals. I tell them how exquisite they are and ask for their help: "How can we stop what hurts you? What can we bring to benefit you and the heart of the Earth?" Sherri Mitchell, a spiritual teacher and indigenous rights activist of the Penobscot Nation, calls women "the water bearers of the Universe."[9] The cycles in a woman's body move in relation to the tides, and throughout history, women in all societies have carried water. Now, water is asking all of us to listen.

The dominant culture is unraveling — and needs to. We are already amid the transition, a cultural fertile darkness likely to be chaotic and unpredictable. May it alter, dismember, and initiate us. Let go of the aspects of dominant culture harming life. Instead, seek to personally and collectively descend into the underworld depths, a mysterious cauldron holding all we do not know.

The act of entering this cave womb is core to Wild Yoga, so that we may grieve and receive visions for our souls and the dream of the Earth.

## A Portal

Opening to the suffering of the Earth creates a portal, pulling us into the heart of the world. I guide others to remember forests that are under assault worldwide and those beings dying in oceans, so many of which have been wiped out — 90 percent of large fish, 50 percent of coral reefs, 40 percent of plankton.[10]

"What if we let this break our hearts, evoke our fear, incite our rage, and call forth a prayer that longs for the impossible?" I ask those who participate in a five-day Prayers in the Dark program.

Sixteen of us sit in a circle in the Utah desert. The sky is blue, and the sun is bright. We are shaded under a large, cave-like overhang. It is late morning, and the desert is silent except for the occasional call of a mourning dove.

Many in the group are quiet, unsmiling, their eyes cast down. When asked, several claim to feel numb. Others continue to maintain silence, and a few, I notice, sit with furrowed brows. Their edginess is palpable. One woman, with a stone in her hand, nervously strikes the ground, as though trying to dig a hole. I am not surprised by their agitation.

"The Earth will be fine," says Jane, a young woman who recently finished medical school. She looks around the group, as though expecting consensus.

"What makes you think so?" I ask.

"Extinctions have always happened," shouts Sam, an older man from New Mexico. "New species evolve." Multiple silver and turquoise bracelets hang off his arm, rattling as he talks.

"Extinctions are occurring a thousand times faster, too rapidly for new species to evolve," I counter.[11]

"We need to focus on human survival," interjects Sam, his eyes glaring, his mouth taut.

"How will our children breathe without trees?" I ask.[12]

"It's the apocalypse," says Mary, a painter from California. "There's nothing we can do," she continues, her voice barely a whisper. Her eyes well up with tears. She rests her face in her hands and sobs, her shoulders shaking.

"Our biosphere is still alive," I say, "and ecosystems, plants, and animals."

"I do my part," says Mark, a graduate student from the University of

Chicago, his tone defensive. "I garden and recycle." Others in the group nod, a validation of their like-minded thinking.

"Individual lifestyle shifts are not enough to stop global empire," I say.[13]

"We'll switch from fossil fuels to solar and wind," Mark retorts.

"Those require mining and destruction of land too. Read *Bright Green Lies.*"[14]

"Technology will come up with something," Sam chimes in. I look around the group. So many are quiet, listening in, and seem unsure what to say.

"Humanity won't survive continued industrial expansion and consumption," I reply.

"It's over," Mary says, her tears continuing to flow silently. "There's nothing we can do." Two other women are also crying. One, sitting next to Mary, reaches over to offer her a hug.

That night, in my sleeping bag, I lie awake feeling dread. A shiver runs through my body, not from the cold, but from fear of where we are. Covid-19 has given us a glimpse of what many face daily — food shortages, loss of civil freedoms, totalitarian leadership, and deaths. But the ecological crisis is far worse. It's hard to be with the devastation already happening and the awareness of more likely to come. Rolling over in my sleeping bag, I say a silent prayer that our fear gives rise to courage. That we may let go of Western culture's destructive ways, descend into the unknown, listen from within the belly of the Earth, and ask her to guide us.

## Into the Heart of the World

Whatever we love and may lose carries us into the world's heart. Many people prayed for me when I had cancer. Their good wishes healed me and brought me joy. I was surprised by how well I felt, despite the physical pain. Later, I wondered if their prayers had helped me feel good. Prayer is part of my soul's calling. It connects us to the moment and invites us into a cocreative partnership with life. In the yoga asana classes I teach, I invite our movements to be prayer and our bodies a doorway to the sacred.

I pray with others in nature, guiding people to let go and listen. To feel their unmet longing to find deeper meaning and purpose, to become whole and live a soul-centered existence. Sometimes the prayers we live can feel intensely tricky. In the cave womb of transformation, visions can emerge, and the dark nights of our soul can pull us toward the holy mystery at the center of our lives. I have shared in these pages a few times I have been in a fertile dark-ness: having cancer, seeking my soul, ending my marriage. So many visions came as I let go of my old ways and surrendered to the dream of the Earth. I have written about twisted tree, Junie and Star, bear, and the dark waters.

I am in alignment with my soul, and I know others who are too. Yet eco-systems are collapsing under the greed of global capitalism, and more species and lands die each day. Our prayers need to stretch beyond the individual. Soul making is a collaboration tied to the fate of Earth, asking us to descend into the collective dark night of our planet. If we can open to the tremendous sorrow of our failure to protect oceans, forests, and rivers, this can bring us into the world's heart, dismembering our sense of self and what we have be-lieved about the world. We can receive visions for the Earth through a collec-tive descent into the underworldly depths.

On day two of the Prayers in the Dark program, Alicia, a young woman who lives in a yurt in southwestern Colorado, places her forehead and hands on the red soil of the desert. "This isn't yours," she cries, fierce and mournful. "This belongs to all of us." She repeats this phrase over and over, her voice increasing in intensity, her hands slapping the ground.

The same sixteen Prayers in the Dark participants are sitting in another circle underneath the cave-like overhang. Today, we are engaged in a cere-mony similar to the Truth Mandala practice developed by Buddhist teacher Joanna Macy, expressing our feelings about what is happening to the planet.[15] Mary stands up and opens her mouth in a bloodcurdling scream.

The group is silent, frozen, taking in her scream. It pierces us and the land and is both disturbing and relieving, as if we had all howled, shrieked, or wailed.

Alex says, "I grew up on the Boundary Waters," a wilderness area in Min-nesota that is part of the Superior National Forest. He talks about canoeing as a child and all the birds he saw. "Trump has granted leases to mining com-panies," he points out, referring to a past American president. "The land and water will be poisoned."

Thomas, from Wyoming, is trembling and in tears. I ask him if he'd like to share his thoughts with the group. He shakes his head no. "I can't speak," he says, choking. "It's too sad."

I feel my longing. For cement, metal, and tin to melt away. For machines that mine the Earth to be dismantled. For rivers to run clear and be full of salmon. Flocks of birds to darken the sky. Ancient trees to cover the land. Oceans to teem with whales, dolphins, and coral. People to stop extracting and start honoring. The Earth to breathe herself alive.

"Close your eyes and root in the Earth," I suggest to the group. "Imagine you are liquifying in a cocoon or hibernating in a cave. Descend into your despair and listen for what emerges. Ask for visions of how we can respond."

Our souls are linked to the underground heart of the world. Deeper under the surface of our planet than water is fire. Magma, a hot, semifluid material, can move up to the surface and be ejected as lava. The Earth is a fire planet. When humans suppress all wildfires and incessantly burn fossil fuels, they upset the role fire plays in bringing ecological balance.[16] Our feelings are linked to what is happening on our planet. Our fire — our rage — is an active and receptive grief cry. We can speak and listen, surrender and serve, and offer ourselves. We can embody what we receive as responses arise from our depths through images, emotions, words, dreams, or sensations. To live and die the visions we are given is a prayer.

## Death

An ongoing relationship with death kept me close to the Mystery. My scare with cancer did not end once I was in remission. Symptoms I felt when I had cancer — pressure in my chest, a chronic cough, nausea — sometimes returned. I had frequent CAT scans after I recovered, checking to see if it had reappeared. Statistically, the odds of a reoccurrence were high. I was told the remedy would be a bone marrow transplant: six weeks in the hospital taking in chemicals so toxic that 6 percent of people die from the procedure. I worried cancer would come back. I am incredibly grateful it did not and glad I never had to do a bone marrow transplant.

After five years, the doctors said I no longer needed to do CAT scans. Yet death still felt near. A reoccurrence was still possible, although less probable.

On my thirty-fifth birthday, I went to a clinic with chest pain.

In his office, the doctor's eyes widened when he saw my EKG results.

"What?" I asked, looking at him across an old mahogany desk. "Am I having a heart attack?"

"Maybe you already had one," he said. "Could someone drive you to the emergency room?"

Hours later, I was admitted to a hospital and was given another CAT scan. "Your cancer may have returned," the emergency room doctor said.

The familiar metallic taste of dye filled my mouth. They had me stay the night to undergo a barrage of tests. Four thousand dollars later, science had no explanation for my abnormal EKG.

Long-term effects of radiation on the heart and lungs include an increased risk of disease. Feeling close to death has changed my life. Death will claim all of us and those we love one day. It *preys* on us, bringing us to our knees in humility and inspiring us to *pray* and listen. Death initiated me into the mysteries and connected me more deeply with my soul and the sacred.

Our death can feed the spirits if we offer our lives to what matters. According to Martín Prechtel, young people in the Tz'utujil Mayan village where he lived "wrestled with death" during their initiation ceremonies. They tried to court their souls back from death with eloquence. Death was likely to agree to give them their souls only if the initiates committed to "ritually render a percentage of the fruit of [their] art, [their] eloquence, and [their] imagination to the other world."[17] The Earth and Spirit are fed by how we live and die. I imagine them starving and grieving for people to listen, create beauty, and give back. When we live and die eloquently, our lives and deaths nourish the spirit world, like a grandmother tree nourishes a forest in her life and death.

I am reminded of a friend who recently died. After being diagnosed with Lou Gehrig's disease at thirty-five and becoming paralyzed, she grappled with the chronic and terminal illness with grace and even wrote a book about her journey.[18] Junie and Star also showed me what it looks like to step toward death with love. Guiding on the river, I sometimes feel close to death. Praying for my life, I am surprised by the images that arise and remind me of what I love and value — the sacred beauty of wild places; quiet moments alone with my body and my muse; being with loved ones, my dog Xander, friends; swimming or rafting; water.

On quests, I guide others to put their lives on the altar if they are emotionally and developmentally ready. Seeking a psychospiritual death is part of their prayer to receive a vision of their life's purpose. People sometimes encounter soul on their deathbed, but they have no time left to live it. Intentionally letting go of the familiar and stepping into a liminal unknown is a kind of death, and visions of soul or other extraordinary or numinous possibilities can come. Some questers seek an initiatory dismemberment, hoping to receive what David Whyte calls

your own truth
at the center of the image
you were born with.[19]

In a meadow in the Colorado high country, twelve people stand at the edge of a portal made of sticks, pine cones, and flowers. A deer peers out from behind a ponderosa pine. Quaking aspens, lupines, and bluebells surround us. Each person reads their prayer before walking across the threshold to fast solo for three nights.

Initiation ceremonies like these were common in ancient cultures of indigenous and nature-based peoples, and some still do them. Yet, as Martín Prechtel explained, when an entire culture "refuses to wrestle death with eloquence, then death comes up to the surface to eat us in a literal way, with wars and depression."[20] Perhaps if modern Western culture supported its people to grow and face death, it would stop consuming life.

## Cultural Dismemberment

The dominant culture will not last. Founded on the principles of individualism, capitalism, human supremacy, white supremacy, and colonialism, this mainstream culture is incompatible with the Earth's living systems. Yet industrial civilization continues on the path of futile addiction to an unsustainable lifestyle, in denial of its impending collapse.

The world will be healthier once the dominant culture ends — animals, plants, water, soil, developing nations, indigenous cultures, and rural people. The sooner it comes to a halt, the more animals, fish, trees, and rivers will remain, and the more likely it is that we will have sustainable food sources for future generations. Waiting for things to unravel may make the crash worse for humans and nonhumans who live through it and for those who come afterward.[21]

Author Charles Eisenstein wrote, "Ecological deterioration is but one aspect of an initiation ordeal propelling civilization into a new story." It "provides initiatory medicine for the world's dominant civilization" to change.[22] If only the ecological crisis would catalyze radical change that would compel industrial civilization to let go of harming the natural world to keep itself alive. Government and corporate leaders and the systems of power that rule society do not seem willing to put global empire on the ceremonial altar, despite how much harm it causes. The global empire has been going on for a long while, with no sign of any significant shift. Individuals and communities need to reclaim the power to take the necessary courageous steps to ensure the global empire is put on the altar. We can let go of what we don't believe in and know isn't working and of what we enjoyed. We can align with what and who truly matters.

When we let go, we don't know what is next. We descend into our prerational instincts, listen and attune to our planet home, and invite our visionary selves to guide us. A caterpillar surrenders her life in the cocoon, not knowing she will metamorphose into a butterfly. We can liquefy in the cave womb of our imaginations and pray within the dark Earth. Feeling our watery souls and the water flowing under the ground, we can pray for a vision to help us restore forests, birds, oceans, and justice. Yearning for a world where the holy is blended with all we do, we can partner with the dream of the Earth. Will the universe hear us and respond?

I close my eyes and remember visions — mine and others' — that have sprung forth from the depths of wild nature and dreamtime. I remember springs I have drunk from in the wild, my lips on a mossy rock, my mouth filling with the sweet flavor and vibrant texture of waters that have long gestated in the dark Earth until they were ready to rise. I lean in and receive the generosity of water, longing for her elixirs to stir visions of ways to halt the human-caused harm and restore and nourish her ecosystems back to life.

## Wild Yoga Practices for Praying within the Dark Earth

Go out at night or find a dark place in nature, be present in your body with all your feelings, and listen, wait, and pray.

- Find a cave or other wild place where you can sit in darkness. Imagine yourself deep inside the Earth. See if you can sense the place where water arises or feel her heartbeat. Imagine you are gestating in the underground heart of the world. Wait and listen. Notice what you feel and what arises.
- Lie down in a dark place and gestate in the cave womb in your imagination. Invite in the most potent dream or mythic images of your life. Do not decide which images. Make space and see what emerges. Explore whatever comes with all of your senses and see what you

discover. What is it like to feel images arise inside you? Draw, paint, or collage the images.

- Visit a place on the Earth that is being harmed. Bear witness to what that place feels. Sense into the larger story of ecological devastation on our planet and notice what you feel or imagine. Tell the place what you are experiencing and see what happens next.
- Reflect on your relationship with death. Have you had near-death experiences or been close with someone who did? What feelings were stirred? Visit a place in nature where death is present. Tell it what you notice and have experienced and listen for a response.
- Create a ceremonial cocoon, a space where you can liquefy in your imagination. Invite in the possibility that you are part of a cultural dismemberment. Remember the joys and sorrows of your life and the world. Imagine yourself letting go into the underworldly depths of the mysterious unknown. Ask to receive visions for the Earth.

## *A Yoga Pose for Praying within the Dark Earth*

### RABBIT POSE

Rabbit Pose (Sasangasana) relaxes your nervous system, releases neck, back, and shoulder tension, and provides relief from depression and insomnia. In addition, it stretches your spine, strengthens your back, boosts your immune system, and stimulates your intervertebral disks, thyroid gland, and digestion. An easy inversion, with your head lower than your heart, this pose helps you increase circulation and energy, calm your mind, and connect to the Earth.

*To get in the pose:*

- Beginning in Child's Pose, bring your hands back to grab your heels, thumbs on the outside and fingers on the inside.
- Draw your forehead down toward your knees. Firm your grip on your heels to counterbalance the rest of your body going forward.
- Inhale, lift your hips off your heels, and roll onto the top of your head.
- Keep breathing. At first, you will feel a stretch only in your neck and

upper spine. However, with more practice, you will feel the stretch all the way from your tailbone to your neck.

- Make sure there is no pressure on your head as you pull on your heels to stretch your spine. If you need more support, move your hands lower on your feet, grabbing closer to your arches.
- The stronger your arms are, the more your back will stretch. Firm your bicep muscles while softening and relaxing your shoulders.
- Work your heels together, so the fingers of both hands touch between your feet.
- Hold the pose for thirty to sixty seconds.
- Exhale, lower your hips back to your heels, and release your hands forward.
- Relax in Child's Pose.

This pose teaches us to be calm, attentive, and aware of our breath in tight or uncomfortable situations. It challenges us to breathe into the sides and backs of our lungs and builds respiratory health. We tone our abdomen, stretch our back body, and enhance the spine's mobility and elasticity. Stimulating the endocrine function, Rabbit Pose balances hormones and emotions and improves memory and focus while relieving mental fatigue and aches in our head, neck, and back.

Rabbit Pose is playful and easy. Children come into it naturally. Once in the pose, relax your jaw, face, and neck and breathe deeply, expanding your side and back ribs. Plant your crown chakra in the ground and visualize your head extending deep into the Earth, stimulating your capacity to vision and cocreate. Our crown chakra connects us to a universal consciousness. Feel this energy center activated — igniting new ideas and possibilities — while feeling soothed and held. Amid the intensity of our ecological and biodiversity crisis, this pose brings relaxation that can nurture and restore us.

This pose mirrors an intensity we may feel in the world and asks us to go inward and plant ourselves in the Earth. Here, we can breathe and listen for visions. We can connect to the rabbit, which lives close to the ground, as we strengthen our torso. The weight of the world often lives in our head, neck, and shoulders. As we place our crown chakra on the Earth, we can unite with her and imagine we are liquifying in the cave womb. Feel your head intermingling with the dream of the Earth and see what visions arise.

Praying within the dark Earth invites us into our deep imaginations, where we can let go into the heart of the world, grieve, and watch for visions that can guide us. Yet these times of ecological devastation may incite us to take a still more active role in dreaming the world. Our dreams are not only for our souls. They are for our communities and the Earth. Radical dreaming guides us in aligning with our visionary nature to help the Earth by listening for how we can protect land and species. We will explore how in the following chapter.

# CHAPTER SIXTEEN

# Engage in Radical Dreaming

The sun lights up the expansive slopes of the Sonoran Desert, dotted with prickly pear, saguaro, and cholla cacti. Cottonwood trees shade the little river. In Aravaipa Canyon, a gorge in the Pinal Mountains of southern Arizona, I prepare thirteen people for a three-day solo fast. The river bubbles in a playful chorus, churning around boulders and rippling over gravel. *Aravaipa* means "laughing waters" in Apache.

I marvel at the joy of flowing waters and remember the Apache who lived in this canyon for five hundred years, until they were massacred in 1871. Settlers descended on their camp before dawn that April, killing 150 Apache women and children while the men were away hunting. They clubbed to death those asleep and shot those awake.[1] Remaining Apache were relocated to the White Mountain Apache Reservation.[2] Worldwide, indigenous societies have been attacked for six thousand years. That is how industrial civilization expanded and acquired the resources it needed to exist.

*Radical* means "root" in Latin. To me, it means challenging systems and societies at their foundation. For years, I had asked nature and my dreams to help me find a multidimensional response to ecological devastation. A dream comes while I am in Aravaipa Canyon. (*Trigger warning: This dream mentions rape, and there is some discussion about rape in the chapter.*)

> I see a woman about to be raped. She's yanked out of the driver's seat of her car by a man. He holds her captive, pressing her against the car while undoing his pants. A male friend turns to me and asks if he should try to stop it.
>
> "Yes," I say.
>
> My friend picks up a club that resembles a baseball bat and moves toward the rapist. My stomach tightens. What if my friend is killed or

193

*hurt? I decide to join him and approach the rapist from behind. My friend moves toward him from the side. As we get closer, the rapist stops. He turns around and holds up his hands in surrender.*

I had had dreams about rape before, but none where I stopped it. That morning, after I awaken, I return to the dream in my imagination, asking what it wants me to experience. The dream seems to be suggesting that together we can stop the rape.

## Stopping the Rape

I have been listening to women share stories of rape my whole adult life as a therapist, guide, and friend. Rape is part of the everyday violence of our culture that is considered normal. It is the most underreported crime in the world, notoriously underinvestigated and largely unpunished: Fewer than 1 percent of rapes end in a felony conviction.[3] Rapists rarely receive jail time, especially if they knew their victim. Eight out of ten rapists are known to their victims, as are 93 percent of child sex abusers.[4]

Many do not notice the rape of the Earth. Like so many women, I know how it feels to be physically overpowered and have no one see the desecration. I am glad for the deep care I have experienced from other humans and nature and the opportunity I've had to heal. The rape of the Earth — bombs exploded in her belly to create mines, plowed and paved cities, soils and streams poisoned — should be a crime. Yet it is legal.[5] "The ordinary response to atrocities is to banish them from consciousness," wrote psychiatrist and researcher Judith Lewis Herman.[6] "Denial, repression, and disassociation operate on a social as well as an individual level.... Like traumatized people, we need to understand the past in order to reclaim the present and the future." Silencing perpetuates trauma, and healing begins with telling the truth. I can feel the rape of the Earth in my psyche, but how can we stop what so many can't see?[7]

Three saguaro cacti surround us in Aravaipa Canyon, each about thirty feet tall, with barrel appendage arms. I am sitting in a council ceremony with the group that is preparing to solo. I glance at a desert mountain some distance away and see several moving dots that I decipher as five bighorn sheep.

"Will you help me stop the rape?" I ask when it is my turn to speak. I don't expect an immediate response. In council, each person shares what is in their heart. Everyone has a turn to speak, but no one responds directly to anyone.

I asked the question, not seeking an answer, but to reenact the role I played in my dream.

Later in the day, after the council is over, Paul, a grad student in his thirties, comes over and asks if it is okay if he responds. We share our views over dinner, sitting at a picnic table as the desert sky turns orange and purple. Others in the group do not hear us. They are engrossed in their conversations.

"The Earth created us this way," he says. "There's not a problem. She's dreaming us."

*This guy isn't aware of ecological devastation,* I think. "What about the mass extinctions?"

"Extinction is Gaian," he responds. "It's part of her plan. She's shape-shifting."

My chest tightens at this retort. I think of other conversations I've had with intellectuals who consider their thinking to be ahead of the times. While aware of my frustration, I also value listening, and I commit to both hearing what Paul has to say and standing firm in my beliefs.

"This is extermination by capitalism," I counter, borrowing a phrase from Truthout, a nonprofit news organization commenting on various social justice issues.[8]

"Humans are nature." He flashes a calm smile. "Industrialization is a mysterious phenomenon being expressed through humans."

*Seriously? Industrialization, natural — how could he believe that?* "Earth is dreaming us," I say, "but our dominant culture has stopped listening."

"We shouldn't treat the Earth like a victim." His voice exudes confidence. "She can take care of herself."

Taking a moment to consider his stance, I notice a red-tailed hawk flying in the distance, soaring against the setting sun.

"It's possible to be powerful and harmed by another," I say, my tone more assertive.

"Maybe there are evolutionary wonders that would not be possible without this story of separation." He scoops the last bit of pasta into his mouth.

"Do you imagine the Earth wants her rivers poisoned and dammed, her mountains blown up and mined, her ecosystems and biodiversity destroyed?"

"We're not in control."

"Humans can take down what humans have made." I refill my glass with water.

"We can't save the world. We can only belong more fully."

"Stopping the harm and restoring ecosystems is what humans who belong would do," I point out.

"Ecologies do not need us to do anything for them."

*That might be true if humans weren't destroying them.* "There are forests alive today because people cared enough to save them."

"Ecologies adapt," he says. "They take on other shapes or ways of functioning."

"Adapting is not always good. We should *not* adapt to abuse."

"All of this is part of the mass reshaping of Earth's interconnected ecologies," he concludes.

We carry our dishes to the washing station but glance at each other briefly and smile. I like to debate, and sense he does too, no matter the frustration involved. I remind myself that respectful disagreement is essential to mutual growth and collaboration.

## Dreaming for the World

We live in an embedded relationship with a conscious, feeling world. Dreams arise from the Earth. They are alive and more intelligent than our waking ego and offer possibilities that our minds could never come up with. We listen to dreams and the land for our souls and the world's soul. We dream for ourselves, our communities, and the Earth. Dreams enable us to experience possible futures. Arising from what psychotherapist Stephen Aizenstat, founding president of Pacifica Graduate Institute, calls "the World Dream," they offer us a glimpse of the desires of the world so we can "act in the world, on behalf of the world ... in Archetypal Activism."[9] To the Iroquois, the dream world is real, and "dreaming is one of the most important ways to acquire and accumulate authentic power" by which we can "shape-shift the world."[10] Traditional Tz'utujil Maya communities elected officials based on the number of villagers dreaming of that person in office.[11]

Dreams come when we are asleep. Yet they invite us to live in conversation with the waking dream of life. Surprising images or daydreams can also arise at the edge of consciousness while awake. Whether they arrive when we are asleep or awake, dreams hold multiple meanings related to our call and the seeds of our collective imaginings.

Radical dreaming brings together our visionary and revolutionary natures. We can ask our dreams for clues about how to protect land and species and act on what we receive. Listening to nature and dreams for the Earth, future generations, and the world is central to Wild Yoga.

Dreams invite us to step beyond the veil of consensual reality. They can help us inhabit the poetic consciousness of our mythos, connect us with the land and our ancestors, and inspire us to protect the Earth's ecosystems. We can act both mythically and directly. Embodying what dream images reveal imbues us with their mysterious powers. Through dream incubation, some artists ask their dreams to guide what they create.[12] Just as dreams can give artists clues about how to embody a character, paint a picture, or write a book, we can ask our dreams to show us how to protect wild places or stop systems of power that are harming the planet.

Being in a whole relationship with the planet means caring for our mother. Modern culture has separated us from our land and the instinct to protect it. Yet loving the living world means attending not only to wild places, but to the wilderness beneath lands that have been cleared for cities, agriculture, and mining. In a loving relationship, we stay present with who and what we love, even in hard times.

It takes courage to speak or act against those in power. Those who defend land risk being threatened, attacked, arrested, and losing their lives. Max Wilbert, a grassroots organizer and coauthor of *Bright Green Lies: How the Environmental Movement Lost Its Way and What We Can Do about It*, first invited me and others to Thacker Pass in Humboldt County, Nevada, several months before the lithium mine protest began.

## Dreaming with the Earth

Breathing in the scent of sage grass, I relax in the hypnotic silence of one of the last wide-open spaces in America. Between 5 and 8 percent of the global population of sage grouse live here, although up to 99 percent of their population has already been lost. The threatened Lahontan cutthroat trout makes its home in the watershed, and a rare endemic snail dwells in the fourteen springs that burble in the southern Montana Mountains.

There's a misperception that green technology can help the planet: many of those technologies rely on extractive processes that are incredibly damaging to the Earth. Take electric cars, for example, which require lithium for batteries.

Three of us sit amid the sagebrush, finishing up dinner, and watch the first stars come out in the night sky while listening to Max Wilbert talk about the proposed mine.

"Lithium mining is increasing," Max tells us, "mostly because of the growing electric vehicle market." Thacker Pass is the first of many proposed lithium mines in Nevada. Multiple active placer claims (7,996 as of February 2020) have been located in eighteen different hydrographic basins.[13] Lithium is only one ingredient needed to make electric cars. Cobalt, neodymium, dysprosium, coltan, and copper must also be mined and smelted.[14] Cobalt is extraordinarily toxic.

"If we choose cars over the wilderness," Max asks, "what does that say about our values?"

A nightmare flashes before me: a vision of sagebrush replaced with bulldozer treads, smoky toxic air, and a massive open pit. But why oppose a lithium mine? Why not fossil fuels? I dislike them too. Yet the impact on the Earth is not that different between a lithium mine and an open-pit coal mine. "Both require bulldozing entire ecosystems. Both use huge amounts of water. Both leave behind poisoned aquifers. Both are operated with heavy machinery fueled by diesel."[15]

The Thacker Pass lithium mine would use "more than 1.4 billion gallons of water per year."[16] Lithium Nevada Corporation, a subsidiary of Canadian-owned Lithium Americas, is downplaying the effects their mine would have on drawing down water. Its environmental impact statement is misleading. Classifying year-round creeks as "ephemeral" and underreporting the flow rate of the fourteen springs, Lithium Nevada is claiming there is less water in the area than there is to hide the impact their mine would make.[17] Wastewater would "contaminate local groundwater with dangerous heavy metals, in particular a 'plume' of antimony, for at least 300 years."[18]

That night, I gaze up at the stars and the Milky Way from my sleeping bag. Free from artificial lights and the noise of highways, I listen to the distant yips and barks of howling coyotes. In the morning, the sky glows orange-red. Max comes over holding up a red-tailed hawk feather while I'm refilling my water bottle at my car.

"Did you put this here last night?" he asks. "It was sticking out of the ground a few feet away when I awoke."

"No," I answer. "Unless I did it in my sleep."

He shows me a prairie falcon feather and then a raven feather. "How about these?" His tone is somewhat terse. He stares at me intently.

"No. Were these feathers all together?"

"The hawk feather was the first thing I saw upon waking, quite close to where I was sleeping. The other two feathers were sticking out of the ground a short distance away. But I'm certain they weren't here last night."

Goosebumps rise on my arms. I take a deep breath, feeling my heart lift. I think the spirits of the land may be offering acknowledgment, gratitude for our presence.

"And your dreams?" I ask, curious to see what other visions may be coming to Max.

"I dreamed of a woman leading three hundred people to defend this mountain. I have been imagining many people camped here, standing watch and lying in front of machines."

The dream images of others can speak to us as powerfully as our own. Closing my eyes, I put my hands on the ground and let my imagination swim in Max's dream. I see a community planting their bodies on the land, listening to their dreams for guidance, and protecting this mountain's "16 million years of sacred silence."[19] But dreams are a seed, easily lost in the wind. What they reveal unleashes a responsibility to act.

## Dreaming at a Protest Camp

On January 15, 2021, the Bureau of Land Management approved the environmental impact statement for Lithium Nevada's proposed $1.4 billion open-pit lithium mine. That day Max Wilbert and Will Falk established a protest camp at Thacker Pass.[20] Later, they joined the movements of local tribes like the Reno-Sparks Indian Colony and Atsa koodakuh wyh Nuwu (People of the Red Mountain).[21] Paiute-Shoshone ancestors are buried on the land. I volunteered at the camp for a couple of weeks that April. As camp manager, I welcomed people and helped the camp run smoothly. I was also there to learn, to apprentice in how to protect land.

"Protecting land and species is the most important thing we can do," John, a writer from North Carolina, said one day. Four of us sat in the kitchen, surrounded by plywood windbreaks, eating lunch.

I agreed with him, but I also thought the situation was far more complex. "How will we get people to help?" I asked.

"We probably won't," he said. "We'll just have to work harder."

Heather, a woman who lived nearby in Reno, Nevada, chimed in: "Working harder doesn't always work."

"Activist strategies alone aren't enough," I concurred.

"Some people try to help but can cause harm if they lack vision and awareness," Heather added.

I liked the direction she was heading. "If people could perceive nature's intelligence, they'd do something," I offered. "If they listened to dreams, they might have an idea what to do."

"We need to collaborate across disciplines, strategies, cultures." Heather took a bite of bread, then looked toward me. "Like you, Rebecca — what you're doing with Wild Yoga."

John got up to wash his plate. "There's no time for Wild Yoga," he said dismissively. "There's too much work to do."

I bristled inside, disappointed that John could not see how this practice could open people, support the Earth, and strengthen their efforts.

A failure of imagination is just as possible — and potentially damaging — as a failure of action. Our dominant culture does not seem imaginative enough to consider a path forward that does not cause illness, pollution, or species extinction. Listening to dreams and nature gives us access to a creative intelligence far brighter than our human minds. Dreams show us how to act smarter, if we listen to them and relate our actions to what they reveal.

One morning, I sat on a huge boulder amid the sagebrush with another activist, Andrew, a lawyer from Vermont. A red-tailed hawk, which had been nesting in a nearby canyon, circled above. Looking up at the snowcapped peaks surrounding us, Andrew recounted a nightmare from the previous night. I guided him back into his dream.

"The smell is horrible," he described, his eyes closed. "My nostrils are burning. The land has been poisoned. The sagebrush is on fire. Pronghorn are lying on the ground, dead. Everything is hurting." Bringing his knees up to his chin, he wrapped his arms around his legs, as though seeking stability.

I could feel my heart clench, aware of his pain. Not far from where we sat, Lithium Nevada was planning to blow up this mountain. My fingers touched a lithium rock in my pocket. *Why is this mineral worth such devastation?* I wondered, envisioning a sprawl of treatment ponds and tailing piles.

"What else do you see?" I was concerned he might feel uncomfortable with the intensity of emotions and images.

"Meadowlarks are trying to fly, but they keep falling."

"What do you feel?"

"My body is shuddering. I am struggling to breathe." His mouth crumpled as tears sprang to his eyes.

I was curious to keep exploring this dream with him. "And the meadow-larks?"

"They suffer too. Everything is in agony."

"Where does the dream take you?"

"Falling," he said, his hands clenching, "uncontrollably."

"Stay with that," I suggested.

"It wants to carry me up to the stars. But I keep going down."

"Stay with the feeling of being pulled down," I repeated.

"I want to get away from this awful smell." He looked like he was about to gag. "But I can't."

"What happens next?"

There was a long pause during which he began to shake and cry. I shared his pain as tears welled in my eyes. Then I heard the flapping of a raven's wings above us and looked up.

"The grief," he managed to say, "it's too much. It's so dreadful, the devastation planned for this land."

"Raven is here," I whispered. "He sees you."

Andrew's dream invites us to feel the heaviness of what the mountain faces. As of this writing, construction of the lithium mine was scheduled to begin in 2022. Raven reminds us we are connected to the land and need to stay strong. Perhaps if everyone could experience Andrew's dream, it would inspire them to help.

Although the Bureau of Land Management issued permits for Thacker Pass Lithium Mine, their approval is being challenged in federal court by local indigenous tribes, environmental groups, and a local rancher. Thacker Pass would be the largest lithium mine in the United States but is only the first of many proposed lithium mines. In April 2022, an archeological firm began to excavate, digging up the remains of Paiute-Shoshone ancestors. The Bureau of Land Management had issued the necessary dig permits in December 2021. The excavation must be completed before construction of the mine can begin. So far, six tribes and the Inter-Tribal Council of Nevada have sent communications to the Bureau of Land Management "stating they were not consulted and expressing their opposition to 'the desecration of the sacred site.'"[22]

In 1865, a brutal massacre was committed by the U.S. Army at Thacker Pass in the middle of the night. Now tribes fight to preserve the graves of their murdered relatives.[23] Several tribes, including three Great Basin tribes of the Reno-Sparks Indian Colony (Paiute, Shoshone, and Washoe), went to court "in efforts to halt excavation and construction at Thacker Pass," but a judge ruled against them. The Reno-Sparks Indian Colony has appealed to the archeological firm "to stop digging at a site considered sacred to Nevada tribes." The tribes say the "BLM failed to engage in government-to-government consultation with all tribes who attach religious and cultural significance to Thacker Pass, thus violating federal tribal rights." Because of solid indigenous opposition to the excavations, the tribes view them as disrespectful, a corporate "looting and grave robbing" of ancestral lands for profit.[24] Executives at Lithium Americas are poised to make millions ruining the land and hurting poor people who have already been profoundly wronged.

## Dreaming the Future

The environmental movement is failing. As eco-philosopher and activist Derrick Jenson said, "Part of the problem is that we've been victims of a systematic campaign of misdirection. Consumer culture and the capitalist mindset have taught us to substitute acts of personal consumption (or enlightenment) for organized political resistance."[25] For example, we often hear the world is in a water crisis, so we should reduce personal consumption. Mainstream sources like the US Environmental Protection Agency coach us to take shorter showers.[26] But that advice ignores the fact that globally "more than 90 percent of water used by humans is used by agriculture and industry. The remaining 10 percent is split between municipalities and actual living breathing individual humans. Collectively, municipal golf courses use as much water as municipal human beings."[27]

Some argue that those who protest lithium mines are not credible if they drive cars or use lithium products. But if people who oppose lithium mines can't use lithium products, we can't reach out to others on social media, publish articles and books, or drive to protests. I am typing this on a computer. Writer and activist Alex Eisenberg warns us not to fall into the Personal Responsibility Vortex (PRV): drive ourselves crazy obsessing about making responsible consumer choices and "disempower ourselves in making effective changes on the scale they need to be made."[28] Evolutionary theorist Brett Weinstein coined the term *PRV*. He says making good consumer choices is appealing, but "the choices individuals make trying to do right can often be ineffective and harmful."[29] Individuals "spending more for more responsible products" can "cause the system to evolve more quickly in the direction of ruthlessness." He suggests we redirect our energy away from personal responsibility and toward collective action, including creating a more benevolent system that restricts the market from putting the population at risk.

Writer and activist Will Falk said that rather than ask, "What can I do?" we should ask the question "What needs to be done?"[30] Corporations know the source of their power comes from exploiting the natural world for short-term benefits. Throughout history, those willing to exploit have destroyed cultures that do not. So how can we protect the natural world? We have seen what happens to traditional communities that try to stand in the way of "progress," but what do you imagine the natural world wants? We need to develop strategies that will be genuinely effective in supporting the health of the wild world for the future generations of all species.

Those who protest lithium mines get asked: "If electric vehicles aren't the solution, what is?"[31] One day, Max Wilbert and I talk about this while walking up a dry creek bed leading out of the protest camp and into the mountains.

"We could reduce the size of the economy and the size of our population — and especially the amount we consume — and reduce and eventually eliminate cars," Max says.

"Many people can't imagine this," I respond, "but cars haven't been around long."

"My great-grandparents didn't have cars," he points out while climbing a boulder in a steep part of the wash. "In 130 years, we've transformed our society. People once walked everywhere, but now they own cars and drive wherever they want."

I reflect on my experience with transportation. As a guide, I have spent much of my life in the backcountry, far from roads. Living at an off-grid eco-farm in Costa Rica for several winters, I had no car, and I walked, biked, or rode a public bus. I loved living simply in nature and longed to help wildlife survive. "Protecting and restoring wild lands is a primary need," I say.

Max agrees. "We need to replace extractive industry jobs with land restoration jobs."

Envisioning this major change excites me. "It would create a massive shift in the economy."

"If we reduce consumption, the economy will cease to exist," he says.

We pause our chat to scramble up a rock face. I peer into crevices hoping to see a horned lizard or pika. It is early evening, and a few bats fly overhead.

"People will need to be taught ecosystem restoration, watershed health, small-scale organic agroforestry," he continues. "And permaculture."

*Yes!* For a long time, I've felt these lessons need to be part of public education. "Without a global economy, we would need to rely on local food sources," I say.

"One reason we need healthy biotic communities is to have local food sources," he says. "That's part of why protecting and restoring ecosystems is a priority."

I think back to the eco-farm in Costa Rica. We did not have a telephone, internet, or flushable toilets. We grew our food, ate native plants, or purchased local food. I taught yoga as a work trade in exchange for food and lodging. Today, in Colorado, I live close to nature on a small community farm in a tiny home. I listen and pray for ways to influence change on a larger scale.

"Do you think this massive transformation can happen fast enough to halt the ecological crisis?" I ask Max.

"Not likely. Ecological collapse is underway, and social collapse isn't far behind."

"So much seems uncertain," I say, "and out of our control." The heaviness weighs on me most days. I often find myself questioning what is worth doing and being in these times.

"Local and regional efforts can help mitigate the worst outcomes," he says.

"If we 'do the hard work of opening to mystery,' as Martin Shaw says, and listen to our dreams and nature, perhaps visionary ideas and a remembering of ancient forms can emerge," I offer.[32]

Max says our stories need to change. The narrative has to move "from domination to cooperation, respect, and gratitude for our place in the natural world."

My feeling is we can go further. "We must deepen into the uncertainty, listen to those more intelligent than us, and let the Earth reseed and reimagine us."

Max's focus is on the practical. "We need to understand how to live with ecological collapse and deal with the challenges we face and the changes we have to make."

By now, Max and I have arrived back at camp. I am left with a lot of questions. How do we address the urgency of the ecological crisis and slow down to listen to nature, soul, and what remains in the mystery? How do we make collective change happen, in an Earth-rooted way? These questions are complex and challenging to address, but essential for us to contemplate in deciding how to move forward. We can wrestle with them, bring them to nature and our dreams, and listen for responses about what actions to take.

## *Wild Yoga Practices for*
## *Engaging in Radical Dreaming*

Attend to the world around you and notice the suffering of the wild world. Ask the Earth for help in dreaming for the world.

- Before you go to sleep, ask to receive a dream for the world. Perhaps create a ceremony to call in the dream. Speak to the Earth and the place from where dreams come. Explain why a dream would be meaningful to you. Once you awaken, write down any dreams in the present tense. Later, return to a dream in your imagination. Consider its significance in the world context. Journal about what you discover.
- Go for a walk near your home, your street, or your town. Look for signs of the rape of the Earth. What is it like to bear witness? Talk with and listen to a place about what you see. Imagine what coming together to stop the rape might look like, in one place or many.
- Before you go to sleep, ask to receive a dream to guide you in stopping the desecration happening to the Earth. Speak aloud to nature and the dreamtime. Say why you would value receiving such a dream. Jot down whatever dreams come, again in the present tense, even if you can't see how they relate. Consider what ideas or clues they give you in either direct or mysterious ways. Journal about what you discover.
- If you feel strong enough, contemplate ecological devastation. What losses or harm do you feel most strongly? Whom do you care about? A particular place or species? Go to a wild place and spend time with the beauty of what you love while bearing witness to any harm. Let the place or being know you value them and can see the damage.
- Before sleeping, ask to receive a dream about the particular place or being with whom you have just spent time. Speak to them in your imagination and explain why receiving a dream would be worthwhile. Upon waking, again writing in the present tense, record the dreams that came, whether you see a connection or not. Consider what ideas or clues they may reveal about how to relate to or assist the place you are in conversation with.
- (*Trigger warning: This practice invites sensitive reflection about rape.*) If you are supported enough, contemplate the parallel between the rape of women and the rape of Mother Earth. Recall your experience with rape or those of friends, family, or other loved ones. Then, imagine what it might look or feel like if you could stop the rape.

## A Yoga Pose for Engaging in Radical Dreaming

### TWO DOGS FLOW

Two Dogs Flow is the ongoing back-and-forth movement between Downward Facing Dog (Adho Mukha Svanasana) and Upward Facing Dog (Urdhva Mukha Svanasana). This dynamic exercise can improve health, energy, strength, coordination, and circulation, as well as offer relief from joint pain and stiffness. One of the Five Tibetan Rites created by Tibetan Buddhist monks, it is more than twenty-five hundred years old. These rites were first introduced to Western culture by Peter Kelder in his book *Ancient Secret of the Fountain of Youth*.[33]

As you move back-and-forth between the two poses, focus differently on the basis of your experience. If new to yoga, let the transitions be slow and careful. Take your time getting into and out of each pose. If you are comfortable with both poses, let yourself play with the nuances of the more challenging transition between the two poses.

*To get in the pose:*

- Come into Downward Facing Dog. If you are new to this pose, begin in Table Pose (Bharmanasana), as we did in chapter 10. Starting on your hands and knees, spread your fingers wide while stacking your shoulders over your wrists. Then, move into Downward Facing Dog by pressing your palms into the floor, gently curling your toes under your feet, and raising your knees off the mat. Bring your chest toward your thighs, extend your arms, and walk your feet farther back (if needed). Find a comfortable position. Relax your shoulders while keeping your hands flat, with no air between your hands and the floor (if able). Keep your toes pointing forward. Finally, lift your hips and bring your sit bones toward the sky while extending your heels down as close to the floor as you comfortably can. Straighten your legs if you are able or maintain a slight bend in your knees. Return to Table Pose for a gentle transition out of Downward Facing Dog.

- Come into Upward Facing Dog. If new to this pose, lie on your stomach, bend your elbows, and bring your hands beside your chest. Press your palms to the floor while pulling them slightly back. Lift your torso and pelvis off the ground, keeping your legs straight, and draw your belly button toward your spine to protect your low back. Tilt your head back slightly, press into the floor through the tops of your feet, and keep your arms straight and legs strong. Return to lying on your stomach for a gentle transition out of Upward Facing Dog.
- If you have practiced coming in and out of both poses before, try moving directly from Downward Facing Dog to Upward Facing Dog. Bring your shoulders over your wrists without transitioning back to Table Pose or lying on the ground.
- In Upward Facing Dog, draw your thighs up and back to create length in your spine.
- Inhale, press your hands into the ground, and move your hips up to place your body back into Downward Facing Dog. Bring your chin toward your chest and straighten your back.
- Exhale back into Upward Facing Dog. Arch your spine and feel the fronts of your legs on the ground, noticing where they begin to rise slightly above the floor closer to your hips. Drop your head back and keep your neck long and your collarbones broad.
- Move back and forth slowly and gently. Keep your breathing steady. Perhaps roll over your toes in transitioning from one pose to the other (if you can do so without causing pain).
- Once you build stamina, you may pick up momentum and move between the two poses faster. Do up to twenty-one repetitions.

- Throughout the flow, keep your lower belly slightly engaged to protect your low back. Soften your knees (or bend them if you need to).
- Rest and allow your breath to settle when you are done. Feel the energy you have created.

The Five Tibetan Rites are said to foster eternal youth and health. Practice Two Dogs Flow to build and maintain energy, so you can listen to your dreams and help create radical change. Do this flow in the morning to give you power for the day. Even a few minutes of practice can have a positive effect. Go at a comfortable pace and focus on your breathing as you move back and forth between the two poses. Consider studying the other four Tibetan Rites.[34]

Two Dogs Flow can be challenging. Feel free to create a gentler version that suits you. For example, some people switch Cobra Pose (Bhujangasana) for Upward Facing Dog. Cobra allows you to lie on your belly, pressing down lightly into your hands and lifting your head and chest while rolling your shoulders back and down.

Some people move back and forth rapidly, but Two Dogs Flow can be done slowly. Listen to your body and do what is best for you.

In Two Dogs Flow, imagine yourself gathering the strength to move between the world of your dreams and the physical living planet or between the realm of your imagination and of our society. Make the transition from one to the other with grace. Notice how you embody each pose and how you move between them. Imagine these two poses as two wings of a bird that together can enable you to take flight.

In Downward Facing Dog, remember to turn inward toward your dreams, and in Upward Facing Dog, imagine turning outward and acting in the world. When you are in Downward Facing Dog, ask your biggest questions about the world, the Earth, and future generations. Linger long enough to notice if any images, sensations, or emotions arise. Aim to carry whatever arises into your Upward Facing Dog. Find a way to express or enact what comes and see what happens next. When you are back in Downward Facing Dog, notice if another question arises. Continue back and forth in this way as long as you like.

As you feel the strength and stamina you are building in Two Dogs Flow, imagine the monks who created these poses twenty-five hundred years ago. What would they say if they could see what is happening on the Earth now? Imagine twenty-five hundred years into the future — will the Earth still exist? What will be happening? Embrace deep time, a sense of time vastly greater than human lives. Elder Joanna Macy guides people "to reconnect with ancestors and future beings" for guidance and inspiration.[35] Ask your dreams to guide you. Engage in radical dreaming with the distant past and future. What essential elements of the past should we remember? What future do you envision for all beings on Earth?

Radical dreaming invites us to listen to our dreams for the Earth, ask questions about how to stop the harm and protect wild places, and enact what the dream invites. To stay present in the heart of Wild Yoga, let us keep stretching our consciousness and expanding our perception. In the following chapter, we will practice this by reflecting on the impact of the collective shadow, tuning in to how forests are conscious, and considering how to reconcile masculine and feminine energies.

## CHAPTER SEVENTEEN

# Stretch Your Consciousness

Every river has tributaries, but the Copper River in Alaska has multiple streams moving *within* the larger river. Chunks of ice from the surrounding glaciers drop off and splash in, causing waves. Currents of melted ice flow under the surface, weaving in and around and through one another. The Copper is wide and feels as expansive as an ocean.

We float in the Copper on a raft for ten days in late summer. The water temperature is less than fifty degrees, too cold for us, but the brown bears swim. We see them standing on rocks, peering into the water, scanning for salmon, and diving in. I have never been around so many. A mama is playing with her two cubs on the far side of the river. A short distance from our raft, a huge bear is staring at us from atop a high perch at the river's edge. He pees on the rock.

We are guiding a small group to raise funds to protect the river basin. There are mosquitoes and rainstorms, sand dunes and ice sculptures, and so many salmon. We drop our net in, and within a couple of minutes it's full, no bait needed. All rivers were once full of fish. I hold a salmon and stare into his dark eyes. He looks as wise as a buffalo. I feel the millions of years his ancestors have lived in the river. I wonder what he sees and what it is like to be him. My friend takes him and with a sharp knife slices him open, handing me the heart. It is still beating. I kneel on the ground weeping, holding it between my palms. It keeps beating. I hold it until it stops. It hurts to see his life taken. Yet I appreciate the nourishment he gives.

"Thank you," we say to the salmon and the river. We eat his flesh raw.

The Copper River basin is vast — rugged mountains, glacial rivers, and expansive boreal forests. It brings together multiple worlds and perspectives. Under the surface, I feel rivers mixing and mingling. Navigation looks easy, like flat water without rapids. Yet powerful currents move under the surface, and you can get stuck. Helicopters have had to rescue boats. So I study the subtle clues on the surface, trying to see and avoid dark patches of water where the current moves differently.

I relate the landscape to the human psyche. I can get stuck in drama. Appear fine on the surface while turbulent underneath, spinning in a vortex of suffering — my own, others', or the Earth's. When I do, I go back to the wild and swim in the landscape. Or lose myself in the night sky. Or return in my imagination to places I have been, like the Copper River.

Rocks of all sizes cover the shore: graywacke, slate, greenstone. I can't take my eyes off them. Looking down, I am mesmerized by their colors, patterns, shapes, and designs, wondering how far they have traveled. This river is stretching my consciousness. All rivers and any truly wild place can alter us. The Copper offers an image of what stretching my sense of reality looks and feels like. Rivers within rivers, and each one its own world.

Which landscapes stretch you? Where do you feel many streams of consciousness flowing at once? I sense it in ecotones, like where ocean and rain forest mingle or desert and mountain meet. Dreams stretch us to perceive multiple realities. What if we could sense this in waking life and perceive the world through the sense organs of bear, salmon, multicolored rock, and glacier?

In our imaginations, we could experience the world as they might. Multiple streams of consciousness are flowing all the time. The world needs us to broaden our perspective and recognize what is calling in any given moment, like a red-tailed hawk flying over a canyon and zeroing in on its prey. The wings on the tree of my mythos flap as I write, the tree moving through the cosmos, rooted in the Earth. Rivers flow within rivers, and where and how we pay attention matters. We can stretch ourselves to take it all in and let ourselves be pulled down into what is ours to do.

## Plant Self

The vegetal world perceives many things at once and acts with discernment. Plants receive and respond to a multitude of messages in the places they grow. Their photosensitive receptor cells and tissues tune in to eons worth of data. Navigating soil, rock, water, bacteria, and the roots of other plants, they juggle up to twenty environmental factors at a time.

Humans think we are the most intelligent form of life, with the highest consciousness. Yet other modes of existence seem more intelligent and conscious, particularly in how they cooperate. Plants communicate with one another, care for the health of their community, and make collaborative decisions for the well-being of all.

"But don't certain plants choke out other plants?" my friend Thomas asked me on a hike in the Colorado high country.

"Plants fight for sunlight, water, space, and nutrients," I agree, "mostly when they are planted near nonsibling plants."[1]

"Plants can poison their neighbor," he emphasized.

We sat down in a field of mountain bluebells. Taking a leaf from each flower and a few blossoms, we said, "Thank you" and made a wild salad. It tasted fresh and sweet.

"Reciprocal relationships are what are most common in forest ecosystems," I said. Thomas pointed out that plants can be parasites. But I insisted on the reciprocity of their relationships: "Mycorrhizal fungi help plants get phosphorus, and plants give fungi carbon."

He dug into his competition argument. "A tree sends out millions of seeds, but only one will grow to reach the canopy."

Competition is part of nature, but scientific research shows that mutualism is the overarching principle and the primary way ecosystems grow and assemble themselves.[2] Trees in a forest sense the life around them and seem to grasp the connections linking all life-forms. They live in a complex, cooperative web of relationships with underground networks of roots, fungi, and bacteria. Having consciousness means being aware of one's surroundings. Trees in a forest often seem more aware of their communities than humans do. They have complex social relationships not only among themselves but with other creatures and animals. Ancient mother trees shape future generations by giving nutrients to their young and those in need of healing, even if they are ill, dead, or a stump.[3] Trees give to everyone. They do not leave anyone out. Even in their death, mother trees send nutrients to the trees that surround them.

Forests give us the air we breathe. Yet most humans do not grasp the inner lives of trees. If we did, perhaps we could relate to them and learn what they know about community. Trees live on a different timescale than we do and move and act in ways we hardly notice. They calculate and choose, learn and remember, sleep and signal to one another. Plants have twenty different senses to monitor their environment: senses that roughly correspond to the five human senses of sight, hearing, taste, touch, and smell, plus additional ones that do things like "measure humidity, detect gravity, and sense electro-magnetic fields."[4]

Human-centrism leads people to believe their experience of life is what defines consciousness, but forests and ecosystems are conscious and intelli-gent in their own way. Most humans are not smart enough to see their bril-liance. Stuck in cultural misperceptions, like rafts caught in the undercurrents of the Copper River, humans have forgotten how to share and live in interde-pendent relationship. They take more than they give. In slaughtering forests, humans take their own breath, looting the oxygen they themselves and trees need.

Some believe humans are the only creatures with self-reflexive conscious-ness. Yet "we can't know if plants are self-conscious, because we define both the *self* and *consciousness* based on our human selves and limitations."[5] We need to consider what a "plant self" might be, advises Michael Marder, author of *Plant-Thinking: A Philosophy of Vegetal Life*. "Marder points out that plant cuttings can survive and grow independently," writes journalist Ephrat Livni. "That suggests that if plants do have a self, it is likely dispersed and uncon-fined, unlike the human sense of self."[6]

If we let go of our ideas about what particular biological or psychological structures are needed for self-consciousness, the communication strategies and mechanisms of trees "may be considered analogous to what we, humans, define as self-consciousness," writes Marder. Imagine "the possibilities of see-ing and thinking otherwise than with the eye and the brain," and maybe we will "finally become conscious of plant consciousness."[7] If we could grasp a plant's sense of self, maybe we could perceive the interdependence between us and the vegetal world. Perhaps what scientists and mystics say about the human sense of self — an individual within a body — being illusory is true. Maybe if we could learn to be more conscious in the way plants are, we could grow the ability to sense our connection to the web of life, make collaborative decisions, and live in balance.

Our intelligence is not the problem. It is not the consciousness we have that trips us up as much as the consciousness we lack. To survive, we need to perceive the intelligence of others: plants, trees, the sea. To stretch ourselves to listen, understand, and learn how to be more like they are. Perhaps then we, like plants and forests, can develop the capacity to live in the world in a way that cares for and tends everything.

I have slept on the forest floor and communed with trees a lot. Nourished by the generations that came before, they tend those who come after. The roots of a tree are linked in an underground network that functions like a brain. When I am with trees, I experience them as elders. They often seem to understand more than me. We are family, and together we share the sun, moon, and stars.

When I inhabit the tree of my mythos, I feel more conscious of the world around me. Lie on a forest floor. Imagine yourself as a plant or a tree. Stretch how you think, feel, and sense and try to imagine how a plant self may be conscious. Ask the forest for help in sensing and perceiving the world in a manner closer to how trees and plants do.

## Shadow

Our individual shadow is everything we are not conscious of, and our collective shadow is what a group or entire culture is unconscious about. Carl Jung, the pioneering twentieth-century Swiss psychologist, coined the terms *shadow* and *collective unconscious*. The shadow comprises the unconscious parts of the personality that our conscious ego does not want to identify as itself.[8] This includes destructive parts as well as creative capacities that can empower us.

We can observe cultural shadow by finding out who a group sees negatively — who is a sacred scapegoat. If an organization is unaware of a problem and someone who does not share the group shadow names it, they are called a whistleblower. I am blowing a whistle to alert the dominant culture about the intelligence of plant consciousness. Plant consciousness is in the collective shadow of humanity.

The collective shadow, or collective unconscious, holds myths, archetypes, symbols, ancestral memory, and whatever is in the shadow for all humans, including what humans are not yet capable of. It is a source of our potential: everything humans could be. We can remember what humans once were or encounter things that have never been. The practices of Wild Yoga invite us to listen to voices often in the shadow of the dominant culture: trees, dreams, soul, darkness, muses, imagination.

Awakening to what we are not conscious of is challenging. Parts of us do not want to see what has been repressed. No matter how intelligent we are, a lot remains hidden, individually and collectively. Our dominant culture believes nonhumans lack consciousness, or if they have it, it's not as highly developed as human consciousness. This is a negative projection, a splitting off from self-awareness and seeing in others what we cannot see in ourselves. Perhaps humans lack consciousness that others have. Many in modern society see nature as unruly and dangerous. This fuels ecocide and inhibits humanity's ability to sustain life. Becoming aware of what we do not know is vital. Defense mechanisms block perceptions from our waking minds, because if we were to take these perceptions in, the way we see ourselves and the world would change.

To start, work with your personal projections. You know you are projecting when you have a substantial charge toward someone, either positive or negative, and the feelings of love or hate outweigh the circumstance. The tricky part is that negative emotions can also arise from boundary violations, disrespect, abuse of power, misogyny, ecocide, and racism. The concept of negative projection can be overemphasized in personal growth circles and used unethically to dismiss real concerns by someone saying that the other person is projecting. This can inhibit people's capacity to address collective dynamics. Every charge is not a projection. Strong feelings can arise as reflexive or intuitive sensory responses to what is happening around us.

I wrote about reclaiming positive projections in chapter 8, "Romance the Mystery of What You Love." With negative projections, consider what you do not want to identify with — and how it could be true about you. Negative projections have hidden strengths, although they can take time to discover. For months, I had been exploring a negative charge around lying. One day, working with a wilderness therapy client, a liar, I noticed he was a creative storyteller. Suddenly, I understood storytelling to be a gift I needed to claim. I began to seek meaningful stories and practice telling them aloud.

Charges arise when there are qualities in our depths we need to reclaim. In my early thirties, I projected on a woman in her fifties who I thought talked too much. I felt annoyed and wished she would be quiet. Later, it struck me: I had silenced myself. Her presence was asking me to find my voice.

Exploring the collective shadow awakens a greater awareness of social dynamics. The colonizers thought indigenous peoples were savage, but they acted horrendously toward the indigenous and still do. The civilized world views wild nature as messy, but Western civilization has made the most enormous mess, resulting in massive ecological devastation. Yet the wild lives in us, and it is life-giving. The practices of Wild Yoga stretch our consciousness to reclaim our wild nature and honor the wilderness around us and in us.

## Reconciling with the Goddess

In the eyes of the dominant culture, women, like nature, are deemed substandard. The feminine aspects of the world and in ourselves have been suppressed. This is a cultural shadow I wish to blow the whistle on. The practices of Wild Yoga call us to honor women and cultivate qualities of the inner feminine: love, nature connection, creativity, ferocity, mystery, vision.

Sarah, an Irishwoman in her midfifties, reenters a dream in a session on Zoom. She is sitting by her wood-burning stove as the winds and rains of Irish winter blow outside her window. She closes her eyes, and I guide her back into a dream where she encounters a baby alone in a field and a woman standing off in the distance. As she picks up the baby and holds her, she begins to cry.

"I am remembering the three children my mom miscarried," she says. "She was sad but was never allowed to talk about it." Sarah feels her mother as she holds the baby. "It's like I'm crying tears she never got to."

"And the other woman in the dream?" I ask.

"A foreigner with money. I've always hated women like her."

"Cuddle the baby," I suggest, "and be with the woman."

After a moment, she reports: "Now I am holding her too. My mom, the baby, *and* the foreigner."

"Notice what it's like to hold them all."

She is silent and then responds, "Calm, like polarities melting away." Sarah's eyes are still closed. She has stopped crying and seems relaxed.

"Stay with that and see what happens next."

"Something wants to get me." Sarah seems alert and curious.

"Can you see what?"

"It's been trying for a while."

"Who's there?"

"She reminds me of the Cailleach, the Celtic goddess."

I saw a picture of the Cailleach once: white hair, dark blue face, rust-colored teeth, a single eye in her forehead. She was fearsome. "What's it like to be with her?" I ask.

"An honor," Sarah says. "She's the voice of the Earth — guardian, hag, shaper of the land."

"Does she see you?"

"She's poking me with a fire stick." Sarah chuckles.

"You're smiling. Do you like it?"

"Yes," she says, smiling more. "It's playful and fierce."

"Do you know why she is poking you?"

"I'm not sure."

"Has she come before?"

"No. I don't think I was calm enough." Two months earlier, Sarah had left her job as a psychotherapist in the school system, after two decades of service. "The land is who I need to listen to now."

After our session, Sarah began wandering in nature in search of the Cailleach and heard the Cailleach speaking to her in Old Irish.

"Her words hit me like a spear," Sarah reported in a later session, "and touch me so deeply I cry."

She told me she felt the presence of the Cailleach in the mossy Irish soil, now a grassland, but once covered in ancient oaks, pines, hazels, and willow trees. "The Irish are a forest people without a forest," she said.

My ancestors are Irish, and talking to Sarah, I felt closer to them.

"I'm your Irish ancestor," Sarah told me. "If you go back far enough, we're all connected."

A while later, Sarah's dog, Cali, went missing. She and her family searched for three days and nights. Finally, they found the dog on a tree farm near their home. Oak stumps from the original Irish forest sat amid farmed, nonnative Canadian lodgepole pine and Sitka spruce trees. Sarah sensed the Cailleach in the fallen trees.

"They don't know how to be here," she said. "The soil is too moist. Their resin weeps, and they live displaced and half-alive."

Finding her dog on the tree farm felt like a call to Sarah, like the land wanted her to come and listen. So she decided to go every day for forty days and informally invited a few friends to join her. Some days, they did. To Sarah, the land is still a forest. She sat with the old oak stumps and could feel the memory of the ancient Irish forest.

"I'm not trying to find my soul," she said, "I want to know her, the land, the forest."

One day, when Sarah and her friends arrived, the trees had been cut. Men with bulldozers had come.

"The trees seemed relieved," she said. "That surprised me. The land is tired of being a factory. It wants to rest."

Another day, she noticed some fallen trees forming the shape of the Irish cross, four quadrants with a sword going through the circle.

"The toxic masculine is chopping," she said, "and the sacred masculine is rising."

"What is the sacred masculine?" I asked.

"I don't know," she confessed. "I'm wondering how it can walk hand in hand with the sacred feminine." She paused before saying more. "I think you have to be willing to put your body on the cross, to speak out, even if everyone ridicules you."

Soon after, Sarah felt the presence of Jesus while she was sick with Covid-19. He had brown skin, brown hair, and brown eyes and was the last person she expected to see. She's not a Christian and dislikes male-centric religions. Yet she wept and wept.

"He's a representation of the sacred masculine," she explained. "He openly expresses love to his disciples, marginalized people, his enemies."

The Cailleach still speaks to Sarah, but now she is guided by both the sacred masculine and the sacred feminine. The sacred masculine reveres the feminine, women, and the Earth. The sacred masculine has reconciled with the goddess. In old Celtic stories, the generative feminine is the essence of the universe, and women hold the spiritual and ethical center, always with a foot in the other world. Up until the sixteenth century, to become a king in Ireland meant having a ceremonial marriage to the goddess and vowing to protect the land. Writer and teacher Sharon Blackie wrote, "When there is mutual respect between two partners, between the goddess and the king, between land and the people, between nature and culture, between feminine and mas-culine — then all is in harmony and life is abundant."[9] When the contract is broken, everything suffers. Restoring and honoring the voices of the feminine are keys to healing the land, as is healing the relationship between the sacred masculine and feminine.

New and ancient myths emerge from the depths, sometimes connecting us to old stories meant to be passed down. Dreams hold our individual and collective shadows, including lost aspects of the feminine. A young man I guide encountered the feminine in his dreams as water: waves, rivers, lakes, the ocean. Once she came as a dry riverbed, asking him for water. In waking life, he communes with her while sitting beside a lake, and her presence soft-ens him.

Water is a feminine principle in Norse mythology. Dew arises in the val-ley when the past is praised. Urd, the goddess of fate, gathers the water to feed the well of memory and keep the Tree of Life alive. Without Urd, the sun, a masculine principle, would shine too brightly and evaporate all the water. Central to Norse mythology is reconciling the male sky gods and the feminine nature spirits. Urd is a village matriarch. In matriarchal societies, mothers and children are honored and protected, and people remember their ancient stories. Like plant consciousness, matriarchal societies are egalitarian, with neither women nor men dominating, but rather mother trees giving to the forest.

North American buffalo are matriarchal.[10] The males are physically stronger but defer to females for the right to mate. The grandmothers, mothers, and aunties lead the herd to find food and water and avoid predators. The sacred masculine reveres the holy feminine. We can restore her in our psyches and the world and reclaim her within ourselves and our societies by remembering the nature spirits, hags, and goddesses in ancestral myths and by being with those that arise in our dreams.

In Norse mythology, a *blót* is a blessing ceremony invoked to restore the balance between the masculine sky gods and the feminine Earth spirits and bring humans back into harmony with the Tree of Life. Storyteller Andreas Kornevall leads blót ceremonies between and among groups of people who are having conflicts, such as those who practice Earth-based spiritualities and Christians.[11] In them, no one judges or critiques the person speaking. Everyone listens and tries to understand. During one ceremony, an older woman in the group who feels the most upset is invited to speak first. No one will analyze her to determine her issue or problem. All will be tuning in to the collective shadow. The group invites her to speak because they recognize she may be holding it. Giving words to long-suppressed feelings can create transformation for all people and the land.

I would love to see these ceremonies occur in society, so we may honor and listen to the feminine again. I wish women were invited to disagree and emote more often in families, organizations, and governments. When women can't speak the truth to those in power, the collective shadow of patriarchy remains ingrained. If women were invited to speak and be heard, knowing that what they said would not be used against them, perhaps the wild feminine could live. And we could uncover the underbelly of what goes unseen in the world, on the land, and in dreams. Perhaps we could recognize those we put beneath us and take care to listen to the pain they express, shining a light on what needs to be altered.

## Wild Yoga Practices for
## Stretching Your Consciousness

Be gentle with yourself as you expand your perception, tune in to the collective shadow, stretch toward tree consciousness, and become open to revering the feminine.

- Close your eyes and remember wild landscapes. Invite the places where you feel multiple streams of consciousness flowing at once. Perhaps a prairie meeting a forest or a place with multiple plants, animals, and perspectives. Ask your deep imagination and see where you are pulled. Notice how it feels to be amid many streams flowing at once.

- Return to the place with multiple streams in your imagination and let yourself be pulled down into one — bear, salmon, multicolored rock, glacier. Envision yourself as this one. Experience the world as they might. Notice what it is like to see the world through their eyes. What do you offer? How do you engage? What do you need?

- Spend time in a forest. Lie on the ground, look up at the canopy, and sense the underground network below you. Imagine what it would be like to be a tree. Ask the forest to help you perceive and understand tree consciousness. Let yourself be surprised.

- Track your negative projections and, if you can, seek the hidden resource in their depths. Tune in to the collective shadow by noticing how scapegoats or those targeted in families or organizations often hold what is in the collective unconscious. Consider the qualities being projected.

- Remember ways the feminine has come in your dreams or nature — spirits, goddesses, grandmothers, mothers, aunties, hags. Choose one who still feels alive and spend time with her regularly in your deep imagination. Attend to whatever she wants to show you.

- Wander on the land and ask to find a place or being that will stretch your consciousness. A place where multiple perspectives merge. Follow your heart and belly. Let yourself be surprised by where you end up. Spend time and notice how the different streams come together. Ask the place to help you stretch. Offer gratitude for whatever happens.

## *A Yoga Pose for Stretching Your Consciousness*

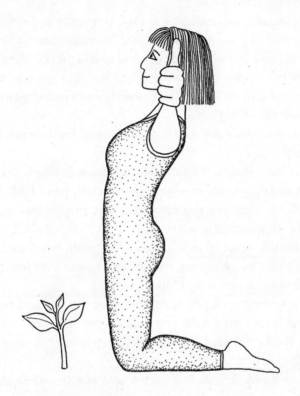

### SEED TO A TREE FLOW

Seed to a Tree Flow is a Self-Awakening Yoga Pose that lets you experience the belly- and heart-opening effects of backbends without compromising your low back and neck.[12] As you lengthen the front side of your body, your back bends in a way that increases your awareness of how to anchor in your center, so you can stay relaxed and protect your low back.

*To get in the pose:*

- Begin in a kneeling stance. Place your knees beneath your hips and position your lower legs so they are parallel.
- Extend your arms in a T position. Make a fist with your hands and extend your thumbs up like the emoji that symbolizes agreement.
- After pointing your thumbs up, roll your arms forward to point both thumbs down.

- Repeat the movement, inhaling as your thumbs come up and exhaling as you roll them down.
- Make significant movements as you roll your arms and shoulders. Let your head and eyes move in sync with your shoulders. With your thumbs up, look up and extend your face toward the sky. Move your hips forward, tighten your buttocks, and feel your spine lengthen. When your thumbs roll down, tuck your chin into your chest as your upper back rounds slightly forward.
- Each time you inhale and your thumbs come up, try to stretch backward a little more.
- Each time you exhale and your thumbs go down, come a little closer toward Child's Pose until eventually you curl fully into Child's Pose.
- In Child's Pose, imagine you are a seed. Tighten your fists and feel yourself as tiny and full of potential.
- On the inhale, sprout from seed into a full-grown tree. Open your chest, roll your shoulders and thumbs up, squeeze your lower buttocks together, and press your hips forward.
- Continue moving back and forth (tree back to seed, seed to tree, repeating) until your breath and momentum carry you. Imagine growing from a tiny seed to a whole tree in one burst of movement and breath.
- Then, slow down. Try moving from a seed to a tree while staying present with each stage of life.
- Pause and kneel in stillness. Breathe with your eyes closed. Experience the effects on your whole being. Notice your mood. Are you playful or energized?
- Lower yourself back into Child's Pose. Notice how quickly you relax. Lengthen your spine on the inhale and relax on the exhale.
- As you come back into sitting, feel each part of your spine move in sync with your whole body.

Seed to a Tree Flow integrates the motions of being curled into Child's Pose with opening your torso as in Camel Pose (Ustrasana). As you move from front extensions down into Child's Pose, remain connected to your center. Notice if you feel a flow of energy, an increased heart rate, or a pulse in your belly.

Imagine yourself a seed in the forest, planted deep in the Earth's soil, slowly growing the courage to sprout into the light and extend upward into a mature tree. Feel your trunk thicken as you endure all the seasons and weather, night and day, year after year. Notice your roots extending deep into the soil, sending out nourishment. As you grow into a big tree, watch over the forest and become a home for birds, insects, and animals. When you feel your life ending, let go. Fall back into the soil. Feel your decomposing body nourishing the life of the forest.

Begin again in seed. Deepen into living in the soil, a bundle of energy bursting with possibility. Feel yourself tiny and in the dark, receiving nourishment from the community. Risk extending out of the comfort of the soil to become a small sapling. Feel how little you are, with so many towering over you. How do you find a way to receive the light? Experience yourself growing into a big tree and then let go of life.

Back in seed again, explore the next iteration. Come forth from the soil, grow into a tree, become a member of the forest community, and let go of life once more. Spend time in the decomposition. Feel the life you feed in death. Notice how you come back to life in those you feed. Move from seed to tree again and again. Take form, exist, and die, giving to the community in each stage you are in. Many trees live for hundreds, even thousands, of years. Experience time as a tree might. Move from seed to tree, generation after generation, and imagine living through that immensity of time.

Congratulations on stretching your consciousness: sensing the multiple streams, imagining being a forest, facing the collective shadow, inviting in the divine feminine. Now it is time to turn toward action. Central to sustaining life on the planet is the need to become a love warrior for the Earth. To honor or join those fighting to protect the last remaining species of plants and animals, support the health of ecosystems and the Earth's biosphere, and devote ourselves to saving those we care about. We will see how in the following chapter.

# CHAPTER EIGHTEEN

# Become a Love Warrior for the Earth

It is August 2020. Twenty-five people drive up a steep logging road and surround the giant claws of a forest-scraping excavator in an old-growth forest in southern Vancouver Island, British Columbia. With tents, barricades, and a "No Roads into Fairy Creek" banner, they spend the night.

A road crew arrives at 4:30 a.m. to build a logging road into the sacred headwaters of Fairy Creek. Upon seeing the blockade, the crew retreats, and two days later, they remove their equipment.

During the Covid-19 pandemic, hundreds of volunteers built a camp of land-based resistance to hold the line and save a forest of gigantic red and yellow cedar trees from being logged, some as wide as fifteen feet and as old as two thousand years.[1] Part of the Rainforest Flying Squad, a volunteer-driven activist movement, they closed industrial access into Fairy Creek at the River Camp.[2] Some land defenders slept in the tall canopies in tree sits for weeks at a time and spoke about the forest's overpowering beauty, about how salmon spawn in the streams under huge old Douglas fir, hemlock, and Sitka spruce.[3]

Forests like these are irreplaceable. Ancient forests draw down carbon and are home to rare plant and animal species. In our current climate and biodiversity crisis, their lives affect the future of us all. The Pacific Northwest indigenous peoples harvest cedarwood without damage to living trees to make their homes, totem poles, utensils, instruments, and canoes. Humans can live in balance with nature.

Many land defenders are young people, but those who showed up at the River Camp were of all ages, from teenagers to a group of four hundred activists calling themselves Elders for Ancient Forests. On Pacheedaht and Ditidaht First Nations territory, blockades were led by elder Bill Jones, an eighty-one-year-old Pacheedaht man.

"The forest is a place of prayer and contemplation, to decide what you want to be and do in this life. A place you are going always," he said. "A place for Pacheedaht members to remember their songs. Like the sockeye song: we come to the river, we ask for what we need, and when we are given the sockeye, we say thank you and please, and when we eat the sockeye, we bring the bones to the river. Reseeding, fulfilling our contract of looking after the river and where the river comes from — the forest."

The equivalent of more than five hundred soccer fields of old-growth forest is cut down in British Columbia daily. In 2020, this generated CAD$11.5 billion in total exports and $1.3 billion in government revenue. Only 2.7 percent of intact ancient forest remains in British Columbia outside of parks, and less than 1 percent of forests are made up of big trees.[4]

"Teal-Jones is now cutting down one-thousand-to-two-thousand-year-old trees at a furious rate," Dr. Robin June Hood told me. Robin is an academic activist who lives close by on Vancouver Island, and the world tree has come to her in multiple dreams. "Every tree branch holds a species which has its own song and purpose, reminding me of the sacredness of all life-forms and giving space for the mystery."

In May 2021, Royal Canadian Mounted Police (RCMP) began violently enforcing a court injunction granting the lumber company Teal-Jones the right to keep logging. Hundreds of forest defenders were assaulted.

For days, hundreds of activists chained themselves to giant tripods made from the trunks of felled trees.[5] Some lay down on the logging road with their arms chained inside devices cemented into the ground. Police used jackhammers, mechanical tools combining a hammer and a chisel, to dig protesters from the roadway. They operated the heavy equipment "within inches" of people while their arms were locked into the ground. They plucked activists out of tripods with cherry pickers; some fell when they were pulled off the tripods. Their vehicles and other possessions were confiscated by the logging company, the RCMP, and the secret Community Industry Response Group (CIRG) attached to the RCMP, who specialize in protecting the logging industry and who often hide their identities to avoid accountability for their brutality.[6]

"The police moved in and destroyed their camps and apprehended everyone's equipment," said Robin. "RCMP made exclusion zones to block media access so the public couldn't see what was going on."

In 2021, four people demonstrating with the Fairy Creek blockade lost their lives. Two of those people went missing and were presumed dead. The

RCMP blocked land protectors from searching for them. The tragic death of two other forest defenders occurred just days after they left Fairy Creek. Both had suffered trauma due to the violent police enforcement of the Teal-Jones injunction. In addition, more than 1,200 protesters were arrested and 101 were charged with criminal contempt, making the blockade the most significant act of civil disobedience in Canadian history. Yet the threat to the forest and the clear-cutting practices of the province remain unchanged as of this writing. The industry continues to run chainsaws through thousand-year-old trunks of trees. Almost two years later, land defenders are still fighting the same fight.

We are a part of the Earth and only as healthy as she is. We strengthen ourselves so we can give back to her. We must remember to act on our love for the one who provides life to all, especially when so many humans have forgotten. A core practice of Wild Yoga is advocating and fighting for the protection and restoration of our Mother Earth.

## Love Warrior

I feel incredibly moved when I hear about people fighting back against injustices toward Mother Nature. The Earth and future generations of all species need people to protect those we care about: the last remaining forests, prairies, oceans, and other ecosystems. As a child, I wanted to learn how to defend myself — karate, boxing, fencing — but fighting was frowned upon. In ancient times, however, training to be a warrior was revered and necessary.

The name I received on my first solo fast, Brave Heart, asked me to be a warrior. As a wilderness therapist, I confronted families with difficult truths. Now, as a soul guide, I live in the cave of my mythos where the Earth's heartbeat echoes, bringing people into the depths. Brave Heart guides me down inner and outer rivers and calls me to speak, write, and act for the Earth.

Being a warrior is part of the healthy masculine aspect of our psyche, almost as suppressed in our culture as the healthy feminine. Toxic masculinity dominates and has no connection to the Earth and soul, raping women and pillaging the land. Our world needs healthy warriors, but men and women in our culture who are not toxic masculine are taught to be toxic feminine — polite, yielding, submissive, sweet — although inside they are often seething.

A warrior is forceful, but not abusive. Her effort, energy, and initiative are harnessed for a good purpose. A warrior decides her attitude. With self-control and discipline, she chooses her battles and is not afraid to die. She is decisive and committed and has skill, power, and accuracy. She is a creative destroyer, taking down what harms to make room for what brings life.

The Buddhist elder Joanna Macy talks about the prophecy of the Shambhala warriors, an epic tale from twelve centuries ago that predicted a time on Earth when all of life would be in danger. A warrior will emerge inside us "to dismantle the weapons," which have been "made by the human mind and can be unmade by the human mind." It will take compassion and "insight into the radical interdependence of all phenomena."[7] The smallest act of care will have repercussions. These are the practices of Wild Yoga, which invite us to attune ourselves to the world and engage with a felt sense of our inherent connection. This takes discipline, courage, and love.

## Sustainable Community

The Congo River drains an area almost half the size of the US. The Congo Basin rain forest is the world's second largest contiguous tract of tropical rain forest, home to endangered species and surviving indigenous communities, Bantu ethnic groups and aboriginal Pygmies — 150 distinct cultural groups. Many are traditional hunter-gatherers. The story is familiar: once the systems of power that rule society have disempowered indigenous people, there is no one to protect them, and the forests rapidly disappear.

Godi Godar Moteke Molanga grew up in the Bantu Ntomba community of the Congo Basin, in the village of Ikongo Boginda, at the edge of Lake Tumba in the Democratic Republic of the Congo. Grandson of the chief, Godi had a boyhood vision that foretold he would live in an unknown land and return to protect his people. When Godi was sixteen, in 1985, a Habitat for Humanity volunteer, Dean DeBoer, came to Ikongo Boginda. Godi's grandfather invited the volunteer to live with them, as family.

At the end of Dean's three-year stay, he invited Godi to travel to the US with him. Godi was nineteen when he accepted Dean's invitation. He has lived in Durham, North Carolina, since his arrival in 1988. Two years later, in 1990, Godi met Candor Soraya Bourne. She was sixteen years old, and he was twenty-one. They became lifelong friends.

In 2011, Godi's mother pleaded with him to protect the land, waters, and forests surrounding their village. Logging companies were destroying the livelihood of his people, endangering wildlife, and polluting the air. He felt his purpose in leaving his tribe had become clear. In response to his mother's pleas, Godi started Go Conscious Earth (GCEarth) in 2012, asking Candor to join him as a founding member.[8] GCEarth helps protect the Congo Basin rain forest by partnering with forest-dependent communities, honoring them as part of the forest ecosystem, advocating for their legal rights to the land they have lived on for generations, and developing sustainable, conservation-oriented initiatives.

Candor served on the board of directors for six years before becoming the executive director of GCEarth. She now works as an adviser to the organization. "In my midforties, I realized I can't spend my life doing things only relevant to humans," she said, her eyes fiery and her face bright. "My efforts need to make a difference to nature."

Candor has participated in multiple nature and soul programs, and the soul name she received from nature is EarthSong. I decided to share Candor's story because Wild Yoga brings together individual soul work and Earth activism, encouraging the need for both, and Candor does both. Her soul name inspires her to honor and celebrate the Earth, acting as a conduit and catalyzer of life-serving creations. "In these times, honoring means protecting," she said. "The Earth needs everyone to act."

Candor has always felt a deep love for and sensitivity to the suffering of the Earth. For many years that sensitivity fed an immobilizing grief. Now, she endeavors to integrate the grief into action. "I couldn't have become a leader without turning toward the grief," she said. "In caring for the Earth, we face constant overwhelm and defeat. There's so much destruction, the issues are complex, and we don't have it figured out."

As many of us who care for the Earth know, facing her grief for the world meant facing her own personal pain. "As is the case for far too many women, my life has been undeniably altered by the experience of being physically overpowered, used, and stripped of my sacred sovereignty as a young woman," she said. "This left me feeling irrelevant and humiliated, like I am nothing. Without a lot of personal work, deep care, and attention, I could have lived a whole life feeling that way."

As Candor healed and strengthened herself, she grew curious and wanted to understand more about the nature of defeat.

"Defeat is pervasive," she observed. "We need to collectively face where we are to be in the world effectively and listen for how to respond. Our wounding can desensitize us to the desecration we witness and even participate in.

When aligned with feeling, we can't help but love and care and therefore act. Health is having the capacity to respond. Being 'response-able' to our purpose and our surroundings is what defines a mature human."

## Instinct

Protecting what we love is an instinct. Some say it's already too late — that we are in the apocalypse or the sixth mass extinction, a result of current and ongoing human activity. That there's nothing we can do. Or nothing we should do, because this is a natural Gaian event.

The rapid loss of species we see today is estimated to be between one thousand and ten thousand times higher than the natural extinction rate, higher than any mass extinction in the Earth's geological history.[9] Humans established industrial civilization, but it has never been sustainable. The structures of our society destroy the Earth every day. I believe humans are responsible for stopping other humans from causing harm. Humans can take down the structures that other humans have created. Defending what we love is an innate response in healthy humans. The biosphere is at risk of collapsing, but forests, bears, buffaloes, and rivers are still alive and can be helped.

When ecosystems are restored, they recover. In chapter 3, I mentioned the Elwha Dam removal and the recolonization of fish that followed. Once the San Clemente Dam on the Carmel River was removed, the California steelhead began to return. Thriving ecosystems can support marine and animal life, provide local food, and reduce carbon emissions. The Great Green Wall is an African led-project aiming to restore 100 million hectares of degraded land. Since 2007, Ethiopia and Nigeria have restored millions of hectares.[10] Restoring ecosystems improves the climate. Trees and plants remove carbon dioxide from the atmosphere and lock it away in their tissues.[11] All over the world, countries need to restore forests and allow them to reach old-growth levels of biodiversity.

When I had cancer, the odds were that I would die. Doctors and loved ones could have rolled me aside and let it happen. Instead, they tried to save my life, even though they didn't know if it would work. My doctor created a treatment plan based on the latest research. My dad took me to the hospital and sat beside me while I received chemotherapy. My mom took care of me in the days after, when I was throwing up. Friends and family loved and prayed for me.

The Earth is suffering. She does not want her rivers poisoned or dammed or her biodiversity destroyed. If she were to receive the care I did, perhaps she could recover. What if people challenged systems that cause harm and acted to restore forest and ocean ecosystems? Like my parents and friends did for me, people could pray for and support the Earth. The most painful part of abuse is when no one notices. Dismissing the harm that is happening to the Earth makes us complicit. If it's a reflex to help the endangered humans we love, we can grow the capacity to care more deeply about our nonhuman relatives — bears, prairie dogs, mountain lions, oceans.

Social psychology reveals that individuals commonly find ways to ignore those being harmed when they are not our loved ones or those we otherwise care about. Consciously or unconsciously, people align with those in power, because it is safer. We need to support people who are working to save the last remaining species and wild places. Humans can listen to the Earth, not only for their mythos and rewilding, but also for the needs of those in our natural community, to hear what species, land, and ecosystems want. Humans can live within the Earth's boundaries.

Visit a clear-cut forest, plowed prairie, or concreted wetland. Ask them what they need. Ask the squirrels, rabbits, owls, and blue jays that once lived there. Ask the bears in Asia, who have been tortured since 1980 in a cruel farming system designed to keep them alive while extracting bile from their gallbladders.[12] Ask the wild buffalo or horses that are routinely slaughtered. Ask the remaining birds, orcas, polar bears, rhinos.

"Please help us," they tell me.

The narratives and people who inspire me most are those committed to listening to the animate natural world, honoring it, and keeping it alive. A real friend is with you not only in good times but also when you are suffering. Having a deep connection to nature means helping to prevent our beloveds from being harmed.

The bear of my mythos is a love warrior for the Earth. He guides me to inhabit my power with vulnerability and to bridge the worlds of the burning forest and the underground river. I invite Earth activists to listen to and be moved by visions that arise from their depths and remind those who do soul work that protecting the forest is all of our work. Sometimes I feel like the forest and the bear, being consumed by the fire. That, too, inspires my actions.

## Forest Management

We can't trust the systems of power that control society to help the Earth, because they are causing much of the harm. Even so-called green policies that say they support the Earth most often do not, like the plan to mine lithium — usurp water, poison land and water — to make electric cars.[13] "Green technology" usually means more consumption, which means more mining and production that leave behind a wake of pollution and environmental degradation. The idea that technology will save the planet is destroying ecosystems and displacing hundreds of thousands of people as industrialists around the world extract more minerals and metals.[14]

In Colorado, not far from where I live, the Rocky Mountain Restoration Initiative (RMRI) has partnered with forty public agencies to "mitigate fires" and "improve forest health."[15] The idea of felling trees to haul to lumber mills has deceptive names: *fuel reduction, forest health, ecological restoration, thinning, reforestation.* The US Forest Service began using these terms in the mid-1900s, after the public became aware of widespread old-growth clear-cutting in the Pacific Northwest.[16]

"Thinning" involves the use of feller bunchers and dozers to mechanically scrape and destroy the forest soil through compaction and suffocation with mulch and to remove living trees, underbrush, and "snags," or dead trees. Flora and fauna, vital to the forest ecosystem, thrive on the forest floor and in dead trees, which are habitats for birds and mammals. The RMRI plans to thin three hundred thousand acres near my home in southwest Colorado.

"I can't imagine the machines digging up that many acres," said Deanna Meyer, founder and executive director of Prairie Protection Colorado.[17] She had been listening to her neighbor's 192 acres of forest being killed with heavy equipment for six months.

"An awful noise and the snapping of trees startled me the first morning," said Deanna. "Walking toward the sound, I saw a piece of equipment with tires taller than me thrashing through the forest. Plants were being flattened and ripped out. Trees were being knocked over and pushed into piles."

Deanna walked over to the man driving the tree masticator. His blade was scraping up and down a tree trunk, until the tree snapped. Then, the machine rolled forward, scraping and snapping more trees. He paused when he saw her coming.

"Please don't kill my neighbors," she said, referring to the trees.

"I'd like to stop," he said, "but this is how I earn money to feed my family."

I remembered the land Deanna was referring to. I had walked on the trails with her the previous summer, through the aspen, spruce, and ponderosa pine forest where she brings the prairie dog communities she rescues. We had visited neighboring properties, and Deanna had pointed out the difference between a natural forest and a thinned one. Thinned forests look manicured. They have a sparse population of trees and no undergrowth.

"I whispered goodbye to all the trees with a swath of blue painted on them," Deanna said, "and looked down at the forest floor and thought about the insects, spiders, squirrels, and voles and asked for their forgiveness."

The US Forest Service clears trees in Colorado and forests all over the country to mitigate fires on public (Forest Service) and private lands. Yet research shows that the more trees you remove from a forest, the more severely a fire will burn. And the biggest fires historically "often burned through thinned forests, clearcuts, overgrazed rangelands, and previously burned acreage."[18] Ecologist Chad Hanson says dense forests are less likely to burn, because they have more shade and moisture and a cooler microclimate; removing trees creates "hotter, drier, and windier conditions" that intensify fires. Why is thinning so popular then? Hanson says that forest management agencies are about "selling public trees to private logging companies, which generates about $150 million each year," and "logging also brings in more than $1 billion in annual Congressional appropriated funds."[19]

"A research study analyzed fires in the Western U.S. and found protected forests burned less," said Deanna, "a lot of the hottest, fastest fires were in forests that had been thinned."[20]

The government cuts down trees in the name of fire mitigation, but "fire ecologists say that far more land burned each year during the 1800s and earlier, than in recent years."[21] Some fires started naturally from lightning strikes, and others were lit intentionally. Prior to colonization, indigenous fire stewardship, also called cultural burning, led to increased biodiversity and lowered risk of high-severity fires.[22] In contrast, the US Forest Service suppressed all fires from 1935 until the late 1960s, when it began to realize firefighting scars the land and retardants poison waterways and wildlife.

Forests are healthier when they manage themselves. Yet the Forest Service is still attempting to suppress fire by logging, even though logging in US forests now causes greater carbon dioxide emissions annually than the amount of greenhouse gas from residential and commercial sectors combined. "Carbon emissions from logging in the US are ten times higher than the combined emissions from wildland fires and tree mortality from native bark beetles."[23] Industrial logging, even thinning, results in a massive net loss of carbon storage. Logging destroys ecosystems and intensifies climate change, and "few realize that more logging occurs in the US, and more wood is consumed here, than in any other nation globally."[24]

"They chop trees to 'reduce fuel load,' but that has nothing to do with fire. Fires are driven by wind and climate. In the huge fire recently in Boulder," Deanna said, remembering the Marshall Fire in December 2021, "there was no forest."

Deanna has warned her neighbors about the harms of forest thinning, but her land borders on Forest Service land at high risk of being thinned. The forest service recently received grants to log 3.5 million acres of Front Range public lands.[25] Josh Schlossberg of the Eco-Integrity Alliance expressed outrage. Taxpayer dollars are being used "to cut down our National Forests to the tune over $3.3 billion (under the new infrastructure bill)."[26] Deanna has requested information about the targeted places in her area under the Freedom of Information Act.

"I'm afraid they will kill the forest behind my house," she said. "I would probably die for that forest."

In July 2022, I returned to Deanna's land to guide a Soulcraft for Earth Activists program. I visited the land near her that had been thinned and was stunned to see how few trees remained. More than 50 percent of the forest was gone. Dead tree trunks were stacked in piles in several places. The soil was flat and vacant. Nothing grew on it besides the few remaining trees. I am sad this is happening to so many forests and angry it's being called "restoration."

## Ecological Revolution

The 1995 Mel Gibson movie *Braveheart* is roughly based on the life of Sir William Wallace, a Scottish knight in the late thirteenth century. Wallace's courage moves me. He revolted against the invasion of Scottish lands and the rape of women, although doing so condemned him to a brutal death.

In a hidden graveyard in a small town near Dingle Bay, Ireland, I visited the tombs of my ancestors. Large earthen mounds and gravestones covered the uneven terrain. A rock wall covered with blackberries surrounded the remnants of two churches, an older Catholic and a newer Protestant one.

*What was it like for my ancestors during the Irish rebellions?* I wondered. *What would they tell me about being a warrior in these times?*

Our world has been invaded by global empire. The systems that control society punish those who fight back, unless they are the police or the military, while exerting a violence so brutal that ecosystems are crashing. Many people are enslaved by the system or lulled into society's addictive way of life. People are taught not to notice everyday violence. Most of what we own was made through resource extraction and enslaved labor: clothes, beds, houses, cars, computers, food. Revolution is the courageous response of a warrior. To belong to the Earth is to stand up for her.

Elder Joanna Macy has named three dimensions of ecological revolution.[27] First is the taking of holding actions to stop or slow the damage to the Earth and its beings. This includes all political, legislative, and legal work to reduce destruction and direct actions — blockades, boycotts, civil disobedience. Second is understanding the dynamics of global empire and creating alternate structures in our communities, such as collaborative living, community gardens, and watershed restoration. Third is shifting our consciousness and affecting the way people perceive the world through philosophies and practices like deep ecology, ecofeminism, or yoga.

As a soul guide, I foster human development, ushering an inner revolution whereby nature and soul can overthrow the egocentric regime of our psyches. Individuals encounter their soul and become initiated to live guided by their mythos. Yet more is needed. Soul making is collaboration tied to the fate of the Earth. We need to dream communally, organize collectively, and strengthen our sociopolitical consciousness so we can respond appropriately and effectively.

Our culture teaches us not to notice the way power operates, how it oppresses some and privileges others. The indigenous, the poor, women, people of color, and the natural world are treated as subordinate. Our global industrial-agro-corporate-military complex uses force — armies, courts, prisons, taxes, the media — and increases it whenever they need to, as in the deployment of British Columbia's CIRG.[28] Sometimes we can work to change existing structures, like Godi Godar Moteke Molanga and Candor Soraya Bourne do. Yet we need to consider all strategies, as author Max Wilbert writes, from "revolutionary law-making to strategic non-violence to coordinated sabotage of industrial infrastructure."[29]

People often fail to challenge power in wealthy countries. Most do not want to risk losing their privileges. Those who defend wild places are often imprisoned or killed. Indigenous peoples protect 80 percent of global diversity, even though they comprise less than 5 percent of the world's population.[30] In 2021, 358 deadly attacks on land protectors were reported. Almost a third of the killings were of indigenous peoples. "The majority of those killed, 59%, worked on land, environmental and indigenous rights, where their activities disrupted the economic interests of corporations and individuals in mining, logging, and other extractive industries."[31]

## Loving Community

I wander through a grove of young and old spruce trees in the Colorado high country. A tiny sapling is kept alive by the love of an ancient tree. Old trees feed their young the nutrients they need to survive, varying the ingredients in response to climatic conditions. Suzanne Simard, author of *Finding the Mother Tree*, researched the underground networks of forests and discovered how, through roots and fungi, trees communicate their needs and share nutrients.[32] Now, she and others are creating Mother Tree learning communities to steward forests. We need human societies as nurturing as forests. And Earth love warriors who oppose what harms the Earth while creating and supporting life-enhancing alternatives. It matters how we get along, educate our children, and relate to those around us.

Most of my friends and those I guide and work with long to live in a soul-rooted community. We tap into it in multiday programs or flowing down a river. We may hold virtual connections with those we have met. Yet we long for a physical, living community with the natural world and deeply rooted humans we can see and touch every day. This dream is a reality at Springhouse, a school for regenerative culture building.

Springhouse, an intergenerational learning community in rural Appalachia, sits in a field of long grass surrounded by mountains and forests. It has five guiding principles: take care of vulnerability, cultivate personhood, build a beloved community, respect the wisdom of the Earth, and love and serve others. Springhouse has a day school for seventh through twelfth graders, coming-of-age programs, and adult programs to explore the mysteries of nature and soul.[33]

"To create a sustainable culture, we need to take back education," said Jenny Finn, founder of Springhouse. "As adults, we need to embody in ourselves what we hope to see in young people."

Springhouse is an eco-soulcentric community engaging in practices that integrate author Bill Plotkin's visionary eco-psychology of human de-velopment, a model to help us mature with nature and soul as our guides. In Plotkin's model, which he calls the Eco-Soulcentric Developmental Wheel, at every stage of life we are asked to complete particular developmental tasks, in the realms of nature and culture, that help us grow.[34] Those in the Spring-house community notice and honor when each child makes their passage to adolescence.

"Education is where we decide what is important enough to pass down," Jenny said. Rather than grades and tests, Springhouse's educational approach holds relationships at the core. By tending to and listening to what emerges, the residents balance cultivating the uniqueness in each person with living in community. "We are an example of a bunch of people who stuck with it. Practicing together over years, we have rooted like trees, holding hands and stepping into the unknown."

Springhouse works with any family that wants to give their methods a try. Mentorship is central, and with additional groups available for restorative justice, each person in the community — child or adult, student or staff — is welcomed to talk about issues that arise. Jenny mentors each of her staff, and her staff mentors each of their students. Everyone has someone to talk to.

"We nurture vitality, not perfection," Jenny explained. "Because we are together day in and day out, we can heal."

Springhouse offers mentorship to people all over the world who want to turn the dream of eco-soulcentric community into reality.

"In an effort to dismantle the notion of education as a commodity," Jenny explained, "Springhouse does not charge for their services. They operate on prayer and contribution."

The eleven-acre farm that is their school was a gift.

"There is an open flow of resources coming in and offered out," Jenny said. "This is the economic model of the future."

When I hold together in my imagination the contributions of all the Earth warriors I have mentioned and so many others I have not, I envision communities rooted in the Earth who nurture the well-being of all, weaving together love, prayer, and protection, dismantling systems that cause harm, and creating new ways of being together that can breathe our world back to life. Honoring the intelligence of nature and the contributions we each make, we can love and protect our planet home and receive and offer in the sym-phony of life.

## *Wild Yoga Practices for*
## *Becoming a Love Warrior for the Earth*

Bear witness to love warriors fighting to protect our last remaining lands and species. Consider how to support them or become one.

- Become aware of how ecological devastation impacts the places you live and love — rivers, forests, prairies, oceans. Find out what organizations or people are working to protect wildlife. Reach out to local grassroots environmentalists and traditional Native peoples fighting to protect wild places. Ask them to tell you more about what they are doing and think about how you can support them or get involved. Perhaps visit a camp or community where people are protecting land or species.

- Strengthen your sociopolitical consciousness by attuning to injustice, oppression, and the suffering of all humans and the animate natural world. Observe how power operates in your families, communities, organizations, and the world. When it is helpful to the Earth and others, consider taking the risk to speak out about the injustices you see.

- Take stock of the resources you have been gifted: money, time, connections, passion, health, land, wholeness, maturity, soul, friends, community. Remember what the Earth has given to us and those we love and consider how you can give back. Take the risk to speak and stand up for who you love. Act in your sphere of influence and collaborate with others of varying approaches, beliefs, cultural backgrounds, and skill sets.

- Track the lies of the green movement and find books and sources of information that are accurate. Consider what sustainability truly means. Downsize your life. Reduce consumption. Restore ecosystems. Develop small-scale, ecologically minded local food sources. Teach children these skills. Tear down destructive infrastructure and restore natural communities.

- Care enough to save those in danger — fish, bears, forests, oceans. Visualize a world where humans care for their land base. Imagine the radical changes needed. The buildings, roads, and structures that need to fall. The restoration of ecosystems and the rewilding of human-use-only land. Imagine what is yours to do and begin it now.

- Build soulcentric community, schools, and relationships. Honor the uniqueness in each person and learn to live and work together on far less energy than our modern culture uses. Prepare for and support the collapse of civilization. Create local, sustainable food systems and pray, honor, and protect the Earth together.

## A Yoga Pose for Becoming a Love Warrior for the Earth

### HALF MOON POSE

Half Moon Pose (Ardha Chandrasana) is a challenging balance posture that strengthens the body (particularly the legs and ankles), teaches coordination, increases flexibility, and helps build focus. It can be beneficial for lower back problems and relieving sacrum pain, sciatica, and lumbar aches.

*To get in the pose:*

- From Mountain Pose, move into Extended Triangle Pose (Utthita Trikonasana): First, lightly jump your feet out wide. Turn your left foot out, toes facing the short end of your mat, so your left foot is at a 90-degree angle with the edge. Then, extend your arms out to your sides in a T shape parallel to the ground. Your right (or back) toes are at a forty-five-degree angle. Next, on your exhale, bend at the hips to lower your torso and extend to the side over your left leg. Keep the sides of your waist long and lengthen your tailbone. Place your left hand on your outer shin, ankle, or a block. (Or on the floor to the outside of your left shin.) Your right arm reaches toward the sky. Turn your gaze up, toward your right arm.

- If you are new to yoga, practice Extended Triangle Pose for some days, weeks, or months before attempting Half Moon Pose.
- To go into Half Moon Pose, start in Extended Triangle Pose, place your right hand on your hip, and turn to look at the floor. Move your torso and hips as needed to maintain balance.
- Bend your front knee slightly and bring your weight onto your front foot.
- Reach your front hand a little forward and place it directly beneath your front shoulder on the floor or, if you can't touch the floor, use a block or place your forearm on a chair. Press down through your fingers to help you maintain balance.
- Lift your back leg and make your thigh parallel to the floor. If you can maintain balance, reach your top hand to the sky and slowly open your chest and pelvis toward the sky too. If you are unable to reach up toward the sky, keep your hand on your hip.
- Either keep your gaze at eye level, your neck straight, or slowly turn your head to look up upward toward your top hand (which is more challenging). Keep a slight bend in your standing leg to protect your knee.
- Exit Half Moon Pose the same way you came into it and return to Extended Triangle Pose. Repeat on the other side.

Half Moon Pose brings together strength and grace and balances the masculine and feminine — the calm cooling of the moon and the fiery intensity of the sun. Root down with your standing leg and stabilize your lower arm while lifting and extending your raised leg and opposite arm. Feel how this active pose is guided by subtleness and intuition. Listen to your soul, dreams, nature, and your muse and let them inspire your physical expression. Feel the energies of the masculine and feminine working together. Imagine being a love warrior for the Earth. Allow your practice to be infused with resilience and soft power. Visualize how your actions can help the Earth.

Half Moon Pose is said to resemble the moon floating in the sky. Part of its Sanskrit name, *chandra*, refers to the brilliant shine of the moon. Half Moon Pose can help us find balance and brightness, but we may need support to begin, a block or a chair. If you lose your balance, reconnect with your breath and try again. Wobbling means your body is learning. Lift your back leg until your thigh is parallel to the floor. Focus your eyes softly on a single point to help you stay balanced. Lengthen and expand. Engage your abdominals for more stability and to align your pelvis. Imagine pressing the foot that is in the air against a wall. Lift your bottom hand away from the floor. Perhaps bring movement and play into the pose by picking something up off the floor while in the pose.

Traditional mythic, animistic, and astrological systems show the moon plays an active role in governing the daily rhythms of life. Scientists are now finding a lunar influence in all bodies, aquatic and terrestrial. All living cells have tidal structures that pulse and breathe. Our lunar somatic ancestry reveals our connection to an animate natural world across time and space.[35] Half Moon Pose is a ritual to make this dance conscious as we root in the depths of feminine darkness and stand in our strength, radiating light. Most of your weight is on your standing leg, with one hand on the floor. With your back leg lifted, open your pelvis and extend your torso. Feel the connection between the work of your limbs and the extension of your spine.

If you need more support than a chair or a block, you can do Half Moon Pose with your back against the wall. This gives you automatic balance and enables you to work on alignment. Or instead, you could press the sole of your top foot against the wall. Once you can do the full pose without wall support for your back or foot, become aware of the alignment of your back. Imagine your back and foot are both against a wall. Your back needs to become as strong as the wall. If this pose is too challenging, spend time in Extended Triangle Pose to build strength. You can make Extended Triangle Pose easier, if needed, by narrowing your stance and placing your hand on a block or a chair.

Congratulations on becoming a love warrior for the Earth, one who feels into the challenges of ecological devastation and acts to help the wild world. We will conclude this exploration of the practices of Wild Yoga by bringing together our connection to the wild, the journey of soul and spirit, and our ongoing relationship with the beloved world. We will look at ways to carry these practices into our lives in support of the Earth and future generations.

# CONCLUSION

# Wild Yoga, Revolution, and Cocreation

In temperate Tasmanian rain forests of myrtle, leatherwood, sassafras, and Huon pine, I feel strangely at home guiding a paddle raft on the Franklin River through cathedral-like mossy gorges. The water is tea brown, stained by tannins from the surrounding vegetation — tea tree shrub, button grass. We spend the first of nine nights at Angel Falls in a huge, shallow cave and stay dry watching rain fall through sunlight. Every time I go down this river, I am humbled by the challenge of weather and rapids and in awe of the raw, unspoiled beauty.

With no settlements in its catchment, the water here is pristine. We drink from our boats, ladling the river water into our cups, no filtration needed. Water is everywhere in the Franklin-Gordon Wild Rivers National Park, trickling down mountain creeks, cascading through rocks. Apart from Ice Age Aboriginal paintings in the Kutikina Cave, there is little human impact. Yet in 1978 this intact ecosystem came under serious threat, endangered by the Tasmanian Hydro-Electric Commission and its planned construction of a massive dam complex, approved by the government. Were it not for Bob Brown and the Tasmanian Wilderness Society leading a nonviolent blockade, the Franklin would have been destroyed. In 1982–83, twenty thousand people marched the streets of Hobart in a rally against the dam, an estimated six thousand land defenders joined the camps in Strahan, and nearly fifteen hundred people were arrested for simply being present at the blockade.[1] Protesters impeded machinery and occupied construction sites. Nearly five hundred were imprisoned for breaking the terms of their bail. The overflow of prisons drew international attention.

As tributaries flow in, the river's volume increases, and after a couple of days, the gradient steepens. On paddle rafts, river guides from Water by Nature Tasmania, Wild Yoga participants, and I work together to navigate

243

and hold on. Paddling helps us balance and stay in the boat. In unison, we lean forward and dig in, navigating rapids with names like Thunderrush, Jaw Breaker, the Cauldron, the Churn, and Nasty Notch. Several days in, we encounter impassable rapids and need to portage. Unloading the boats, we hike our gear across land along the shoreline and set up a rope system secured to high rocks to pull the boats through. The river is changeable. Too little rain, and it is so low you are rock hopping. Too much, and tricky sections become so dangerous you have to wait for the river to go down. What is evoked on the Franklin is at the core of Wild Yoga: reverence for wilderness, deep tranquility, leaning into challenge, working together, a mysterious landscape, the urgency to protect wild places.

The geology of the Franklin dates back 500 million years, to when Tasmania was under a shallow sea. Volcanoes and tectonic activity created mountains, and glaciers carved the land. Amid the dark, towering gorges where there are more than a dozen ancient caves, I feel like I am floating in the underground river of my mythos. As we sleep under the overhang at the Newlands Cascades, the moon lights up the river. I dream of Aboriginal and Torres Strait Islander people, the custodians of this land, and a fire-breathing dinosaur-dragon. The next morning, everyone in the group is wandering in nature to see where they are called. I paddle across the river and crawl into a cave. Water drips over its mouth as I imagine the dinosaur-dragon. His fiery response reminds me of the fire in my mythos consuming the forest. He invites me to breathe fire.

On slippery, wet rock, I exit the cave and then paddle back across the river. A platypus playfully zigzags from bank to bank, his tail slapping the surface as he dives under. His presence reminds me to relax. Back on shore, I take a deep breath and do some gentle yoga asana in the sun. Others join in as two white-breasted sea eagles circle above. Lying on our backs with feet planted on the Earth, we gently rock our knees back and forth to massage our sacrums, or sacred bones. Holding our elbows in opposite hands, we roll our arms in one direction and our heads in the other, releasing our necks and shoulders. Finally, in Bridge Pose, with our pelvises higher than our heads, we imagine our shoulders and heads merging into the Earth.

Feeling relaxed and at home in our bodies no matter what is happening comes most easily in nature. Being immersed in an intact wild place is an indescribable pleasure. The Earth was once like this everywhere.

Degradation to the Earth's ecosystems has increased since 1983, when people rallied to protect the Franklin River. At the same time, legally and politically protecting the environment has become harder. Most political leaders are not prioritizing the environment over development, and an increased risk of serious fines and other criminal penalties means large numbers of protesters are unlikely to turn out, denying a campaign the needed momentum.

"The Franklin would be dammed if it were today," said Bob. "It would be just a dead moat around [nearby] Frenchman's Peak."[2]

In 2014, the Parliament of Tasmania passed laws increasing financial and criminal penalties for those who protest. Bob Brown won a court case against harsh Tasmanian forestry laws threatening fines up to AUD$10,000 and up to four years in jail for anyone obstructing a "business activity." Yet the court found the aims of these laws to be legitimate and affirmed the right to target protesters who interfere with business operations.[3] Similarly, New South Wales introduced laws that "imposed a tenfold increase in fines for people protesting against coal seam gas and mining developments and increased penalties to a possible seven years in jail for 'hindering the working of equipment belonging to or associated with a mine.'"[4]

Antiprotest laws limit fundamental rights to assemble and make it difficult to interrupt the destruction of wild places. Since 2017, dozens of statutes restricting the right to protest have been enacted around the US, and more are pending.[5] These laws penalize people for participating in a democratic process and seek to make the public see protesting as criminal rather than as an exercise of our First Amendment rights. I have witnessed these dynamics play out in the protest against the lithium mine at Thacker Pass. The US Bureau of Land Management fined two lead organizers, Max Wilbert and Will Falk, nearly $50,000 for creating a camp on public land where the mine is planned, alleging trespass. Max and Will had made temporary latrines and a plywood windbreak at the request of indigenous elders who needed them to participate in ceremonies.[6]

The laws and policies of our culture ignore the scientific and mystical reality that the Earth is alive and intelligent. The forests, prairies, and wetlands are her organs. Soil is her skin, and water is her blood. We and other animals are her cells. The Earth is in a fragile state. Her organs have been damaged and her tissues poisoned. To be whole, ecosystems need all their parts. Our love for the Earth is sacred. Connecting to nature incites the desire to protect wild places. Ecocide is one of our biggest challenges, but we can remain aware, expand our strategies, and listen to what our grief and uncertainty unveil. Restoring nature can heal us. We are all responsible. We need to do our work — mature, strengthen ourselves, discover our soul's gifts — so we can care for her. To be effective, spiritual practices, personal growth platforms, and activists need to lead us to a responsible tending of the greater Earth community, helping us protect lands and species.

The practices of Wild Yoga are a pathway to reinhabit our wild bodies and stretch our consciousness to align with forces greater than our minds so we may live in cocreative relationship. Listening to the animate natural world and our dreams, we can encounter and embody our souls and live in spiritual union while following the mystery of what we love and grieve. By being vulnerable, descending into darkness, and playing our unique note, we can court the muse, pray, offer our erotic engagement, dream radically, and become love warriors for the Earth. We can create life-enhancing communities that honor nature and listen to our dreams.

I would not have made it down the Franklin River alone. But together, we are strong. For the last two decades, I have been living in and listening to wild places and supporting individuals to encounter soul and stretch their consciousness. Communities are needed to weave prayer and protection. Some personal growth facilitators belittle Earth activism, and some activists dismiss the need for personal work. Yet prayer and protection are meant to work together. For cultures of nature-based indigenous peoples, they always have. I envision the practices of Wild Yoga carrying us into eco-centric communities.

Wild Yoga assists people in descending into their prerational instincts, into what Thomas Berry calls "the dream of the Earth."[7] The Earth is animate, and through conscious partnership with her, we can help her imagine possible futures, and she can give us ideas about how to end our life-destroying culture and cocreate Earth-centric cultures. Soul-initiated individuals bring vision and delivery systems, like Joanna Macy's the Work That Reconnects or Jenny Finn's intentional learning community at Springhouse. To support creative strategies that enhance life, eco-centric protectors and communities — soul-initiated lovers of the Earth — can dream and act together to end the harm and reestablish reverent balance.

Wild Yoga is a movement of perpetual listening and acting on what we know. We don't know what the future will be, but we can aim to grow in right relationship with the Earth. Eco-centric people are aware of their embeddedness with nature. They understand that the Earth community is central, unlike *ego*centrism, which puts individuals first. Protecting ecosystems is part of being a mature human. Anyone who loves the Earth can listen, develop their imagination, and stretch their consciousness. The Earth needs all of us. There are so many intelligences greater than our minds — muses, dreams, forests, waters, imagination, darkness, mystery. Wild Yoga is an embodied way of engaging with the beauty *and* the devastation, encouraging us to dream and pray for the world, live our mythos, and stretch ourselves.

We can honor our relationship with the greater web of life, vital to all living creatures. Although mainstream society penalizes those who protect nature, we can listen to our bodies, hearts, souls, the land, and dreams for the vitality and impetus to find creative ways to challenge damaging sociocultural structures and stop the desecration of Earth.

The images of my mythic soul — fire, tree, bear, wings, underworld river, cave, the Earth's heart — arose unbidden to show me where I belong, weaving me into the fabric of the world, enabling me to know my thread. Animas Valley Institute has helped me and others understand how to pursue and commit to soul. Being soul initiated does not raise our status; it increases our responsibility. As long as the Earth suffers, anything we have — privilege, connections, money, time, soul — is for giving back to the Earth.

Soul lives in the forest and is never done speaking. And we are never done listening. I live for my soul and to be close to the Earth — birds, grasses, mountains — where I can't help but notice the harm they suffer. I have mixed the telling of my soul story with other elements of life, because soul by itself is not enough. Soul stretches our consciousness by reflecting the beauty of the shape we are called to make. Yet we need to stretch more to nourish those around us as trees do in a forest.

Stretching consciousness is central to Wild Yoga. This book — a mystical stream of consciousness flowing through me — is a guide to the practices and relationships that have stretched me, ones that I believe can help humanity and the Earth. Each set of practices is a little river flowing into a big one. As formidable as the Copper or Franklin River, our soul and muse, informed by our relationship with the wild, can help us partner with the world.

The rapids dwindle as we enter the Lower Franklin, past forests of ancient Huon pine. Paddling is more demanding as the river slows and widens. On the last day, we reach the confluence where the Franklin empties into the Gordon River, which was dammed in 1974. Its headwaters, the Serpentine and Huon Rivers, were dammed in 1972. Protesters lost their fight for the Gordon but brought their momentum to defend the Franklin. The water becomes dark, murky, and cold as we cross over. I can no longer see beneath the surface or drink from the boat. Sad to leave, I wish more of the Earth's ecosystems were as intact as the Franklin River.

We are at a confluence. What kind of world do you want to live in, and what are you willing to do to help create it? Wild Yoga invites us to listen and be in loving, embodied engagement. To live our soul's artistry and let our actions be directed by the Earth and our dreams. To play and relax and let intelligences far greater than ours stretch us. Camped on the Gordon River in Tasmania our last night, each person offers thanks and praise to the river in a council ceremony. Someone shares a dream:

> I am swimming in a tsunami wave and enamored with it. Three children float beside me. I care for and try to keep them safe. A beautiful wall of water is falling in front of me.

Her image, I sense, is for all of us, inviting us to live in the wild flow of the unknown.

The wild world needs our embodied love prayers, and we need her. I call on the forests and trees I have known and those I have never met. "Teach us to create connections," I ask, "like your mycelium networks, which inherently know how to tend air, soil, and water, so we can honor our mutuality and dream for the world." I call on the riverways, oceans, and underground aquifers and bless their life-giving elixirs. "Teach us to revere you," I say. "Help us to nourish life and have the strength to dissolve what causes harm." Each day, I wander outside in the Sonoran Desert where I live and ask the land for the words I need to write.

Today I ask for a note to end on, wandering around the trails at Black Arrow Lodge Hacienda at the edge of Saguaro National Park in Arizona. Looking up at the peak we call Fire Mountain, I ask for guidance. The sun is bright at midday and the breeze cool. As I near the fountain where I often watch birds, I notice the flowers of desert brittlebush exploding in hues of brilliant yellow. Pausing, I bend down to take in her sweet scent. Native to the Southwest, this common flowery shrub is a drought-resistant member of the sunflower family. Sitting beside her, I stare into her blossoms, deeply moved by the bright gold- and ochre-colored shades of her delicate petals. This is her moment to risk opening.

A slight tremor in my chest, I recognize her call. "Show up humbly and courageously — listen and sing," I hear.

Go outside and see who wants to speak with you. Take your deepest feelings and questions about your life and the world. In witnessing the flowers of desert brittlebush blossoming in the dry winter, I feel drawn to bless you as she did me. With tenacity and love, may you root and flower. May we, living the poetics of soul in union with the Divine, come together to protect wild places and live in ways that honor the Earth.

# Acknowledgments

W ild Yoga was born of forests, oceans, and mountains, bears, wolves, and honeybees, and the mystery that lives within all wild places. This book was created in community, evolving from what the animate natural world has shared with me and thousands of people I have guided over the last couple of decades.

Thank you to teachers, friends, Earth activists, soul journeyers, participants, and colleagues who have been in nature with me. You have influenced my perception, and your stories deepen this book. Some people and stories I name. In other stories, identifying details are held in confidence. I am grateful to those I witnessed and those who allowed me to interview them.

To my literary agent, Anne Depue, thank you for believing in me and Wild Yoga and for your gracious and insightful advice about the content and overall approach of this book. To my editorial director, Georgia Hughes, thank you for seeing the value of my writing and for your clarifying questions that offered a powerful and wise influence on the shape and final result of this book. To Kristen Cashman and Diana Rico, who also offered valuable input, and to the entire New World Library team, thank you for your skill and enthusiasm.

I am grateful to colleagues, friends, and writers who graciously reviewed and offered valuable feedback on early versions of one or more chapters or all of them: Nancy O'Rourke, Heidi Mitchell, Mary Carroll Moore, Peter Scanlan, Heather and Mark Timken, Kristine Carter, Liz Shulman, Christine Lissitzyn, Derrick Jensen's writing group, Maya Köbernik, David Ferris, Lisa Ohlen Harris, Kendra Langeteig, Hilary Leighton. Your encouragement and feedback strengthened my writing and enabled this book to become what it is.

To my primary yoga teacher trainers, Brahmanand Don and Amba Stapleton: thank you for helping me discover my yoga and encouraging me to share my ideas and offer Wild Yoga programs. I am grateful to other friends and colleagues I met in the Nosara Yoga Institute community who nurtured the creation of Wild Yoga: Janel Lynn Schullo, Ann Hunt, Robin Patino, Heinz and Maya Köbernik, Horace Usry, Richard Sho Albert, Jeannette Vargas, Naoko Yamaguchi, Meriah Dale McCauley, Nango Murray, Martin Marks, Alana Layne Greenburg, Daniel Richardson, Erika Mehiel, Julian DeVoe, Jane Fryer, Indira Kate Kalmbach, Joy Burch, Kara Jasinski Leupp, and more. Thanks to the owners and managers of the Yoga Farm in Costa Rica, where I lived and taught yoga: Gabriel Schmerler, Klaus Fronius, Patrick McMahon, Christie Carr. And to other yoga teachers with whom I studied: Amy Ippoliti, Scott Blossom, Jeanie Manchester, Darren Rhodes, Christina Sell, K-Lea Gifford, Kathy Curran.

Big gratitude to Bill Plotkin and Animas Valley Institute, where I've trained and guided for two decades. Much of Wild Yoga was inspired by what I experienced while being immersed in Animas's work. Special thanks to those with whom I've guided multiple programs: Doug Van Houten, John Lynch, Jeffrey Allen, Peter Scanlan, Jim Marsden. And to all the guides past and present: Geneen Marie Haugen, Sabina Wyss, Erica Rhinehart, Jade Sherer, Annie Bloom, Bruce Howatt, Laura Gunion, Sage Magdalene, Palika Rewilding, Laura Blakeman, Kate Joyner, Nate Bacon, Mary Marsden, Dustin Timmons, Gene Dilworth, Brian Stafford, Peter Fonken, Cristin DeVine, Bill Ball, Sheila Belanger, Anne Hayden. And to others who have given generously within the Animas community: Donna Medeiros, Becky Maloney, Jeanine Surber, Rachel Posner, Elizabeth Shephard, Chelle Nagle, Jessica Gellings, Preston Edward, Courtney Taglialatela, Tracey Belt, Julian Norris.

Huge thanks to Eleanor Bingham Miller, who invited me to live at and tend Black Arrow Lodge in Tucson, Arizona, between November 2020 and May 2022, and in whose sweet sanctuary I was able to write most of this book.

Gratitude to those who contributed art: the marvelous cover by Doug Van Houten, the eloquent poses drawn by Sarah Brooks. And thanks to Tracy Cunningham, art director at New World Library, for collaborating and bringing it all together.

Thanks to the nature-based indigenous Ngäbe-Buglé community in Southern Costa Rica for welcoming me into their village and teaching me about their culture and language. I am grateful for the opportunity to study with indigenous teachers Martín Prechtel and Ruby Gibson. Thanks to indigenous writers Sherri Mitchell, Joy Harjo, and Linda Hogan and to Andreas

Kornevall for connecting me with my ancestors through Norse mythology. And to Jenny Deane and Brian O'Hare, who've helped me connect to my Irish ancestry.

Thank you to indigenous peoples, the world's greatest conservationists, although they rarely get credit for it, and to anyone who helps protect wild places and species. And thanks to Deep Green Resistance, Protect Thacker Pass, and all the Earth activists who I have learned from, particularly those participating in programs I've led bringing personal and planetary together: Max Wilbert, Robin June Hood, Candor Soraya Bourne, Trav London, Elisabeth Robson, Spencer Hamil, Michelle Martin, Aimee Wild, Deanna Meyer, Julia Barnes, Derrick Jensen, Trinity La Fey, Salonika Neupane, Benjamin Warner, Will Falk, Lierre Keith, Susan Breen.

Special thanks to Michael Pilarski, who organized the Global Earth Repair Conference in 2019 and invited me to participate in panel discussions with ecology-minded leaders like Charles Eisenstein, Dahr Jamal, Laurence Cole, and others.[1] Your work inspires me!

Thank you to the river guides and companies who taught me how to guide a boat and allowed me to guide people down the river: Mountain Waters Rafting, Holiday River Expeditions, Water by Nature Tasmania, Salt River Rafting, Adventure Logic, Safpar Rafting.

Gratitude to the wilderness therapy organizations who taught me how to challenge people with love and fostered a community that invited that: Open Sky Wilderness Therapy, Aspen Achievement Academy, Passages to Recovery, Alldredge Academy.

Gratitude to teachers and trainers of the Hakomi Institute who assisted me in learning to listen deeply to my body and in how to guide others to do so: Phil Del Prince, Melissa Grace, Mukara Meredith, Morgan Holford, Jaci Hull. And thanks to the Vipassana and Dharma Ocean meditation communities that also helped me deepen my capacity to listen to my body.

My heartfelt gratitude goes to the visionaries and writers whose models, philosophies, and ideas have strongly influenced my own: Joanna Macy, Bill Plotkin, Sharon Blackie, Don Stapleton, Robert Bosnak, Derrick Jensen, Robert Moss, Stephen Aizenstat, Martín Prechtel, Ruby Gibson, Martin Shaw, Clarissa Pinkola Estés, Charles Eisenstein, Terry Tempest Williams, Susan Griffin, Mary Oliver, Robin Wall Kimmerer, Chellis Glendenning, and more.

So many others provided insight and support in many different ways. Special thanks to Autumn Leigh, Alix Rowland, Lesley Hudson, Don and

Cyrus Lewis, Tricia Gourley, Chelsey Chapman, Aryeh Margolis, Katrina Blair, Christi Strickland, Susanna Raeven, Alexis Slutzky, Kayla Wexelburg, Evan Meyer, Emily Demong, Robin Brodsky, Caroline Williford, Wendy Robertson Fyfe, David Emery, Claire Dunn, Deb Collins, Brett Fernon, Jean Aspen, Chloe Bovoletis, Cristina San Pedro, Jo-Lynn Park, Norman Elizondo, Julian Misliuc, Ellis McNichol, Isa Vasanti, Ananda Elise Foley, Danny Running Bear, Joy Morris, Anrael Mukanday Lovejoy, Onye Onyemaechi, Laurie Adams, Kelly Ray Matthews, Jen Libera, Cory Arellano, Roger Strachan, Aaron Phillips, John Rosmarin, Amanda Armstrong, Jessie Krebs, Kris Drummond, Joseph McCaffrey, Donald Cooper, Greg and Judy Munch, Dave Talamo, Pam Parsons, Jim Forleo, Coulter Stone, Dixie Hamann, Oley Smith, Anne-Marie Marron, Bell Selkie Lovelock, Harry Leland, Nathan Osgood, Christy Lynne Campbell, Stephanie Marchal, Jim and Suzanne Bolton, Darsi Olson, David Grimes, George Foster, Brooks Barron, Clay Sullwood, Courtney Bowman, Joyce Elizabeth, Sayo Yamaguchi.

I may not have been able to finish without my pup, Xander, who reminded me when it was time to rest and play.

Special thanks to my parents Richard and Linda Kane, my brother Richard, his wife Carrie, my niece and nephew Nico and Greta, and all my grandparents, aunts, uncles, and other ancestors.

There are so many people to thank, more than I can remember. I apologize to anyone I left out and for all the ways this book falls short due to unconscious assumptions or cultural biases. I am grateful to my muse for giving me the ideas and words to finish this now. I share it with a deep prayer for the Earth. May we grow into loving partners.

# Notes

## Introduction: Awakening from the Edge of Death

1. Carey Gillam, "Weedkiller 'Raises Risk of Non-Hodgkin Lymphoma by 41%,'" *Guardian*, February 14, 2019, https://www.theguardian.com/business/2019/feb/14/weed-killing-products-increase-cancer-risk-of-cancer.
2. Eknath Easwaran, trans., *The Bhagavad Gita* (Tomales, CA: Nilgiri Press, 2007).
3. Bill Plotkin's Eco-Soulcentric Developmental Wheel and Nature-Based Map of the Human Psyche; Don Stapleton's Cycle of Transformation through Awareness; Robert Bosnak's Embodied Imagination; cross-cultural indigenous practices and traditions; eco-depth psychology; Joanna Macy's concept of deep time and Active Hope practices; Martín Prechtel's Bolad's Kitchen school; Derrick Jensen's writing and Deep Green Resistance organization; Tibetan Buddhism and embodied meditation as taught by Dharma Ocean; and a variety of other yoga, transformative dance, and body-centered practices, including Hakomi and Ruby Gibson's Somatic Archaeology.

## Part I: The Wild

1. Reni Fulton, "My Wildish Self," Naturally Radiant, accessed September 24, 2022, http://naturallyradiant.michelemarik.ca/my-wildish-self/.

## Chapter 1: Listen to the Intelligence of Your Body

1. "Hakomi," GoodTherapy, last updated February 28, 2018, https://www.goodtherapy.org/learn-about-therapy/types/hakomi.
2. *Dr Ruby Gibson on Somatic Archaeology*, YouTube video, 28:40, posted October 7, 2016, by Freedom Lodge, https://www.youtube.com/watch?v=oDpXMwwpnLE.
3. Rebecca Wildbear, *Wild Yoga: Embody Your Wholeness*, YouTube video, 21:58, posted May 4, 2017, https://www.youtube.com/watch?v=vpWYCuW4Phs&t=2s.

## Chapter 2: Deepen Your Ecological Perception

1. Geneen Marie Haugen, "Wild Imagination," *Parabola*, May 16, 2019, https://parabola.org/2019/05/16/wild-imagination-by-geneen-marie-haugen/.
2. Laurens van der Post, *The Lost World of the Kalahari* (San Diego, CA: Harcourt, Brace, 1977).
3. Richard Louv, "What Is Nature-Deficit Disorder?," October 15, 2019, Richard Louv blog, http://richardlouv.com/blog/what-is-nature-deficit-disorder.
4. Chellis Glendinning, *My Name Is Chellis and I'm in Recovery from Western Civilization* (Boston: Shambhala Publications, 1994), 64.
5. Patrick M. Burns, "Why Wilderness Therapy Works," *Psychology Today*, December 1, 2017, https://www.psychologytoday.com/us/blog/brainstorm/201712/why-wilderness-therapy-works.
6. Bill Plotkin, *Wild Mind: A Field Guide to the Human Psyche* (Novato, CA: New World Library, 2013), 1–9.
7. Laura Sewall, "The Skill of Ecological Perception," in *Ecopsychology: Restoring the Earth, Healing the Mind*, ed. Theodore Roszak, Mary Gomes, and Allen Kanner (New York: Random House, 1995), 203–6.
8. Sewall, "The Skill of Ecological Perception," 204.
9. Sewall, "The Skill of Ecological Perception," 209.
10. "An Overview of Our Offerings," Animas Valley Institute, accessed August 12, 2021, https://www.animas.org/programs/offerings-descriptions/#great.
11. Mary Oliver, "Wild Geese," *Wild Geese: Selected Poems* (Hexham, UK: Bloodaxe Books, 2004).
12. Sewall, "The Skill of Ecological Perception," 211.
13. Sewall, "The Skill of Ecological Perception," 213.
14. Eligio Stephen Gallegos, quoted in Trebbe Johnson, "Finding Your Animal Guides," *Yoga Journal*, no. 109, March–April 1993, 26–32.

## Chapter 3: Flow in the River of Your Heart Waters

1. Derrick Jensen, *Endgame*, vol. 2, *Resistance* (New York: Seven Stories Press, 2006), 596.
2. National Park Service, *Time Lapse of the Removal of Elwha Dam, Washington State*, YouTube video, 1:29, posted July 16, 2013, by Ian Miller, https://www.youtube.com/watch?v=bUZE7kgXKJc.
3. Don Stapleton, *Self-Awakening Yoga: The Expansion of Consciousness through the Body's Own Wisdom* (Rochester, NY: Healing Arts Press, 2004), 41–43.
4. The concept for this pose came from Stapleton, *Self-Awakening Yoga*, 45–46. I have added my own ideas to the original concept.
5. Wildbear, *Wild Yoga*, https://www.youtube.com/watch?v=vpWYCuW4Phs&t=2s, starting at 4:50.

# Chapter 4: Embody Feral Female Ferocity

1. Derrick Jensen, *Endgame*, vol. 1, *The Problem of Civilization* (New York: Seven Stories Press, 2006), 60.

2. Sharon Blackie, *If Women Rose Rooted* (Tewkesbury, UK: September Publishing, 2017), 12.

3. Bill Plotkin, *The Journey of Soul Initiation* (Novato, CA: New World Library, 2021), 431.

4. Susan McGee Bailey, *How Schools Shortchange Girls: The AAUW Report; A Study of Major Findings on Girls and Education*, Wellesley Centers for Women, 1992, https://www.wcwonline.org/Publications-by-title/how-schools-shortchange-girls -the-aauw-report-a-study-of-major-findings-on-girls-and-education.

5. Robert Frahm, "Boys Get More Attention in Class Than Girls, National Study Finds," *Hartford Courant*, February 11, 1992, https://www.courant.com/news /connecticut/hc-xpm-1992-02-12-0000204148-story.html.

6. "2022 State of the Gender Pay Gap Report," Payscale, last updated March 15, 2022, https://www.payscale.com/research-and-insights/gender-pay-gap/.

7. Neha Thirani Bagri, "Child Marriage Is Allowed in More Than 100 Countries — Including the United States," *Quartz*, September 18, 2016, last updated July 20, 2022, https://qz.com/783681/child-marriage-is-allowed-in-more-than-100-countries -including-the-united-states/.

8. Andrew Whalen, "What Is the Lolita Express? Epstein's Infamous Sex Plane In- cluded VIPs Like Bill Clinton," *Newsweek*, July 9, 2019, https://www.newsweek.com /jeffrey-epstein-lolita-express-bill-clinton-flight-logs-1448367.

9. Cecilia Plaza, "Miss Diagnosis: Gendered Injustice in Medical Malpractice Law," *Columbia Journal of Gender and Law* 39, no. 2 (July 22, 2020): 91–139.

10. Contessa Gayles, *The Feminist in Cellblock Y*, YouTube video, 1:15:00, posted April 25, 2018, https://www.youtube.com/watch?v=JYxTzsabkH8.

11. Catherine Clifford, "Global Wealth Inequality Is 'Founded on Sexism,' Says Oxfam International," CNBC.com, January 19, 2020, https://www.cnbc.com/2020/01/17 /global-wealth-inequality-is-founded-on-sexism-oxfam-international.html.

12. "Violence against Women," World Health Organization, fact sheet, March 9, 2021, https://www.who.int/news-room/fact-sheets/detail/violence-against-women.

13. "Domestic Abuse Is a Gendered Crime," Women's Aid Federation of England, accessed August 12, 2021, https://www.womensaid.org.uk/information-support /what-is-domestic-abuse/domestic-abuse-is-a-gendered-crime/.

14. "Violence against Women in the United States: Statistics," National Organization for Women, accessed August 12, 2021, https://now.org/resource/violence-against -women-in-the-united-states-statistic/.

15. Soraya Chemaly, *Rage Becomes Her: The Power of Women's Anger* (New York: Atria Books, 2019), 167.

16. Maureen Murdock, *The Heroine's Journey: Woman's Quest for Wholeness* (Boston: Shambhala Publications, 1990), 59.

## Chapter 5: Receive the Love of Trees

1. Richard Schiffman, "'Mother Trees' Are Intelligent: They Learn and Remember," *Scientific American*, May 4, 2021, https://www.scientificamerican.com/article/mother-trees-are-intelligent-they-learn-and-remember/.
2. Georg Kappen, Elisabeth Kastner, Torsten Kurth, Johanna Puetz, Andreas Reinhardt, and Juuso Soininen, "The Staggering Value of Forests — and How to Save Them," Boston Consulting Group, June 9, 2020, https://www.bcg.com/publications/2020/the-staggering-value-of-forests-and-how-to-save-them.aspx.
3. "Why Is Palm Oil Bad?," Transport & Environment, accessed August 12, 2021, https://www.transportenvironment.org/challenges/energy/biofuels/why-is-palm-oil-biodiesel-bad/.
4. Stefano Mancuso, quoted in Amy Fleming, "The Secret Life of Plants: How They Memorise, Communicate, Problem Solve, and Socialise," *Guardian*, April 5, 2020, https://www.theguardian.com/environment/2020/apr/05/smarty-plants-are-our-vegetable-cousins-more-intelligent-than-we-realise.
5. Alex Gray, "Humans Have More Than 5 Senses," World Economic Forum, January 9, 2017, https://www.weforum.org/agenda/2017/01/humans-have-more-than-5-senses/.

## Chapter 6: Dream in the Cave Womb

1. Robert Moss, *The Secret History of Dreaming* (Novato, CA: New World Library, 2010), 16.
2. Sherri Mitchell, *Sacred Instructions* (Berkeley, CA: North Atlantic Books, 2018), 14–15.
3. Mitchell, *Sacred Instructions*, 15.
4. Moss, *The Secret History of Dreaming*, 16.
5. Plotkin, *The Journey of Soul Initiation*, 18.

## Part II: Holy Longing

1. Regina Sara Ryan, "Praying Dangerously," *Praying Dangerously: Radical Reliance on God* (Prescott, AZ: Hohm Press, 2011), viii.

## Chapter 7: Open to a Sacred World

1. "Catholic Church an 'Empire of Misogyny' — Mary McAleese," *BBC News*, March 8, 2018, https://www.bbc.com/news/world-europe-43330026.
2. Malidoma Somé, *Of Water and the Spirit: Ritual, Magic, and Initiation in the Life of an African Shaman* (New York: Penguin Books, 1995), 20.
3. Plotkin, *Wild Mind*, 13.

4. J. R. R. Tolkien, "Mythopoeia," *Tree and Leaf* (London: HarperCollins, 2001), 83–90.
5. David Whyte, *Crossing the Unknown Sea: Work as a Pilgrimage of Identity* (New York: Riverhead, 2002).
6. Plotkin, *The Journey of Soul Initiation*, 20–24.
7. Jalal al-Din Rumi, "Some Kiss We Want," *Rumi: The Book of Love: Poems of Ecstasy and Longing*, trans. Coleman Barks (New York: HarperCollins, 2003).
8. Thomas Berry, *The Dream of the Earth* (San Francisco: Sierra Club Books, 1990), 211.
9. David Whyte, "All the True Vows," *The House of Belonging* (Langley, WA: Many Rivers Press, 1996).
10. Andreas Kornevall home page, accessed August 20, 2021, https://www.kornevall.com/.
11. Andreas Kornevall, "The Norse Legend of the World Tree — Yggdrasil," *Ancient Origins*, last updated May 10, 2019, https://www.ancient-origins.net/myths-legends -europe/norse-legend-world-tree-yggdrasil-002680.
12. Malidoma Somé, quoted in Leslee Goodman, "Between Two Worlds: Malidoma Somé on Rites of Passage," *The Sun*, July 2010, https://www.thesunmagazine.org /issues/415/between-two-worlds.
13. Nicole Schoolfield, "How to Do the Yoga Goddess Pose (Utkata Konasana)," Be Extra Yoga, November 20, 2019, https://beextrayoga.com/how-to-do-goddess-pose -in-yoga-utkata-konasana/.

## Chapter 8: Romance the Mystery of What You Love

1. Martín Prechtel, *The Smell of Rain on Dust: Grief and Praise* (Berkeley, CA: North Atlantic Books, 2015), 24–26.
2. Trebbe Johnson, *The World Is a Waiting Lover: Desire and the Quest for the Beloved* (Novato, CA: New World Library, 2005), 64.
3. James Hollis, *The Eden Project: In Search of the Magical Other* (Toronto, ON: Inner City Books, 1998), 33–38.
4. Plotkin, *Wild Mind*, 101–3.
5. Kahlil Gibran, "On Love," *The Prophet* (Auckland, New Zealand: Floating Press, 2009), 14.
6. Martín Prechtel, *Stealing Benefacio's Roses* (Berkeley, CA: North Atlantic Books, 2013), 120.

## Chapter 9: Embrace Grief and Despair

1. Somé, *Of Water and the Spirit*, 10–12, 55.
2. Prechtel, *The Smell of Rain on Dust*, 31.
3. Stephen Harrod Buhner, *Earth Grief: The Journey into and through Ecological Loss* (White River Junction, VT: Raven Press, 2022), 14–16.
4. "Waters of the World Threatened by Dumping 180M Tonnes of Toxic Mine Waste," MiningWatch Canada, Earthworks, February 28, 2012, press release, https://www .earthworks.org/media-releases/troubled_waters_press_release/.

5. Melissa Denchak, "Water Pollution: Everything You Need to Know," National Resources Defense Council, April 18, 2022, https://www.nrdc.org/stories/water-pollution-everything-you-need-know.

6. Travis Donovan, "UN Environment Programme: 200 Species Extinct Every Day, Unlike Anything since Dinosaurs Disappeared 65 Million Years Ago," *Huffington Post*, August 17, 2010, https://www.huffpost.com/entry/un-environment-programme-_n_684562.

7. Robert Davis, *Kauai 'o'o*, YouTube video, 01:24, posted March 12, 2009, https://www.youtube.com/watch?v=nDRYoCmcYNU&ab_channel=RobertDavis.

8. Laura Moss, "11 Recently Extinct Animals," Treehugger, last updated July 21, 2022, https://www.treehugger.com/animals-presumed-extinct-in-the-last-decade-4869347.

9. George Amato, quoted in Kai Kupperschmidt, "A Wild Hope," *Science*, June 9, 2022, https://www.science.org/content/article/two-decades-vanished-stunning-spixs-macaw-returns-forest-home.

10. Joanna Macy, "The Bestiary," Work That Reconnects Network, November 26, 2017, https://workthatreconnects.org/resource/the-bestiary/.

11. Damian Carrington, "Humans Just 0.01% of All Life but Have Destroyed 83% of Wild Mammals — Study," *Guardian*, May 21, 2018, https://www.theguardian.com/environment/2018/may/21/human-race-just-001-of-all-life-but-has-destroyed-over-80-of-wild-mammals-study.

12. "Global Assessment Report on Biodiversity and Ecosystem Services," Wikipedia, May 6, 2019, https://en.wikipedia.org/wiki/Global_Assessment_Report_on_Biodiversity_and_Ecosystem_Services.

13. Joanna Macy, "The Greatest Danger," *YES! Magazine*, February 2, 2008, https://www.yesmagazine.org/issue/climate-solutions/opinion/2008/02/02/the-greatest-danger.

14. "Deforestation," National Geographic Resource Library, last updated July 15, 2022, https://education.nationalgeographic.org/resource/deforestation.

15. Barry Yeoman, "Why the Passenger Pigeon Went Extinct," *Audubon*, May–June 2014, https://www.audubon.org/magazine/may-june-2014/why-passenger-pigeon-went-extinct.

16. Aldo Leopold, "Quotes from Green Fire," *The Aldo Leopold Foundation*, accessed August 31, 2021, https://www.aldoleopold.org/teach-learn/green-fire-film/leopold-quotes/.

17. Rebecca Wildbear, "Massive Dam Threatens Spectacular Gorge Downstream of Victoria Falls," *Earth Island Journal*, July 29, 2020, https://www.earthisland.org/journal/index.php/articles/entry/dam-threatens-batoka-gorge-zambezi-river/.

18. Kathy Hughes et al., *The World's Forgotten Fishes: Final Report*, World Wildlife Fund, 2021, https://wwfint.awsassets.panda.org/downloads/world_s_forgotten_fishes__report_final__1.pdf.

19. Gibran, "On Love," 14.

20. Francis Weller, *The Wild Edge of Sorrow: Rituals of Renewal and the Sacred Work of Grief* (Berkeley, CA: North Atlantic Books, 2015), xii.

21. John Hadder, "Thacker Pass Lithium Mine in Humboldt County, NV," Great Basin Resource Watch, last updated June 16, 2022, http://gbrw.org/proposed-thacker -pass-lithium-mine/.

22. The concept for this pose came from Stapleton, *Self-Awakening Yoga*, 156–59. I have added my own ideas to the original concept.

## Chapter 10: Make a Pearl of Your Vulnerability

1. Plotkin, *The Journey of Soul Initiation*, 189.

2. Brené Brown, *Daring Greatly: How the Courage to Be Vulnerable Transforms the Way We Live, Love, Parent, and Lead* (2012; repr., New York: Avery, 2015), 45.

3. Brown, *Daring Greatly*, 45.

4. Plotkin, *Soulcraft: Crossing into the Mysteries of Nature and Psyche* (Novato, CA: New World Library, 2010), 97.

5. Plotkin, *Wild Mind*, 9–18.

6. Plotkin, *Wild Mind*, 16.

7. Plotkin, *Wild Mind*, 47.

8. Plotkin, *Wild Mind*, 48.

9. Plotkin, *Wild Mind*, 48.

10. Brown, *Daring Greatly*, 68–71.

11. Brené Brown, *Dare to Lead: Brave Work, Tough Conversations, Whole Hearts* (New York: Random House, 2018), 126.

12. Brené Brown, *Daring Greatly*, 71.

13. Daniel Deardorff, *The Other Within: The Genius of Deformity in Myth, Culture, and Psyche* (Ashland, OR: White Cloud Press, 2004), 2.

14. Deardorff, *The Other Within*, 40–41.

15. Deardorff, *The Other Within*, 5.

16. Brown, *Daring Greatly*, 52.

17. For example, Meditation Summit, *Pema Chödrön, Tonglen Meditation: News We Can Use, Session 30, June 23, 2016*, YouTube video, 47:52, posted July 2, 2016, https://www.youtube.com/watch?v=j_XPJhGwjbU.

18. bell hooks, *Reel to Real: Race, Class, and Sex at the Movies* (Abingdon, UK: Routledge, 2012), 149.

## Chapter 11: Descend into the Reverent, Dark Mystery

1. Stephen Waldo, "26 Shocking Porn Statistics Most Men Don't Know," Husband Help Haven, accessed August 24, 2022, https://husbandhelphaven.com/porn-statistics/.

2. David Whyte, "All the True Vows."

3. The concept for this pose came from Stapleton, *Self-Awakening Yoga*, 238–40. I have added my own ideas to the original concept.

4. Stapleton, *Self-Awakening Yoga*, 238.

## Chapter 12: Play Your Part in the Symphony

1. "A Bird's-Eye View of Human Language and Evolution," MIT Press blog, January 5, 2017, https://mitpress.mit.edu/blog/a-birds-eye-view-of-human-language-and-evolution/.
2. "What Are Some Common Traits between Birds and Humans?," AmazingLife.Bio, accessed August 24, 2022, https://www.amazinglife.bio/common-traits-birds-and-humans.
3. David Robson, "The Beautiful Languages of the People Who Talk Like Birds," *BBC Future*, May 24, 2017, https://www.bbc.com/future/article/20170525-the-people-who-speak-in-whistles#:~:text=Joining%20just%20a%20handful%20of,to%20each%20in%20their%20forest.
4. "The Land," the Yoga Farm website, accessed August 24, 2022, https://www.yoga farmcostarica.org/the-land-and-punta-banco/.
5. Bruce Chatwin, *The Songlines* (Westminster, UK: Penguin, 1988).
6. Wendell Berry, "Work Song, Part 2: A Vision," *New Collected Poems* (Berkeley, CA: Counterpoint, 2013).
7. Fiona MacDonald, "Scientists Document Wild Birds 'Talking' with Humans for the First Time," *ScienceAlert*, July 22, 2016, https://www.sciencealert.com/scientists-document-wild-birds-communicating-with-african-tribespeople-to-help-them-find-honey.
8. Victoria Gill, "Regent Honeyeater: Endangered Bird 'Has Forgotten Its Song,'" *BBC News*, March 17, 2021, https://www.bbc.com/news/science-environment-56417544.
9. The concept for this pose came from Stapleton, *Self-Awakening Yoga*, 190–91. I have added my own ideas to the original concept.

## Part III: Beloved World

1. "Joanna Macy: A Wild Love for the World," *On Being with Krista Tippett*, podcast transcript, last updated April 25, 2019, https://onbeing.org/programs/joanna-macy-a-wild-love-for-the-world/.

## Chapter 13: Cultivate Wild Eros

1. D. H. Lawrence, *A Propos of Lady Chatterley's Lover* (London: Mandrake Press, 1930).
2. Terry Tempest Williams, *Red: Passion and Patience in the Desert* (New York: Knopf Doubleday, 2008), 106.
3. Williams, *Red*, 106.
4. Williams, *Red*, 108.
5. Williams, *Red*, 108.
6. Susan Griffin, *Pornography and Silence: Culture's Revenge against Nature* (New York: Harper and Row, 1981), 82–88.
7. Derrick Jensen, *Toxic Mimics*, YouTube video, posted January 19, 2020, by Deep Green Video, https://www.youtube.com/watch?v=v--Ry7lGcZI.

8. Julie Bindel, *Feminism for Women: The Real Route to Liberation* (New York: Little, Brown, 2021).

9. George F. Koob, "Hedonic Homeostatic Dysregulation as a Driver of Drug-Seeking Behavior," *Drug Discovery Today: Disease Models* 5, no. 4 (Winter 2008): 207–15, ScienceDirect, https://www.sciencedirect.com/science/article/abs/pii/S174067 5709000279?via%3Dihub.

10. Todd Love, Christian Laier, Matthias Brand, Linda Hatch, and Raju Hajela, "Neuroscience of Internet Pornography Addiction: A Review and an Update," *Behavioral Sciences* 5, no. 3 (September 2015): 388–433, National Library of Medicine, https://www.ncbi.nlm.nih.gov/pmc/articles/PMC4600144/.

11. Scott Christian, "The Brain Scan That Will Tell If You're Addicted to Porn," *GQ*, September 23, 2013, https://www.gq.com/story/british-study-brain-scans-show -porn-addiction-similar-to-alcohol-addiction.

12. Dan Mahle, "My Year without Porn: Some Surprising Lessons," Your Brain on Porn, last updated March 31, 2015, https://www.yourbrainonporn.com/about/your-brain -on-porn-in-the-news/my-year-without-porn-some-surprising-lessons/.

13. "Studies Linking Porn Use or Porn/Sex Addiction to Sexual Dysfunctions and Poorer Sexual and Relationship Satisfaction," Your Brain on Porn, https://www .yourbrainonporn.com/relevant-research-and-articles-about-the-studies/porn-use -sex-addiction-studies/studies-linking-porn-use-or-porn-sex-addiction-to-sexual -dysfunctions-and-poorer-sexual-and-relationship-satisfaction/.

14. Christine Emba, "Consent Is Not Enough. We Need a New Sex Ethic," *Washington Post*, March 22, 2022, https://www.washingtonpost.com/opinions/2022/03/17 /sex-ethics-rethinking-consent-culture/.

15. Melissa Fabello, "3 Reasons Why Sex-Positivity without Critical Analysis Is Harmful," Everyday Feminism, May 14, 2014, https://everydayfeminism.com/2014/05 /sex-positivity-critical-analysis/.

16. Gail Dines, "The Porn Crisis," Dr. Gail Dines website, https://www.gaildines.com /the-porn-crisis.

17. Dines, "The Porn Crisis."

18. Meghan Murphy, "It's Not about You: Beyond 'Kink-Shaming,'" *Feminist Current*, July 10, 2012, https://www.feministcurrent.com/2012/07/10/its-not-about-you -beyond-kink-shaming/.

19. Alys Harte, "A Man Tried to Choke Me during Sex without Warning," *BBC News*, November 28, 2019, https://www.bbc.com/news/uk-50546184.

20. "Do Parents Really Know How Many Teens Watch Porn Online?," Hartford HealthCare, October 26, 2020, https://thocc.org/about/news-press/news-detail? articleId=29384&publicid=469.

21. Dines, "The Porn Crisis."

22. Amy Fleming, "Is Porn Making Young Men Impotent?," *Guardian*, March 11, 2019, https://www.theguardian.com/lifeandstyle/2019/mar/11/young-men-porn-induced -erectile-dysfunction.

23. Jenny White, "People Who Like Kinky Sex Are Just Bad in Bed," *Evie*, January 15,

2022, https://www.eviemagazine.com/post/people-who-like-kinky-sex-are-just-bad-in-bed.

24. Covenant Eyes, "Pornography Statistics: 25+ Facts, Quotes, and Statistics about Porn Use," Clinical Care Consultants, 2013, http://blog.clinicalcareçonsultants.com/wp-content/uploads/2013/12/porn_stats_2013_covenant_eyes.pdf.

25. Mahle, "My Year without Porn."

26. Brian Earp, "Boys and Girls Alike," *Aeon*, January 13, 2015, https://aeon.co/essays/are-male-and-female-circumcision-morally-equivalent.

27. "Female Genital Mutilation," World Health Organization, fact sheet, January 21, 2022, https://www.who.int/news-room/fact-sheets/detail/female-genital-mutilation.

28. Anne-Marie Marron, "What Is Erotic Intelligence and How Do We Access It?," Anne-MarieMarron.com blog, September 3, 2020, https://anne-mariemarron.com/blog/what-is-erotic-intelligence-and-how-do-we-access-it.

29. Amy Weintraub, "Breath of Joy," *Yoga International*, https://yogainternational.com/article/view/breath-of-joy.

## Chapter 14: Court the Muse

1. Alan Yuhas, "Dinosaurs Performed Dances to Woo Mates, According to New Evidence," *Guardian*, January 7, 2016, https://www.theguardian.com/science/2016/jan/07/new-evidence-dinosaurs-performed-dances-mating.

2. "The Nine Muses of the Greek Mythology," Greek Myths & Greek Mythology, accessed July 30, 2022, https://www.greekmyths-greekmythology.com/nine-muses-in-greek-mythology/.

3. Plotkin, *Wild Mind*, 101.

4. Derrick Jensen, *Songs of the Dead* (San Francisco: PM Press, 2009), 37.

## Chapter 15: Pray within the Dark Earth

1. Brian Handwerk, "Underground 'Fossil Water' Running Out," *National Geographic News*, May 8, 2010, https://www.nationalgeographic.com/science/article/100505-fossil-water-radioactive-science-environment.

2. Hannah Ritchie and Max Roser, "Clean Water," Our World in Data, last updated June 2021, https://ourworldindata.org/water-access.

3. Jore, "Forget Shorter Showers," Vimeo video, 11:23, posted August 25, 2015, https://vimeo.com/137294079.

4. James Gaines, "A Strange, Endangered Ecosystem Hides in Underground Waterways," *Wired*, February 12, 2022, https://www.wired.com/story/a-strange-endangered-ecosystem-hides-in-underground-waterways/.

5. Tripp Baltz, "Navajo, Battling Covid, Say Coal Mines Sapped Drinking Water," *Bloomberg Law*, June 17, 2020, https://news.bloomberglaw.com/environment-and-energy/virus-ravaged-navajo-say-coal-mines-sapped-their-drinking-water.

6. Grace Livingstone, "The Farmers Who Worry about Our Phone Batteries," *BBC News*, August 15, 2019, https://www.bbc.com/news/business-49355817.

7. Todd Frankel and Peter Whoriskey, "Tossed Aside in the 'White Gold' Rush," *Washington Post*, December 19, 2016, https://www.washingtonpost.com/graphics /business/batteries/tossed-aside-in-the-lithium-rush/.

8. Carrington, "Humans Just 0.01% of All Life But Have Destroyed 83% of Wild Mammals."

9. Sherri Mitchell, *Sacred Instructions: Indigenous Wisdom for Living Spirit-Based Change* (Berkeley, CA: North Atlantic Books, 2018), 121.

10. Julia Barnes, "They Want to Mine the Deep Sea," *Scuba News*, September 6, 2020, https://www.thescubanews.com/2020/09/06/they-want-to-mine-the-deep-sea/.

11. "Global Assessment Report on Biodiversity and Ecosystem Services," *Wikipedia*.

12. #TheConsciousChallenge, "Oxygen & Deforestation," The Conscious Club website, April 30, 2019, https://www.theconsciouschallenge.org/ecologicalfootprintbible overview/oxygen-deforestation.

13. Max Wilbert, "The Everyday Violence of Modern Culture," Deep Green Resistance News Service, November 30, 2015, https://dgrnewsservice.org/civilization/the -everyday-violence-of-modern-culture/.

14. Derrick Jensen, Lierre Keith, and Max Wilbert, *Bright Green Lies: How the Environmental Movement Lost Its Way and What We Can Do about It* (Rhinebeck, NY: Monkfish Book Publishing, 2021).

15. "Truth Mandala," Work That Reconnects Network, November 26, 2017, https:// workthatreconnects.org/resource/truth-mandala/.

16. Stephen Pyne, "Our Burning Planet: Why We Must Learn to Live with Fire," *Yale Environment 360*, October 8, 2020, https://e360.yale.edu/features/our-burning -planet-why-we-must-learn-to-live-with-fire.

17. Martín Prechtel, quoted in Derrick Jensen, "Saving the Indigenous Soul: An Interview with Martín Prechtel," *The Sun*, April 2001, https://www.thesunmagazine.org /issues/304/saving-the-indigenous-soul.

18. Teri Dillion, *No Pressure, No Diamonds: Mining for Gifts in Illness and Loss* (Portland, OR: Pomegranate Publishing, 2020).

19. Whyte, "All the True Vows."

20. Martín Prechtel, quoted in Jensen, "Saving the Indigenous Soul."

21. Jensen, *The Problem of Civilization*, 92–94.

22. Charles Eisenstein, *Climate: A New Story* (Berkeley, CA: North Atlantic Books, 2018), 8.

# Chapter 16: Engage in Radical Dreaming

1. Ari Kelman, "Murder, Purely," *Chronicle of Higher Education*, April 30, 2008, https://www.chronicle.com/blognetwork/edgeofthewest/murder-purely.

2. Edward Abbey, "In the Land of 'Laughing Waters,'" *New York Times*, January 3, 1982, https://www.nytimes.com/1982/01/03/travel/in-the-land-of-laughing-waters.html.

3. "Statistics," National Sexual Violence Resource Center, nsvrc.org/node/4737.

4. "Children and Teens: Statistics," RAINN, accessed August 24, 2022, https://www
.rainn.org/statistics/children-and-teens.

5. Sean Butler and Will Falk, "Rights for Lake Erie? Why Corporate Rights and
Preemption Must Go," Deep Green Resistance News Service, December 20, 2019,
https://dgrnewsservice.org/civilization/ecocide/agriculture/rights-for-lake-erie
-why-corporate-rights-and-preemption-must-go/.

6. Judith Lewis Herman, *Trauma and Recovery: The Aftermath of Violence — From
Domestic Abuse to Political Terror* (New York: Basic Books, 1997), 1.

7. Herman, *Trauma and Recovery*, 1–4.

8. Justin McBrien, "This Is Not the Sixth Extinction. It's the First Extermination Event,"
Truthout, September 14, 2019, https://truthout.org/articles/this-is-not-the-sixth
-extinction-its-the-first-extermination-event/.

9. Stephen Aizenstat, *Dream Tending: Awakening to the Healing Power of Dreams* (New
York: Spring Journal, 2011).

10. Robert Moss, *Dreamways of the Iroquois* (Rochester, VT: Destiny Books, 2005).

11. Martín Prechtel, *Long Life, Honey in the Heart* (Berkeley, CA: North Atlantic Books,
2004).

12. Robert Bosnak, *Embodiment: Creative Imagination in Medicine, Art, and Travel*
(Abingdon, UK: Routledge, 2007), 86–104.

13. David von Seggern, "Green Energy Meets Mining," *Desert Report*, March 9, 2021,
http://www.desertreport.org/?p=2995.

14. Kate Singer, "Proposing Cradle-to-Grave Evaluations for All Vehicles," *Meer Magazine*, November 3, 2020, https://wsimag.com/science-and-technology/63818
-proposing-cradle-to-grave-evaluations-for-all-vehicles.

15. Max Wilbert, "Thacker Pass and the 'Green' Mining Boom," *The Peace Chronicle:
The Magazine of the Peace and Justice Association*, Climate (Spring 2021), https://
www.peacejusticestudies.org/chronicle/thacker-pass-and-the-green-mining-boom/.

16. Wilbert, "Thacker Pass and the 'Green' Mining Boom."

17. Edward Bartell, letter to the Bureau of Land Management regarding Thacker Pass
Lithium Mine Project Draft EIS, September 14, 2020, http://www.gbrw.org/ftpgbrw
/Thacker%20Pass/EIS-2020/DEIS/Bartell/Bartell%20DEIS%20Comments.pdf.

18. Maya Kapoor, "Nevada Lithium Mine Kicks Off a New Era of Western Extraction,"
*High Country News*, February 18, 2021, https://www.hcn.org/issues/53.3/indigenous
-affairs-mining-nevada-lithium-mine-kicks-off-a-new-era-of-western-extraction.

19. Max Wilbert, "The Cost of a Battery," *Earth Island Journal*, February 1, 2021,
https://www.earthisland.org/journal/index.php/articles/entry/the-cost-of-a-battery.

20. Protect Thacker Pass home page, https://www.protectthackerpass.org/.

21. Reno Sparks Indian Colony home page, accessed August 18, 2021, https://www.rsic
.org/.

22. Jennifer Solis, "Tribe Appeals to Archeological Firm to Stop Digging at Thacker
Pass," *Nevada Current*, April 25, 2022, https://www.nevadacurrent.com/2022/04/25
/tribe-appeals-to-archeological-firm-to-stop-digging-at-thacker-pass/.

23. Geoffrey Deihl, "Showdown at Thacker Pass," *Sane Thoughts for Insane Times*,

September 19, 2022, https://geoffreydeihl.substack.com/p/showdown-at-thacker
-pass?utm_source=profile&utm_medium=reader2.

24. Solis, "Tribe Appeals to Archeological Firm to Stop Digging at Thacker Pass."

25. Derrick Jensen, "Forget Shorter Showers," *Orion Magazine*, July 2009, https://orion
magazine.org/article/forget-shorter-showers/.

26. "Save Water and Energy by Showering Better," Environmental Protection Agency,
EPA WaterSense, February 2017, https://www.epa.gov/sites/default/files/2017-02
/documents/ws-ourwater-shower-better-learning-resource_0.pdf.

27. Jensen, "Forget Shorter Showers."

28. Alex Eisenberg and Elisabeth Robson, "The Personal Responsibility Vortex," Protect
Thacker Pass, February 6, 2021, https://www.protectthackerpass.org/the-personal
-responsibility-vortex/.

29. TEDx Talks, *The Personal Responsibility Vortex: Bret Weinstein at TEDxTheEver-
greenStateCollege*, YouTube video, 16:33, posted June 13, 2012, https://www.youtube
.com/watch?v=SjNRtrZjkfE.

30. Will Falk, "Will Falk on Personal Purity and Asking, 'What Needs to Be Done?,'"
Protect Thacker Pass, February 4, 2021, https://www.protectthackerpass.org/will
-falk-on-personal-purity-and-asking-what-needs-to-be-done/.

31. Max Wilbert and Elisabeth Robson, "Solutions: If Electric Cars Won't Save the Planet,
What Will?," Protect Thacker Pass, https://www.protectthackerpass.org/solutions/.

32. Martin Shaw, "Navigating the Mysteries," *Emergence Magazine*, May 12, 2022,
https://emergencemagazine.org/essay/navigating-the-mysteries/?fbclid=IwAR3
_fN9NSIKtH0jVwpN9vfQemt2OyZYp5PpDnXu3iIoWZMa2WjL5q6jXgjY.

33. Peter Kelder, *Ancient Secret of the Fountain of Youth* (Gig Harbor, WA: Harbor Press,
1985).

34. "Everything You Need to Know about the Five Tibetan Rites," Healthline, September
24, 2019, https://www.healthline.com/health/5-tibetan-rites.

35. Work That Reconnects Network, *Deep Times: A Journal of the Work That Reconnects*
home page, accessed August 31, 2022, https://journal.workthatreconnects.org/#:~:text
=The%20title%20comes%20from%20what,New%20Eyes%2C%20and%20Going%20
Forth.

## Chapter 17: Stretch Your Consciousness

1. McMaster University, "Plants Prefer Their Kin, but Crowd Out Competition When
Sharing a Pot with Strangers," EurekAlert!, news release, November 16, 2009,
https://www.eurekalert.org/news-releases/765128.

2. "Janine Benyus," biography on Omega Institute website, accessed September 1, 2021,
https://www.eomega.org/workshops/teachers/janine-benyus.

3. Peter Wohlleben, *The Hidden Life of Trees* (Vancouver: Greystone Books, 2016).

4. Stefano Mancuso, quoted in Jeremy Hance, "Are Plants Intelligent? New Book Says
Yes," *Guardian*, August 4, 2015, https://www.theguardian.com/environment/radical
-conservation/2015/aug/04/plants-intelligent-sentient-book-brilliant-green-internet.

5.  Ephrat Livni, "A Dispersed Self: A Debate over Plant Consciousness Is Forcing Us to Confront the Limitations of the Human Mind," *Quartz*, last updated July 20, 2022, https://qz.com/1294941/a-debate-over-plant-consciousness-is-forcing-us-to-confront-the-limitations-of-the-human-mind/#:~:text=Green%20philosophy&text=That%20said%2C%20Marder%20admits%20that,might%20be%2C%E2%80%9D9D%20ohe%20says.

6.  Livni, "A Dispersed Self."

7.  Michael Marder, *Plant Thinking: A Philosophy of Vegetal Life* (New York: Columbia University Press, 2013), 151–78.

8.  "Carl Jung and the Shadow: The Hidden Power of Our Dark Side," Academy of Ideas, December 17, 2015, https://academyofideas.com/2015/12/carl-jung-and-the-shadow-the-hidden-power-of-our-dark-side/.

9.  Sharon Blackie, "The Ancient Practice of Marrying the Land," *Uplift*, 2016, accessed September 1, 2021, https://uplift.love/the-ancient-practice-of-marrying-the-land/.

10. Sue Owen, "Female Leadership Nothing New to Buffalo," Politifact: The Poynter Institute, February 11, 2014, https://www.politifact.com/factchecks/2014/feb/11/hugh-fitzsimons/female-leadership-nothing-new-buffalo/.

11. Andreas Kornevall home page, accessed August 20, 2021, www.kornevall.com.

12. The concept for this pose came from Stapleton, *Self-Awakening Yoga*, 181–82. I have added my own ideas to the original concept.

## Chapter 18: Become a Love Warrior for the Earth

1.  Chris Istace, "Rainforest Flying Squad — Fighting for Vancouver Island's Remaining Old Growth Forests," The Mindful Explorer blog, https://www.chrisistace.com/rainforest-flying-squad-fighting-for-vancouver-islands-remaining-old-growth-forests/.

2.  Last Stand for Forests, website of the Fairy Creek Blockade, accessed September 2, 2021, https://laststandforforests.com/.

3.  Just in Canada / Juste au Canada, *Fairy Creek: The Last Stand*, YouTube video, 1:39:26, posted August 4, 2021, https://www.youtube.com/watch?v=C-DitozPh98.

4.  Dr. Karen Price, Dr. Rachel Holt, and Dave Daust, "B.C.'s Old-Growth Forest: A Last Stand for Biodiversity," April 2020, https://sierraclub.bc.ca/wp-content/uploads/bcs-old-growth-forest-a-last-stand-for-biodiversity-report-2020.pdf.

5.  Jesse Winter, "'War in the Woods': Hundreds of Anti-Logging Protesters Arrested in Canada, *Guardian*, June 24, 2021, https://www.theguardian.com/environment/2021/jun/24/british-columbia-logging-ancient-growth-protests.

6.  Molly Murphy and Research for the Front Lines, "Real Climate Action Means Defunding the Police," *Briarpatch Magazine*, November 3, 2021, https://briarpatchmagazine.com/articles/view/climate-action-defunding-police-CIRG-RCMP-Fairy-Creek.

7.  Joanna Macy and Chris Johnstone, *Active Hope: How to Face the Mess We're in with Unexpected Resilience and Creative Power*, rev. ed. (Novato, CA: New World Library, 2022), 95–99.

8. Go Conscious Earth website, accessed September 2, 2021, https://www.gcearth.org/.
9. World Wildlife Fund biodiversity webpage, accessed September 2, 2021, https://wwf.panda.org/discover/our_focus/biodiversity/biodiversity/.
10. Brandon Wiggins, "These 8 Ambitious Ecological Projects Are Helping to Heal the World," Global Citizen, April 30, 2020, https://www.globalcitizen.org/en/content /ecological-restoration-projects/.
11. Eisenstein, *Climate*.
12. "Bear Bile Farming," Animals Asia Foundation, accessed September 3, 2021, https://www.animalsasia.org/us/our-work/end-bear-bile-farming/.
13. Jensen, Keith, and Wilbert, *Bright Green Lies*.
14. Godwin Bosco, "The Idea That 'Green Technology' Can Help Save the Environment Is Dangerous," *The Wire*, December 2, 2019, https://thewire.in/environment/the-idea -that-green-technology-can-help-save-the-environment-is-dangerous.
15. Aedan Hannon, "Conservation Partners Target 300,000 Acres in Southwest Colorado," *Durango Herald*, December 24, 2021, https://www.durangoherald.com /articles/conservation-partners-target-300000-acres-in-southwest-colorado/.
16. Chad Hanson, "Logging in Disguise: How Forest Thinning Is Making Wildfires Worse," *Grist*, April 24, 2021, https://grist.org/fix/opinion/forest-thinning-logging -makes-wildfires-worse/.
17. Prairie Protection Colorado website, accessed September 2, 2021, https://prairie protectioncolorado.org.
18. "Why Thinning Forest Is Poor Wildfire Strategy," Western Watersheds Project, accessed August 3, 2022, https://www.westernwatersheds.org/gw-poor-wildfire -strategy/#:~:text=In%20fact%2C%20mechanical%20thinning%2alone,through%20 the%20open%20forest%20stands.
19. Hanson, "Logging in Disguise."
20. Curtis Bradley, Chad Hanson, and Dominick A. Dellasala, "Does Increased Forest Protection Correspond to Higher Fire Severity in Frequent-Fire Forests of the Western United States?," *Ecosphere*, October 2016, https://www.researchgate.net /publication/309472850_Does_increased_forest_protection_correspond_to _higher_fire_severity_in_frequent-fire_forests_of_the_western_United_States.
21. Ray Ring, "History Is Full of Fire," *High County News*, May 26, 2023, https://www .hcn.org/issues/251/13986.
22. "Indigenous Fire Stewardship Promotes Global Diversity," University of Waterloo News, August 3, 2021, https://uwaterloo.ca/news/media/indigenous-fire-stewardship -promotes-global-biodiversity.
23. Danna Smith, Chad Hanson, and Matthew Koehler, "Logging Is the Lead Driver of Carbon Emissions from US Forests," *Earth Island Journal*, April 4, 2019, https://www.earthisland.org/journal/index.php/articles/entry/logging-carbon -emissions-us-forests/.
24. Smith, Hanson, and Koehler, "Logging Is the Lead Driver."
25. *Confronting the Wildfire Crisis: A 10-Year Implementation Plan*, US Forest Service, US Department of Agriculture, January 2022, https://www.fs.usda.gov/sites/default /files/Wildfire-Crisis-Implementation-Plan.pdf.

26. Josh Schlossberg, "Opinion: Removing Trees from Colorado Forests Will Not Prevent Wildfires from Burning," *Colorado Sun*, August 14, 2022, https://coloradosun .com/2022/08/14/colorado-wildfire-forest-management-opinion/.

27. "Three Dimensions of the Great Turning," Work That Reconnects Network, accessed September 3, 2021, https://workthatreconnects.org/spiral/the-great-turning/three -dimensions-of-the-great-turning/.

28. Molly Murphy and Research for the Front Lines, "The C-IRG: The Resource Extraction Industry's Best Ally," *Briarpatch Magazine*, January 5, 2022, https:// briarpatchmagazine.com/articles/view/the-c-irg-the-resource-extraction-industrys -best-ally.

29. Max Wilbert, "The Everyday Violence of Modern Culture," Deep Green Resistance News Service, November 30, 2015, https://dgrnewsservice.org/civilization/the -everyday-violence-of-modern-culture/.

30. Gleb Raygorodetsky, "Indigenous Peoples Defend Earth's Biodiversity — but They're in Danger," *National Geographic*, November 16, 2018, https://www.national geographic.com/environment/article/can-indigenous-land-stewardship-protect -biodiversity-.

31. Karen McVeigh, "More Rights Defenders Murdered in 2021, with 138 Activists Killed Just in Colombia," *Guardian*, March 2, 2022, https://www.theguardian.com /global-development/2022/mar/02/more-human-rights-defenders-murdered -2021-environmental-indigenous-rights-activists.

32. The Mother Tree Project website, accessed September 3, 2021, https://mothertree project.org/.

33. "Regenerative Cultural Design," Springhouse, accessed September 3, 2021, https://springhouse.org/sourced-design/.

34. Bill Plotkin, *Nature and the Human Soul* (Novato, CA: New World Library, 2007).

35. Joshua Schrei, "Your Consciousness Comes from the Moon," *The Emerald* podcast, May 31, 2022, 1:27:00, https://open.spotify.com/episode/0USKcMV6qf8xIg55b 2dW5b?si=7e4dbee212a744ca&fbclid=IwAR26e2QhPGNrrSOi-heI3KctLKjgPqv IHrGBwjzCw-4iXAiYOH_htIyRkAY&nd=1.

## Conclusion: Wild Yoga, Revolution, and Cocreation

1. Adam Morton, "'The Franklin Would Be Dammed Today': Australia's Shrinking Environmental Protections," *Guardian*, January 29, 2018, https://www.theguardian .com/environment/2018/jan/30/the-franklin-would-be-dammed-today-australias -shrinking-environmental-protections.

2. Bob Brown, quoted in Brendan Gogarty, "Bob Brown Wins His Case, but High Court Leaves the Door Open to Laws Targeting Protesters," *The Conversation*, October 17, 2017, https://theconversation.com/bob-brown-wins-his-case-but -high-court-leaves-the-door-open-to-laws-targeting-protesters-85742.

3. Michael Slezak, "Bob Brown Wins High Court Challenge to Tasmanian Anti-Protest Laws," *Guardian*, October 17, 2017, https://www.theguardian.com/australia

-news/2017/oct/18/bob-brown-wins-high-court-challenge-to-tasmanian-anti
-protest-laws.

4. Slezak, "Bob Brown Wins High Court Challenge."

5. Carrie Levine, "New Anti-Protest Laws Cast a Long Shadow on First Amendment Rights," Center for Public Integrity, December 20, 2021, https://publicintegrity.org /politics/new-anti-protest-laws-cast-a-long-shadow-on-first-amendment-rights; "US Protest Law Tracker," International Center for Not-for-Profit Law, last updated March 31, 2022, https://www.icnl.org/usprotestlawtracker/?location=&status =enacted,enacted_with_improvements,pending,defeated&issue=&date=custom &date_from=2021-01-01&date_to=2021-12-01&type=legislative.

6. Max Wilbert, "Thacker Pass Dispatches: 'Blatant Harassment' — Thacker Pass Activists Fined $50K for Providing Bathrooms to Native Elders," *Sierra Nevada Ally*, September 20, 2021, https://sierranevadaally.org/2021/09/20/thacker-pass-dispatches -blatant-harassment-thacker-pass-activists-fined-50k-for-providing-bathrooms-to -native-elders/.

7. Berry, *The Dream of the Earth.*

# Acknowledgments

1. "Presenters at the 2019 Global Earth Repair Conference," Global Earth Repair Foundation, https://globalearthrepairfoundation.org/presenters-at-the-2019-global -earth-repair-conference/.

# About the Author

Rebecca Wildbear, MS, E-RYT 500, the creator of Wild Yoga®, has been guiding Wild Yoga programs since 2007. She is a river and soul guide who helps people tune in to the mysteries that live within the Earth community, dreams, and their own wild nature so they may live a life of creative service. She was on the faculty at Nosara Yoga Institute for many years and has also been guiding vision quests and other nature and soul programs through Animas Valley Institute since 2006. Her writing has been published by *Earth Island Journal*, *Kosmos Journal*, *CounterPunch*, and Deep Green Resistance News Service. To learn more about Rebecca, visit www.rebeccawildbear.com.

# About the Illustrator

Sarah E. Brooks is a Tucson-based illustrator and craftswoman. She draws with pen and ink and practices the ancestral skills of buckskin tanning and sheep's wool felting. She is inspired by the mysteries in dreams, the magic of the wild, and the funny things that we humans get up to. To see more of Sarah's work, visit www.instagram.com/sarahstickfigures.